POLITICALLY INCORRECT JOKES FROM THE NET

POLITICALLY INCORRECT JOKES FROM THE NET

collected by Phillip Adams
and Patrice Newell

M. SSATIN
732 Lafayette Av
BUFFALO NY 14222

716-886-7620

Souvenir Press

First published in Australia
by Penguin Books Australia Ltd.

First British edition published 1998
by Souvenir Press Ltd.,
43 Great Russell Street, London WC1B 3PD

Reprinted 1998 (twice)
Reprinted 1999 (twice)
Reprinted 2000 (four times)
Reprinted 2001 (twice)
Reprinted 2002 (twice)
Reprinted 2003

ISBN 0 285 63445 3

Printed and bound in Great Britain by
Cox & Wyman Ltd., Reading, Berkshire

To Sandra Blood, who once again gave hers that others might laugh. And to John Glenn, who cast his net very wide indeed.

I am the very model of a modern teenage cyberpunk

I rent my own apartment and it's full of electronic junk.

I own a Vax, a 486, I've even got a PDP

I finished Myst and Doom but I'm stumped by Wing Commander
  Three.

I'm very well acquainted with matters pornographical

I have a list of image sites, both overseas and national.

I'm totally an anarchist the government I'd like to wreck,

Though if they were to get blown up, who'd give to me my welfare

cheque?

When I've learnt what progress has been made upon the Internet,

When I know something more than just a smattering of netiquette,

In short when I can have a worldwide soapbox on which to stand,

I've got no time for other things, like beer and trips to Disneyland.

My life outside the Internet is very, very sad, you see

I cannot get my spots to fade, my social life's a tragedy.

But still, if you need answers that concern your electronic junk

I am the very model of a modern teenage cyberpunk.

A cybersong, to the tune of 'A Modern Major General'

CONTENTS

An Electronic Epidemic

Influenza. Billions have caught it, tens of millions have died from it. Again and again it appears, invading country after country. Unable to treat it, even to explain it, desperate doctors have conferred with astrologists who insist its dread cycles synchronise with the approach of comets. First came the cosmic visitor, astrologists insisted, then the epidemic. The doctors accepted the comet's influence, its 'influenza'. And that became the name of the contagion.

Now, as we approach the end of a century and of a millennium, we confront a contagion far deadlier than the flu. Instead of being transmitted from person to person through the respiratory tract, by such old-fashioned means as inhalation of infected droplets resulting from coughing and sneezing, we have an electronic epidemic with a transmission rate approaching the speed of light. It is called the Internet, and within a few short years 30 million people have been afflicted. Thus far the majority of victims have been the male offspring of the middle class, whose immune systems have been repressed by spending too many hours sitting alone gazing at computer screens or fondling their laptops. However, there are grim signs that the Internet is beginning to infect/afflict females as well.

Searching for an explanation of the outbreak, we looked for the influenza of comets. Halley's was a recent visitor but an unlikely culprit, given that it was a nocturnal display and somewhat feeble. Now, thanks to two amateur astronomers, Mr Hale and Mr Bopp, we know the truth. Coinciding with the launch of William Gates's Windows 95, with the public listing of Netscape, the astronomers discovered a comet a thousand times greater in size and brilliance than Halley's. Suddenly appearing from behind mighty Jupiter it seemed, at first, to be heading straight towards Earth where it would do us in like the dinosaurs. Recent calculations by astronomers – using computers with Internet connections – suggest a near-miss. In about a year's time.

Clearly this comet has been conjured by the epidemic, rather than the epidemic by the comet. Though, if the Internet continues to spread, the gravitational pull of cyberspace will draw the visitor from outerspace and our planetary software, namely human beings, will be emphatically Hale-Bopped.

Not that those infected by the Internet show much concern. As soon as they catch the disease they quarantine themselves in close proximity to their computer and, bathing themselves in the seance-glow of cathode, start showing the familiar symptoms of gee-whizzery and unbridled optimism. Just as many of those who contract multiple sclerosis become pathologically cheerful – 'euphoria' is regarded as a symptom of MS – those caught in the Internet become delirious with joy. While the luddite sees every cog and microchip as a personal threat, those who surf the Internet see their technology as delivering, among other laudable things, an end to the dangerous anachronism of nationalism – marking the dawn of a new age in democracy, of global citizenship in a world without walls, without boundaries, without hierarchies.

Feverish, bright-eyed, the innocent victims of the Internet speak wildly about its promise. Currently connected via keyboard, it's only a matter of time, they insist, before voices replace fingertips. Then instantaneous translation of the spoken word will banish forever the curse of the Tower of Babel, and all the world will be able to communicate instantly. Others insist that barriers of gender will fall as well, since here is a form of communication that, for the moment at least, blurs the issue. Many males create feminine personae for the Internet, whilst women can present themselves as males. Even when the system becomes multi-media, vocal *and* visual, the technologies will allow people to camouflage themselves, to create any voice or face they wish to present to the wider world. Techno-transvestisism, if you will.

Meanwhile, the disabled community hopes that programmers will recognise their special needs, so that they too will be full participants in an electronic world which, unlike the real one, will not deny them access or acceptance.

The Net is deemed to be anarchic, ready to subvert the powers of the powerful, to undermine the monoliths, to mock the secrecy of government and corporation. Experience the ecstasy. Hear the hubris. The tens of millions caught up in this contagion sing its praises louder than all the church choirs in history sang in praise of the Saviour.

But then, the Internet *is* the saviour. How appropriate, at the end of a millennium, that we should be welcoming this microchip Messiah. (Last time a carpenter, this time a laptop.) And the yearnings of the faithful have a poignant beauty, a multi-orgasmic excitement, a transcendental fervour. Verily we say unto you, the information superhighway forms a clover leaf with the road to Damascus.

There are people who go even further, who talk of a synthesis, a fusion of human and artificial intelligence. It is not the meek who will inherit the world in this scenario, but the nerds.

Imagine the planet as a giant brain, with everyone on the Internet a neuron, using their modems as synapses; linked in a vast, collective intelligence; forming, finally, a mighty, unified consciousness. That metaphor is only the beginning. Now that the New Age intersects with the New Physics, you hear another, even more astonishing argument. It goes like this: the death sentence of the second law of thermodynamics is being challenged by the growth of intelligence, of consciousness. It is blossoming on our planet, via technologies like the Internet, and

4

will inevitably, finally, fill the cosmos. So while God didn't exist and doesn't exist, He, She or It is coming into existence.

There's little room for devil's advocacy, for the doubting Thomas, in these rapturous extrapolations. Try as you might to mop their fevered brows and calm them down, the sufferers of the contagion, the devotees of this cathode cult, cannot be soothed or persuaded. The suggestion that there's a dark side to every moon, that no technology has ever lived up to its promoters' promises, falls on deaf ears.

One would wish the new technology a sacred destiny but know that it will be profane. 'Twas ever thus and ever will be. Virtual reality, that oxymoronic term, could deliver imagined experiences of unimaginable beauty and may, for the odd philosopher or artist, do so. But we already know that for most it will be a tawdry and salacious experience; a three-dimensional, tactile computer game of butchery, lechery or both.

Film was to be a great force for good, doing for the human imagination what Esperanto would do for language. Silent movies became the first global medium, the likes of Chaplin and Pickford the most famous people the world had ever known. Then, slowly but surely, cinema became a charnel house, and now most people most of the time troop along to films that are essentially fascist, in which the likes of Willis, Schwarzenegger or Stallone engage in egomaniacal one-upmanship, examples of American triumphalism.

Another small problem was, of course, the cultural dominance of Los Angeles, its great voice drowning out other voices, making (for example) British feature films rarities in their own culture, strangers in their own cinemas. Despite private funding and lottery money in support of local production, box office figures still demonstrate the total dominance of the US, of LA. And when you factor in the video stores, let alone television viewing habits, America achieves a share of market, a share of mind unprecedented in human history. Not even the Roman Catholic Church, at the height of its powers, could claim the reach of the major studios.

Television. It was to be 'the meeting place of strangers', the greatest force for democracy, the greatest educative tool the world had ever known. True, from time to time there was a glimmering of evidence that its contribution was benign, magnanimous. Some held, for example, that it was televised images of carnage that forced Washington to retreat from the Vietnam War. (Just for the record, this happens to be piffle. War and Vietnam got on wonderfully for many, many years, just as war and television get on wonderfully today, as the high ratings and enthusiastic response to Desert Storm remind us.) There were some who said that, without television, the Berlin Wall wouldn't have crumbled and communism wouldn't have collapsed. But you've only to look at the outpourings of America's 5000 channels – a number that's rising by the hour – to realise that the stuff it pumps out would earn you a fine as a polluter should you try to pour it down the drain.

Thirty-three years ago, we argued that we hadn't

had 15 years of television but one year's television 15 times. Much the same needs to be said about those 5000 channels. Given the poverty of original programs, the paucity of quality, the predominance of endlessly repeated movies and series, America doesn't really have 5000 channels at all. It has 50 channels 100 times.

Not even literacy has proved to be the triumph it was touted. Comparatively few people use literacy for literature. Most use the skill to look up the TV programs for the 5000 channels, or to read their astrological charts or the magazines chocker with celebrity stories about Michael Jackson and the life and death of Princess Di. Whilst the Bible remains a best-seller, millions have preferred *Mein Kampf*, Mao's *Little Red Book* or the latest novel by Jeffrey Archer.

Nuclear power promised us infite supplies of cheap energy, and instead gave us Hiroshima, Nagasaki, the Cold War and Chernobyl. Show us a technology and we'll show you a two-edged sword, a broken promise.

A world without walls? Without boundaries? Without hierarchies? Not if Bill Gates can help it. Let his name be a warning. Microsoft intends building tollgates all over the infobahn, and any number of other gatekeepers are muscling in. On Friday, 11 August 1995, Wall Street celebrated the Internet with a 600 per cent rise in the shares of a newly listed, 15-month-old, loss-making company called Netscape Communications. Within minutes they'd valued it at $3.8 billion, more than enough to rank it among the top 30 UK enterprises, and outranking the likes of Woolworths and the second-string banks.

Netscape Communications produces the navigator point-and-click Internet browser software to facilitate cyberspace exploration. Within a nanosecond, the new company was giving Bill Gates a run for his money and reminding us that the free and easy, anarchistic days of the Internet are ending.

In the late '60s, boffins working for the US Defence Department's Advance Research Projects Agency (ARPA) called the Internet into being. The first network, small and secret, started operation in 1969. It was intended to help researchers build networks that could survive technical problems or wholescale attacks. It was hoped that the new system might remain viable even after nuclear war. Because it had no centre, no nexus, the Internet was, and remains, resilient.

Over the next 20 years the Net grew steadily as more and more institutions linked in, hooked up. Soon there was a plethora of interlinked networks, many of them financed by the US government and others by semi-government agencies. And slowly but surely, commercial organisations moved in.

Between the ideal and the reality falls the shadow. Already the idealism of the Internet is being debauched by carpetbaggers, advertisers, marketers, pornographers, conspiracy theorists, paranoid right-wingers, racists, bigots and would-be entrepreneurs. It's no longer the nerds who are the problem.

Online gambling is shaping up as the next big Internet challenge (after pornography) for regulatory authorities, with an absence of safeguards to prevent access by children and lack of security for financial transactions the main concerns. The Caribbean Casino provides a warning at the beginning of its Internet site that it is off limits to people under the age of 18, but it has no mechanisms to enforce his rule. There are concerns that Internet casinos could pose a serious threat to government revenue from legalised forms of gambling. The casino is the brainchild of a 34-year-old Canadian, Mr Warren Eugene, who has set up his operation in the tax haven of the Turks and Caicos Islands, part of the Bahamas. Mr Eugene told the *Wall Street Journal* that he believed the cybercasino could be a 'trillion dollar worldwide business'.

Every day the system, so all-at-once and urgent, so full of possibilities, grows. And with it grow the abuses. As libertarians, we abhor censorship and are reluctant to join the ranks of control freaks. Despite the efforts of Microsoft, Netscape, et al, the Internet remains free of a centre, a backbone, a controlling nexus. There's no transmitter to turn off, no presses that can stop rolling.

It's true that the Internet is the largest, most powerful and efficient network for the storage and transmission of information that we've seen. Only a few years back, it had a guiding philosophy that seemed to guarantee its integrity. Then it became a juggernaut, and now it's a bandwagon. And because anything goes on the Net, it is already being blamed for social problems in the way we previously blamed television.

The Net was recently blamed, in effect, for the Oklahoma City bombing – it was alleged that bomb-building advice, from ultra-right sources, was on the Net. The fact is that any number of paranoid publications and survivalist mags – not to mention a couple of official government publications – explain how to use diesel fuel and fertiliser for explosive purposes. It makes no more sense to blame the Net for our social problems than it does to suggest it's responsible for the Hale-Bopp comet.

Recently it's become patently, painfully obvious that the New Age has been infiltrated by the hard right. The Australian magazine *Nexus* (*Noxious* might be more appropriate) began its life by recycling conspiracy theories, promoting alternative therapies and listing UFO sightings. Latterly it's been giving space to the most rabid right-wingers in the US, and suggesting that the Oklahoma City bombing was the work of ASIO. Slowly but surely Shirley MacLaine has given way to the Michigan Militia, and the same phenomenon has been observed in alternative journals in the UK and Europe. Similarly, Australia's green movement has been subverted by white supremacists, using ecological arguments to camouflage racist immigration policies. So we shouldn't be surprised that the Internet has been embraced by skinheads and neofascist crazies. You can hardly blame the Net for that – any more than you can blame the telephone directory for listing the name and addresses of bigots. Or the roads for encouraging maniacs to buy a car.

Nonetheless, the likelihood is that the

meretricious will drown out the worthy. While
we're told that the Internet will put us in touch
with the Uffizi, the Prado, the Louvre, and the cave
paintings of Lascaux, James Gleick, the author of
Chaos, says, 'It's a wave, and no wave is complete
without its backwash.' And Gleick sees in the
cyberspace democracy the same stresses and
undercurrents that assail real-world society. He's
discovered you can get anonymous, threatening
letters by e-mail even quicker than you can get
them in the post. 'Angry teenagers screech at one
another from behind pseudonymous masks,' says
Gleick. 'Just the other day a young man I've never
met posted a public message expressing the desire
to see my hands blown off in an explosion.'

Luddites like Kirkpatrick Sale, who likes to smash
computers with sledgehammers in front of
audiences in American halls, see the Net turning the
world into a society of loners, devastating the warp
and weft of communities and substituting a mess of
electronic pottage.

The other criticism is, of course, elitism – that
the Net is only for the affluent. Jon Katz, critic for
Wired magazine, admits to this danger but points
out that 'low income earners don't read serious
daily papers or magazines either. They'll probably
have access to computers when digital technology
fuses with television and becomes easier and
cheaper … Everything has a price tag – the car
makes us mobile and pollutes; airplanes get us
places but are noisy and crash; medicine prolongs
life and causes most people to die alone and in
hospital. I think the world has never sorted out

11

its feelings about technology. We fight it every time.'

Recently a University of Michigan sophomore was arrested on charges of transmission of a threat by electronic means, and thus became the first person to be charged with a federal crime for behaviour on the Internet. Needless to say, enthusiasts of cyberspace took close note. The Internet is speech driven – albeit a hybrid form of speech combining elements of talk, broadcast and print publication – and wants to be left as free and unfettered as possible.

The Michigan case was dismissed. For good or ill, cyberspace would remain ungoverned and ungovernable, an electronic Wild West. Like real live speech, Internet speech can incorporate behaviour that is legally actionable by civil or criminal means: fraud, transmission of threats, libel, copyright violation, and the like. Lawyers and users are still trying to work out the ways in which existing laws may be applied to the Net. Software has progressed a little faster. There are 'bozo filters', which roam the Net and cancel things people find obnoxious, and the NetNanny, which filters out adult or other material at the terminal. Meanwhile, commercial services such as Compuserve and American On Line regularly cancel the accounts of users who break sometimes restrictive house rules – as do universities, many of which have banned, for example, pictorial pornography, not only because it may cause offence but because, frequently, it involves violation of copyright.

In Australia the federal government is looking at

ways to clean up the Internet and block
objectionable material, such as child pornography.
Attorney-General Lavarch is proposing that
operators of computer networks be self-regulating
under a broad industry code of practice, and that a
complaints body be set up for the public.

But a very big imp is out of the bottle, and you
can already download a service offering nearly one
million porno images which have been downloaded
8.5 million times by consumers in over 2000 cities
in over 40 countries. Then there's the guy in
Antarctica who's set up a service that sends pictures
of imaginary pizzas. Australian columnist Peter
Goers made contact and ordered, from the
available categories, a 'pizza with kittens, baseballs
and green lollies'.

While still chuckling over that, he surfed the
categories: Anal Sex, Assassins, Baptist Bible Study,
Bifem Sex, Big Tits, Christ, Cricket Talk, Depressed,
Dog Sex, Hottub, Gay Sheep. But it was hard to be
amused by the considerable amount of information
he found under Bombs. How to make explosives
from all manner of freely available household
products, and 'how to kill teachers and other
people you don't like'.

Nonetheless, provided you don't play with it too
much – because you'll go blind – the Internet is no
more likely to destroy society than it is to save it.
It's probably sensible to remember our favourite
aphorism: data isn't information, information isn't
knowledge, and knowledge isn't wisdom. People
seeking wisdom on the Net will face immense
frustrations because it seems to contain an infinity

of dumpbins full of data, whereas nuggets of wisdom, as in the real world, are few and far between.

There are many who will surf the Net seeking answers to the most tantalising questions that humans have ever asked. Where do we come from, why are we here? Others, like us, are more interested in humour. Where do the flies go in the winter time? What happens to the picture when you turn off the television set?

We've often wondered where jokes came from. Some years ago we discovered that many were coming from the Internet. For example, when a space shuttle exploded, killing all on board, it was an Internet wit who immediately proffered the suggestion that NASA stood for 'Need Another Seven Astronauts?' So we went searching and found that, indeed, a great many members of the Internet, mostly American, mostly young and mostly male, are exchanging or creating jokes in little collectives, by raising a topic and asking for contributions.

Take a phenomenon like the Blonde joke. Someone types a few examples on the screen and issues an open invitation. Soon you can scroll through thousands of them, of varying quality, as people desperately try to top each other. Ditto for Polish jokes which, rather than Irish jokes, tend to represent America's favourite form of racial bigotry.

It was once observed that the world would one day be thrown off its axis by the weight of *National Geographic* magazines accumulating in North

America. According to our investigations, the accumulated weight of light bulb jokes represents a more urgent threat. As long as they stay in the Net we may survive, but God help us if too many people print hard copies.

Years ago, an American documentary film on automation revealed that all the light globes in America are manufactured by a total of four people. Now the Internet demonstrates that a great many people are employed, if not gainfully, on the manufacture of light bulb jokes. Whilst only four people might make the bulbs, millions are involved in changing them.

If you judge the unpopularity of a profession by the number of jokes on the Net, lawyers have a major image problem. It would be possible to fill a far thicker book than this with nothing but lawyer jokes, closely followed by attacks on economists and, inevitably, on politicians. And particularly on the Clintons. The anti-Clinton jokes are legion and, by and large, unfunny. Surprisingly, many more are directed at Hillary than at Bill, confirming that right-wingers tend to be misogynists. Sadly, almost as many are aimed at the hapless Chelsea. Whilst the mother is accused of everything from lesbianism to murder, the jokes at the expense of the child emphasise her alleged ugliness and almost invariably involve incest in or around the Oval Office.

We are astonished by the number of attacks on, of all things, viola players. Why this harmless, if not mellifluous-sounding instrument is deemed so vile, we do not know. But the weight of evidence – a total of 2000 jokes, at last count, attacking the instrument and those who play it – reveals a new dimension of bigotry. A popular folksong tells us that there will soon be ten million lawyers in the US, so there are plenty of opportunities for unhappy, abrasive encounters with the profession. But viola players? One doubts that there could be more than 10000 viola players in the US. After all, if you were to multiply the number of viola players in your average symphony orchestra by the number of symphony orchestras in the US, you'd get, at best, a few hundred. In per capita terms, therefore, viola players are many times less popular than attorneys.

Other popular targets include engineers, IBM and Bill Gates. Presumably a majority of cyberpunks are Apple users, which explains why they get so acrimonious about IBM's acronym. The initials are held to signify many a dangerous notion: Insolence Breeds Mediocrity, Institute of Broken Minds, Incredible Bunch of Muffinheads, etc. Microsoft comes a close second, with Bill Gates more demonised than Saddam Hussein.

Mostly, however, Internet jokes are just jokes. They represent the usual attempts to exorcise the normal range of fears and anxieties. Jokes are principally a method of coping with things that embarrass or frighten us – women, sex, race, religion, mortality, flatulence, old age, the penis. Tell a joke and you're almost certainly revealing an anxiety. They confirm what we discovered when compiling *The Penguin Book of Australian Jokes* – that most jokes are global jokes, endlessly localised. Thus a Clinton joke becomes a Howard joke becomes a Blair joke becomes a Yeltsin joke.

Yes, there were daily updates on the O.J. Simpson trial, but these tended to have a half-life of a half-hour. Whilst they could be noted, there wasn't much point in including them. In any case, almost all of them, like almost all the celebrity jokes, are libellous.

More interesting are the little get-togethers of electronic tribes, sub-cultures who tell jokes in secret languages. We discovered a number of jokes being circulated by pilots, airline and private, concerning air traffic controllers, aviation authorities, and cockpit error. Apart from being highly alarming to nervous fliers, they're often so jargon-ridden as to be incomprehensible.

Nuns, penguins and gorillas retain their popularity on the Internet, but we hadn't expected tens of thousands of jokes about elephants, and particularly the social relationships between elephants and ants. Nor had we expected the Net to be such a rich source of aphorisms and canonical lists.

More in line with the known demographics of Net users are the thousands of pages on *Star Trek*. The numbers of Internet users who double as trekkies is astonishing.

Given that America is a born-again culture, that a majority – indeed a moral majority – of Americans are regular churchgoers, we shouldn't have been surprised by the popularity of Heaven jokes. We're not sure how difficult it is for a camel to pass through the eye of a needle – or how hard it'd be for the very rich Bill Gates to pass through the

Pearly Gates – but it's easy to find hundreds of jokes about St Peter vetting new arrivals. We were reminded of the recent rumour on the Net that Microsoft had bought the Vatican – a story so persistent that the corporation had to issue a denial. The Vatican chose to remain silent.

Perhaps this preoccupation with Heaven links back to the aesthetics of *Star Trek*, a program that always looked a tad Pearly-Gatish. Here was the future imagined in terms of a classical past. How odd that so many distant galaxies were populated by people dressed in togas who wandered amongst plaster rocks and doric columns whilst orating like bad Shakespearean actors. Perhaps Heaven is just another cosmic destination for trekkies to visit.

Access, Auspac, Bandwidth, Bulletin board, Chameleon, Click, cracking, cross post, domain name, downstream, e-mail, incription, file, finger, format, freeware, hacking, hypertext, interface, internaut, load, log in, modem, MOO, navigate, password, ping, port, route, scrollback, server, session, site, tyre-kicker, upstream, vandal, vehicle, visit, WWW, zip, zippie: the Internet already has its own language, thousands of words used as code or shorthand by its passionate citizens. This language is rapidly invading standard English and will soon add to the 10000 Americanisms that have recently found their way into *The Oxford English Dictionary*.

So, like television, like cinema, like rock 'n' roll, like rap, like country and western, like the jargon of the junkie, the Internet is, thus far, just another north American culture that is busy colonising the planet. And us. Let us hope that in time the Net does become truly global. But for the time being this global phenomenon, like Marshall McLuhan's Global Village, has an American address. Whatever the Internet's strength, that remains, for us, its weakness.

DUMB AND DUMBER

A painting contractor was discussing a job with a woman. In the first room she said she'd like a pale blue. The contractor wrote this down, went to the window, opened it and yelled out, 'Green side up.' In the second room she told the painter she'd like a soft yellow. He wrote this on his pad and went to the window, opened it and yelled, 'Green side up.' In the third room she asked for a warm rose colour. The painter wrote this down, walked to the window, opened it and yelled, 'Green side up.' The lady then asked him why he kept yelling green side up. 'I'm sorry,' came the reply, 'but I have a crew of blondes laying turf across the street.'

There was a middle-aged man called Steve who decided to return to college to pursue a degree. Not being sure of what he wanted to take, he began to look around campus at all the different colleges. He saw the college of physics, the college of sociology, the college of psychology and the college of assuming. Having never heard of a college of assuming, Steve was puzzled.

While he stood there pondering what it was, the Dean of the college happened by and inquired if he could help. Steve replied, 'I've never heard of the college of assuming. What is it?'

'Well, I'm the Dean of the college. Here in the college of assuming, we take assumption to a new art form,' said the Dean.

'I still don't understand,' replied Steve.

'Let's try this. Can I assume you have a dog?' asked the Dean.

'Why, yes, I do have a dog,' replied Steve.

'And can I assume that you have a backyard for your dog to play in?' inquired the Dean. 'Why yes, I do have a backyard for my dog,' said Steve.'

'Okay, and can I further assume that because you have a backyard you also have a house?' said the Dean.

'Why yes, I do have a house,' said Steve, beginning to be amazed.

'Now, because you have a house and a dog, and a backyard, can I then assume that you have a wife?' said the Dean flatly.

'That's amazing! Yes, I do have a wife,' said Steve.

'Then because you have a wife, can I assume you are not gay?' inquired the Dean.

'No, I'm not gay,' replied Steve.

'There you see,' stated the Dean. 'From the simple fact of assuming you had a dog, I was able to assume you had a house with a backyard, a wife, and you are not gay.'

24

Clearly amazed, Steve enrolled in the class of assumptions. One day about three weeks later, while waiting for class to start, Steve saw a very puzzled man in the halls. 'Can I help you?' inquired Steve.

'Why yes,' replied the man. 'What is the college of assuming?'

Delighted, Steve replied, 'The college of assuming takes assumption to a new art form.'

'I'm not sure I understand,' replied the man.

'Well, let me give you an example,' said Steve. 'Do you own a dog?'

'Well no,' replied the man.

Steve quickly stepped back and said, 'You fag!'

The heaviest element known to science was recently discovered by university physicists. The element, tentatively named Administratium (Ad), has no protons or electrons, which means that it has an atomic number 0 and falls outside the natural patterns exhibited by other elements. However, it does have one neutron, 125 assistants to the neutron, 75 vice neutrons and 111 assistants to the vice neutrons. This gives it an atomic mass of 312. The 312 particles are held together by a force involving the continuous exchange of meson-like particles, called 'memos'. Because it has no protons or electrons, Administratium is inert. Nonetheless, it can be detected chemically, in that it seems to impede every reaction in which it is present. According to one of the discoverers, even a small amount of Administratium makes one reaction which normally lasts less than a second take more than four days. Administratium has a half-life of approximately three years. It does not actually decay. Instead, it undergoes a reorganisation in which a vice neutron, assistants to the vice neutron and certain assistants to the neutron exchange places. Some studies have indicated that its mass actually increases after each reorganisation, although this is yet to be explained. Another phenomenon which has been observed, as expected from the mechanics of minute particles, is that the more one tries to pin down the positions of vice neutrons within the structure of Administratium, the more uncertain those positions become.

Within a short time of the discovery being announced, the existence of the element was confirmed in laboratories around the world. In addition, a team at the University of Utah told a press conference they had been able to create Administratium in fusion experiments conducted at room temperature. Using highly sophisticated probability detectors, the team had Polak-monitored a stream of memos from a fax-mounted device. Dr May B. No and her associate, Dr May B. Yes, said the details of their experiment were being kept confidential, pending further development of the data. But, they claimed, there were definitely more memos that came out of the device than went in!

A city fella takes a ride in the country and heads

along the highway in his soft-top BMW. He turns off and drives along a dirt road in the middle of nowhere and, after a while, comes across a farmer driving a tractor. And the damndest thing – the farmer wasn't wearing any pants.

'Hey, how come you're not wearing trousers?'

'Well, city boy, the other day I went out aworking in the fields and I plum forgot t' wear me shirt. Got back home that night and m' neck was stiffer than an oakwood board. So this here's my wife's idea.'

A student walks into a car showroom and after a long talk with a salesman, he picks the car he wants to buy.

'Do you have the cash to pay for it, sir, or will you be making a hire-purchase agreement?'

'I'll buy it on HP, thanks.'

So the student dictates his details to the salesman, who fills in the HP application. Then, to the salesman's astonishment, he signs at the bottom of the form with a big cross and a little cross.

'What're these crosses?'

'Well, the big cross is my name and the little cross is "BSc Agriculture".'

A guy walks into a bar, approaches the bartender and says, 'I've been working on a top secret project on molecular genetics for the past five years and

I've just got to talk to someone about it.'

The bartender says, 'Okay, but before we talk about that, just answer me a few questions. When a deer defecates, why does it come out in little pellets?' The guy doesn't know. The bartender then asks, 'Why is it that when a dog poops, it lands on the ground and looks like a coiled rope?' The guy has no idea. So the bartender says, 'You don't know shit! And you want to talk about molecular genetics?'

Smitty is interviewing for a new bartender. He asks one guy applying for the job how he became interested in tending bar.

'Actually,' says the guy, 'I learned to appreciate the value of mixing drinks when I was a forest ranger. Before I went off into the wilderness on my first assignment, my fellow rangers gave me a farewell party. As a going-away gift, they gave me a martini-making kit, a bottle of gin, vermouth, a mixer, a stirrer, and a bottle of olives. I was confused. Why would I need a martini set in the woods? A more experienced ranger set me straight: you'll find this to be the most important piece of equipment you have. You might be out there in the wilderness totally alone for weeks, maybe months. Soon you'll remember your martini set. You'll take it out and begin to make yourself a martini, and within 30 seconds there will be someone at your side saying, 'That's not the way to make a martini ...'

A man walks into a pub with a giraffe on a lead. 'I'll have a pint of Guinness,' says the man, 'and ten pints for the giraffe.'

The man then starts to down his pint in one go. The giraffe sees this and starts banging down the ten pints like there's no tomorrow. The race is on, the man gets halfway down and the giraffe's only on number four. Then, with an amazing burst of speed, the giraffe just manages to scrape ahead. But on pint number ten the giraffe gets halfway then collapses dead on the bar. The man promptly finishes his pint and starts to leave. 'Hey,' says the barman, 'you can't leave that lyin' there!' Says the man, 'It's not a lion, it's a giraffe.'

A blonde walked into a hair salon and insisted that the stylist cut around the earphones of her Walkman. The stylist did as she asked.

About a month later, the blonde returned to have her hair styled again. Again, the stylist was told to cut around her earphones.

This happened for months on end. Finally, the hairstylist couldn't contain his curiosity so, while giving the blonde a haircut, he pulled the earphones off. Whereupon the blonde fell to the floor stone dead. The paramedics arrived and took the body away. The hairstylist lifted the earphones to hear what she'd been listening to. He put them on and heard: 'Inhale ... exhale ... inhale ... exhale ...'

Why were blondes made 10 per cent smarter than cows?

So when you squeeze their tits they don't shit on your face.

Three blondes were walking along a beach when they found an old oil lamp made of brass. They rubbed it and, lo and behold, a genie appeared. 'I am the genie of the lamp. I can give each of you as much intelligence as you desire,' said the genie.

'Oh my,' cried the first blonde, 'I guess I would like to be 100 times smarter than I am now!' ZAP. The genie turned her into a brunette.

'Well,' said the second blonde, 'I don't think I need to be that smart. I'd like to be about ten times smarter than I am now.' ZAP. The genie turned her into a redhead.

'Gee,' said the third blonde, 'I think I'm just about okay the way I am. I get a lot of attention and men seem to like me. I guess if anything I'd like to be ten times dumber than I am now.' ZAP. The genie turned her into a *man*.

Why did the blonde get fired from the M&M factory?

She kept throwing away all the Ws.

What's black, blue, red and brown and lies in a gutter?

A brunette who's told too many blonde jokes.

A blonde was tired of hearing blonde jokes and decided to prove people wrong. She spent weeks studying a map of the United States, memorising all the capitals for all the states. The next time someone started telling a blonde joke she said, 'Hey, not all blondes are stupid. I can prove it. Give me the name of any state and I'll tell you its capital.'

'Vermont,' someone suggested.

'V.'

How do you change a blonde's mind?

Blow in her ear.

How do you measure a blonde's intelligence?

Stick a tyre pressure gauge in her ear.

How do you keep a blonde busy all day?

Put her in a round room and tell her to sit in the corner.

How do you get a blonde to marry you?
    Tell her she's pregnant.
What will she ask you?
    'Is it mine?'

How can you steal a blonde's window seat?
    Tell her the seats that are going to London are all in the middle row.

Why is a blonde like Australia?
    They're both down under, and no one cares.

What do you give the blonde who has everything?
    Penicillin.

Why do blondes wear panties?
    To keep their ankles warm.

What's the difference between a blonde and a brick?
    When you lay a brick it doesn't follow you around for two weeks whining.

How can you tell when a blonde reaches orgasm?
She drops her nail file.

How does a blonde commit suicide?
She gathers her clothes into a pile and jumps off.

How does a blonde get pregnant?
And I thought blondes were dumb.

What's the difference between a chorus line of
blondes and a magician?
A magician has a cunning array of stunts.

Why do blondes hate M&Ms?
They're too hard to peel.

What job function does a blonde have in an
M&M factory?
Proof-reading.

Why can't blondes make Coolade?
Because they can't fit eight cups of water into the little packet.

How do you keep a blonde in suspense?
I'll tell you tomorrow.

What happens when a blonde gets Alzheimers?
Her IQ goes up.

Why can't blondes make ice-cubes?
They forget the recipe.

Did you hear about the blonde whose boyfriend said he loved her?
She believed him.

Did you hear about the blonde who robbed a bank?
She tied up the safe and blew the guard.

How many blondes does it take to play hide and seek?
One.

What's the difference between a blonde and a trampoline?
You take off your shoes before using a trampoline.

Why do blondes like lightning?
They think someone is taking their picture.

Why do blondes drive BMWs?
Because they can spell them.

What does the postcard from a blonde on holiday say?
'Having a wonderful time. Where am I?'

Why don't blondes make good pharmacists?
They can't get the bottle into the typewriter.

What do you get when you offer a blonde a penny for her thoughts?
    Change.

What do a blonde and President Gorbachev have in common?
    They both got fucked by ten men whilst on holiday.
What's the difference between a blonde and President Gorbachev?
    He knows who the ten men were.

Why does a blonde keep a coathanger on her back seat?
    In case she locks her keys in the car.

What did the blonde call her pet zebra?
    Spot.

Why are there no dumb brunettes?
    Peroxide.

What's a blonde's favourite nursery rhyme?
Humpme Dumpme.

A blonde went to a library and checked out a
book called *How to Hug*. She got back home and
found it was volume seven of the encyclopaedia.

A cop stops a blonde woman who's driving down
a motorway.
    'Miss, may I see your driver's licence please?'
    'Driver's licence, what's that?'
    'It's a little card with your picture on it.'
    'Oh, duh! Here it is.'
    'May I have your car insurance?'
    'What's that?'
    'It's a document that says you're allowed to drive
the car.'
    'Oh, this! Duh! Here you go.'
    The cop then unzips his trousers and the blonde
goes, 'Oh no, not another breathalyzer test.'

Two blondes are walking through the woods. One
looks down and says, 'Look at the deer tracks.' The
other blonde looks and says, 'Those aren't deer
tracks, those are wolf tracks.' 'No, those are deer
tracks.' They keep arguing and arguing and ten
minutes later they're both killed by a train.

A blonde is telling a priest a joke that is both dirty and Polish. Halfway through the priest interrupts her. 'Don't you know I'm a priest? And that I'm Polish?'

'Oh, I'm sorry,' the blonde apologises, 'do you want me to start over and talk slower?'

A young blonde is asked out on a date. The boy picks her up and they go to a nearby carnival. They ride a few rides, play a few games and seem to be hitting it off. During a sort of romantic lull, the boy says, 'What do you want to do now?'

'I want a weigh,' she says. Well, okay, thinks the boy. They walk over to the fortune scales and weigh her. They play a few more games and stop for food. 'What do you want to do now?' asks the boy again.

'I want a weigh,' she says. Mmm, a little odd, but I'll go along with it, the boy thinks. Again they get her weight and fortune.

After a few more games and a marvellous fireworks show, the boy repeats, 'What do you want to do now?'

'I want a weigh,' she says. Damn, thinks the boy, she's just too weird for me. They get her weight and fortune again and the boy drives her home.

As she walks into the house her sister says, 'How did your date go?'

'Wousy,' says the girl.

A young businessman rented a beautiful office and furnished it with antiques. But no business was coming in. Sitting there, worrying, he saw a man come into the outer office. Wanting to look busy, he picked up the phone and pretended he was negotiating a big deal. He spoke loudly about big figures and huge commitments. Finally he hung up and asked the visitor, 'Can I help you?'

The man said, 'I've come to install the phone.'

Jack and Jill have both been perfect employees, much valued by the company. Owing to the downturn in business, one of them has to go. But which one? The boss decides on a plan. He'll watch Jack closely for a day and, having monitored his performance, will similarly monitor Jill's. Then he'll make the decision.

The next day, Jack arrives early, works hard all morning and doesn't even take time off for a pee. He skips lunch and works very, very hard all afternoon. There are no private phone calls, no coffee breaks, and he leaves around 7 p.m.

'If they're both such diligent workers,' thinks the boss, 'the choice will be very hard indeed.'

Next morning, Jill comes in half an hour late complaining of a headache. She pops some aspirin, hangs around the water fountain talking to her friends, takes a very long coffee break, leaves early for lunch, comes back late, makes lots of private phone calls, and bores all her colleagues by telling them how miserable she feels. Then she takes some more aspirin and leaves around 4 p.m.

Next morning the boss calls her into his office. He says, 'Jill, you know I have to either lay you or Jack off.'

She says, 'Well, you're going to have to jack off because I've got a headache.'

Three blondes were attempting to change a light bulb. One of them decided to call 911.

BLONDE: We need help. We're three blondes changing a light bulb.

OPERATOR: Hmm. You put in a fresh bulb?

BLONDE: Yes.

OPERATOR: The power in the house is on?

BLONDE: Of course.

OPERATOR: And the switch is on?

BLONDE: Yes, yes.

OPERATOR: And the bulb still won't light up?

BLONDE: No, it's working fine.

OPERATOR: Then what's the problem?

BLONDE: We got dizzy spinning the ladder around and we all fell and hurt ourselves.

A young man gets a job as a circus roustabout. The circus owner, thinking he might be able to recruit him as an assistant lion tamer, takes him to the practice cage. The head lion tamer, a beautiful young woman, was just starting her rehearsal. As she entered the cage, she removed her cape with a flourish and, standing in a gorgeous abbreviated costume, motioned to one of the lions. It crept towards her, licked her knees and rolled over twice.

'Well,' said the owner to the young man, 'think you could do that?'

'I'm sure I could, sir,' said the young man, 'but you'll have to get that lion out of there.'

A young bloke started work in a supermarket. First day, a customer asked him if she could buy half a grapefruit. He excused himself to ask the manager. 'Some ratbag out there wants to buy half a grapefruit,' he began, only to see that the customer had entered the office behind him, 'and this lovely lady would like to buy the other half.'

Impressed with the way the clerk had resolved the problem, the manager later asked him, 'Where are you from?'

'Lancaster, Pennsylvania,' replied the clerk, 'home of ugly women and great hockey teams.'

'Yes? My wife is from Lancaster,' said the manager menacingly. And the clerk asked, 'What team was she on?'

Two male engineering students meet on campus. One says, 'Hi, where'd you get the new bike?'

'Well, I was walking to class the other day when a

pretty co-ed rode up, jumped off it, took off all her clothes and said, "You can have anything you want!" '

'Right,' said his friend, 'her clothes probably wouldn't have fit you anyway.'

One morning Daddy Bear came down to breakfast, to find his porridge bowl empty. 'Somebody's been eating my porridge,' said Daddy Bear.

'Someone's been eating my porridge!' said Baby Bear.

At that moment Mummy Bear came out of the kitchen and said, 'You stupid bastards. I haven't made it yet!'

On his first date with a beautiful woman, a bloke decided to impress her with his abilities in wine tasting. He told the wine steward to bring a bottle of 1985 Sterling Cabernet Sauvignon from the Cameros district vineyard. Upon tasting it, the young man berated the wine steward. 'No, no, no! This is a 1987 vintage from the North Coast vineyards near Calistoga. Please bring me exactly what I ordered.'

The second bottle was poured and, once again, the man was very annoyed. 'No, no, no! This is 1985 all right, but it's from the Mount Helena vineyards!'

Watching the drama from the bar, an old drunk

staggered over to the couple's table and said, 'Wow! That's an impressive ability you've got. Can you tell me what's in this glass?'

Not wanting to pass up an opportunity to impress, the man sipped at the drunk's glass. 'Christ, that tastes like piss,' he yelled as he spat the mouthful out.

'That's right!' exclaimed the drunk. 'Now tell me where I was born and how old I am.'

A girl comes home from her first semester at college. She yells, 'Mom, Mom, I've got a case of VD.'

'Put it in the cellar,' says her mother, 'your old man will drink anything.'

A piece of bacon and a sausage are in a frying pan being cooked. The sausage says, 'It's hot in here, isn't it!' and the bacon replies, 'Wow! A talking sausage!'

A bloke walks into a very expensive cake shop, goes up to the counter and asks for a donut. The assistant picks up a pair of elegant silver tongs, retrieves a donut and places it on a doiley.

The customer is impressed. 'That's very hygienic – using a pair of tongs.'

'Oh yes sir, this is a very clean shop.'

'Well, in that case I'll have a chocolate éclair as well.'

Once again the assistant picks up the silver tongs and retrieves a chocolate éclair, placing it on a paper doiley. While he's doing this the customer notices a piece of string sticking out of the assistant's trousers. 'What's the string for?'

'Well sir, it's such a hygienic shop that when I go to the toilet I mustn't touch my penis. So I pull it out with the string.'

The customer thinks about this for a moment and asks, 'How do you put it back again?'

'Oh, that's easy,' says the assistant, 'I use the tongs.'

A guy in a restaurant says to the waiter, 'I'd like the fried lobster with french fries and broccoli.' The waiter says, 'Sorry, sir, we have no broccoli.'

'Never mind,' says the bloke, 'I'll have the roast duck, roast potatoes, cabbage and broccoli.'

The waiter says, 'Sir, we have no broccoli today.'

'In that case, I'll have the chicken, sprouts, the carrots and broccoli.'

'Listen sir, how do you spell dog, as in dogmatic?'

'D-O-G.'

'How do you spell cat, as in catastrophe?'

'C-A-T.'

'How do you spell fuck, as in broccoli?'

'There's no FUCK in BROCCOLI!'

'That's what I've been telling you for the past ten minutes, you stupid git.'

A guy was stuck on a desert island for years. Then, from the depths of the ocean, came a stunning dark-haired beauty equipped with scuba gear. She walked slowly, voluptuously, up to the guy and asked very softly, 'Would you like a cigarette?' His eyes filled with wonder as he answered, 'Sure.' She unzipped a pocket on the sleeve of her wetsuit, pulled out a pack of cigarettes and a light. She offered him a cigarette, took one herself and lit them both.

As they smoked their cigarettes, she asked, 'Would you like a martini?' 'Wow! Yes,' he responded with immense enthusiasm. So she unzipped another pocket, pulled out a shaker of martinis, a couple of glasses and poured them both a drink.

She watched him as he sipped the drink and, with a breathtakingly beautiful smile, whispered into his ear, 'Would you like to play around?'

Amazed at his good fortune, he said, 'You've got to be kidding! You've got golf clubs in there, too?'

After a long day on the course the exasperated golfer turned to his caddy and said, 'You must be the absolute worst caddy in the world.'

'No, I don't think so,' said the caddy. 'That would be too much of a coincidence.'

A lady goes into a hardware shop and asks for a hinge. The man at the counter gets one and asks, 'Do you want a screw for that hinge?'

The lady says, 'No, but I'll blow ya for that toaster over there.'

Juan and Jose were shopping for horses. When they'd each found the horse they wanted, they were in a quandary.

'How will we tell which horse is yours and which is mine?' asked Jose.

'I know. You crop your horse's ears and I'll leave mine as they are,' answered Juan.

'No, that would hurt the horse.'

'Okay. I'll cut my horse's tail and you keep your horse's tail long.'

'Nooo! Horses need their tails long to brush flies off.'

'I know. Branding! I'll put a big X on the rear of my horse. And you put a big Y on yours.'

'No, no. My horse is too beautiful to mark up like that.'

'I've got it,' said Jose. 'You take the black one. I'll take the white one.'

A guy walks into a bar and sits down on the barstool. 'Hey, barthendther, gifth me a beer.' The bartender walks over with a tall cool one. 'Here'sth your beer.'

The other guy sits up straight. 'Heey, you're imithating mee.'

'No, I talk thith way too.'

'Okay, I guesth itth okay.'

Later, a big burly guy walks in and sits down at the other end of the bar. 'Yo, bartender. Gimme a beer.' The bartender responds, 'One beer comin' up, man.'

The little guy gets ticked off and yells, 'Heey, you were imithathing mee!' The bartender comes over close and replies, 'No, I wasth imithathing the other guy.'

Why do farts smell?

For the benefit of the deaf.

Do you know what mothballs smell like?

Yes.

Really. How do you get their little legs apart?

Why did the couple stop after three children?

Because they read that every fourth child born is Chinese.

What is bright orange and sounds like a parrot?

A carrot.

What's the difference between a university and a polytechnic.

At a polytechnic they teach you to wash your hands after going to the toilet. At a university they teach you not to piss on your hands in the first place.

Many an American tourist around Windsor Castle has been heard asking, 'Why did they build it so close to the airport?'

ENGLISH TOURIST: Hello. Do you farm around here?

CORNISH FARMER: Aye.

ENGLISH TOURIST: Fantastic day, isn't it?

CORNISH FARMER: Aye.

ENGLISH TOURIST: Have you lived here all your life?

CORNISH FARMER: Not yet.

Going through his wife's bedroom drawers, a farmer discovered three soya beans and an envelope containing $30 in cash. He confronted his wife, who promptly confessed. 'Darling, over the years I haven't been completely faithful to you. But when I do fool around, I put a soya bean in the drawer to remind myself of my indiscretion.'

The farmer admitted that he hadn't always been faithful either and, therefore, was inclined to forgive and forget a few moments of weakness. 'Where did the $30 come from?' he asked.

'Oh that,' his wife replied. 'When soya beans hit $10 a bushell, I sold out.'

A ham sandwich walked into a bar, ordered a drink and the bartender said, 'No, we don't serve food here.'

man entered a barber shop and said, 'I'm sick of looking like everyone else. I want to be different. Give me a part from ear to ear!'

'Are you certain?'

'Absolutely,' said the man.

The barber did what he was told and the satisfied customer left the shop.

Three hours later he came back. 'Put it back the way it was,' he said.

'What's the matter?' asked the barber, 'are you tired of being a non-conformist already?'

'No,' he replied, 'but I'm tired of people whispering in my nose.'

n English tourist is on holiday in a Cornish village when he spots what is obviously the village idiot sitting next to the horse trough. In his hand is an old stick, and tied to the end is a piece of string which is dangling in the water. The tourist decides to humour the fellow and asks, 'Have you caught anything yet?' The village idiot looks up and studies the stranger before saying, 'Aye, you be the seventh today.'

Three vampires walk into a bar and order drinks. The first vampire asks for Blood. The second vampire asks for a Blood Light. The third vampire asks for some hot water. The bartender is baffled. 'Why don't you want Blood, like everyone else?' 'Because,' says the vampire, pulling out a tampon, 'I'm making tea.'

INTERSEX

How do you know when a female yuppie achieves orgasm?

She drops her briefcase.

A woman decides to buy a new cupboard, one of those you have to assemble yourself. Back home she reads the instructions very carefully and manages to assemble the cupboard in the bedroom. It looks great. Then a train passes and the damn thing collapses. Undaunted, she rereads the instructions and reassembles the cupboard. Another train passes and the cupboard collapses again. Convinced she's doing something wrong, she rereads the instructions and reassembles the cupboard. A train passes and the cupboard collapses for the third time. Finally, fed up, she calls the store and is told they'll send along a technician to have a look.

The technician arrives and assembles the cupboard. Whereupon a train passes and the cupboard collapses. Baffled by this unexpected event, the techo decides to reassemble the cupboard and sit inside it, to see whether he can find out what causes the cupboard to collapse.

About an hour later the woman's husband comes home, sees the cupboard, says, 'That's a nice looking cupboard,' and opens it. 'You won't believe this,' says the technician, 'but I'm standing here waiting for the train.'

A strikingly handsome man and a very beautiful dark-haired woman were having dinner in a fine restaurant. Their waitress, taking an order at a table a few steps away, noticed that the man had stopped smiling and now had a rigid facial expression. Moreover he was slowly sliding down his chair and under the table. Strangely, his dinner companion seemed unconcerned. The waitress watched fascinated as the man slid all the way down his chair and out of sight under the tablecloth. The woman remained calm and unruffled, apparently unaware that her dining companion had disappeared.

After the waitress had finished taking the order, she approached the table and said to the woman, 'Pardon, M'am, but I think your husband just slipped under the table.'

The woman looked up at her and calmly replied, 'No, he didn't. He just walked in the door.'

A bloke goes into a bar carrying a small box. He asks the bartender. 'If I show you the neatest thing you've ever seen, will you give me a free beer?'

The bartender says, 'Sure, but I've got to warn you, I've seen a *lot* of things in my time.'

'Yeah, but you've never seen anything like this,' says the man, opening the box to reveal a tiny little person at a piano, jamming away. 'He plays Bach, he plays Stravinsky, he plays John Cage, he plays it all.' The bartender is mightily impressed.

'That *is* the neatest thing I've ever seen. Where did you get him?'

'Well, I was walking on the beach, found this brass lamp and rubbed it, and a genie came out and granted me a wish.'

'Do you think I could have a wish, too?' the barman asks.

'Sure,' says the man, producing the lamp from his coat pocket. The bartender gives it a rub, the genie pops out and the bartender says, 'I want a million bucks.' POOF! The bar is full of ducks. They're flying around. They're crapping on everything. They're everywhere.

The bartender screams at the man, 'Why didn't you tell me your genie was defective?'

'Yep, hard of hearing. I didn't ask for a 12-inch pianist, either.'

A prostitute goes into a bar and spots a koala on a stool. They talk, they flirt, and the koala takes her home. After a night of passion the koala climbs out of bed and ambles towards the door. 'Where are you going?' yells the prostitute. 'I haven't been paid.' Suspecting that a koala mightn't understand the nature of her profession, she reaches for a dictionary and shows him the definition. 'Prostitute: n. a woman who performs sexual services for money.' Whereupon the koala grabs the dictionary and shows her a definition: 'Koala Bear: n. a furry marsupial. Eats bush and leaves.'

Elvis, Liberace and John Belushi are sitting around in Heaven bored out of their heavenly lives. They go to Gabriel and ask if there's any way they can get out. Apprehensively he agrees to let them return to Earth for a short while, telling them that if they even think of committing a sin, they'll go straight to Hell.

So, zap, they're on Hollywood Boulevard. As they're walking, Elvis sees a bar. He heads towards the door and the moment he touches it, poof! He's gone. The others realise that Gabriel was serious.

A little while later John Belushi sees a little packet of white powder lying in the gutter. He thinks for a moment and bends over to pick it up. Poof! Liberace disappears.

Why does Mike Tyson cry after sex?
The mace.

Three women were sitting in a bar talking about their lives. The first one said, 'My husband is an architect. When we make love it has power, it has form, it has function. It is incredible!'

The second one said, 'My husband is an artist. When we make love it has passion, it has emotion, it has vision. It's wonderful!'

The third woman sighed and, sipping a marguerita, said, 'My husband works for Microsoft. When we make love, he just sits at the end of the bed and tells me how great it's going to be when it gets here.'

What do you get when you cross a computer with a prostitute?

A fucking know-it-all.

Once upon a time an explorer in a distant land was granted an audience with the king, who was an impressive figure except for one unusual feature – his head. It was tiny, about the size of a grapefruit. After talking with his majesty for some time, the explorer couldn't contain his curiosity a moment longer and asked the royal personage about the size of his cranium.

After a pause, the king explained that he hadn't always been a king and that, in fact, he'd once been a fisherman. One day, whilst pulling in his nets, he found he'd caught a mermaid.

57

'From the waist up, she was a very beautiful woman. From the waist down, a fish. I was preparing to take her to market to sell as a curiosity when she spoke to me and said that she was a magic mermaid. And she said that if I let her go, she would grant me three wishes. I agreed to this and asked for gold, jewels and other riches. Immediately these appeared. Next, I asked to be made a king and have a kingdom to rule, with a great castle. As you can see, this wish was granted.

'The mermaid then asked me what my third wish was. I said I found her very beautiful and that I wanted to make love. She replied that as she was only half woman, this wasn't possible. That's when I made my mistake. "Well, in that case,' I said, 'can you give me a little head?" '

A man rushes into his house and yells at his wife, 'Brenda, pack your things. I've just won the State Lottery.'

Brenda replies, 'Shall I pack for warm weather or cold?'

'I don't care,' says the man, 'just as long as you're out of the house by noon.'

'Well, I was playing golf with my wife. I'd been having a great game but unfortunately she wasn't. On the 15th tee I hit a beautiful shot, 270 metres straight down the fairway. My wife steps up and hits a tremendous slice that leaves the course and lands in the pasture out of bounds. We both went looking for the ball and just as we were about to give up I spotted a glint of white coming from a cow's behind, just under its tail. I lifted the tail to make sure, and then called to my wife saying, 'Here, honey, this looks like yours.' That's the last thing I remember.'

What did the leper say to the prostitute?
You can keep the tip.

Why was the leper caught speeding?
Because he couldn't take his foot off the accelerator.

Two guys want to buy two tickets to Pittsburgh. They go to the ticket counter and notice that the ticket agent is very, very beautiful, with large breasts and prominent nipples. Fixating on them they say, 'We'd like two pickets to Tittsburgh.' Overwhelmed with embarrassment, they run away and don't know what to do. Then they see a priest walking by and explain that, for reasons they can't articulate, they're unable to buy two tickets to Pittsburgh. Can he help them?
He immediately agrees, walks up to the counter

and, like the boys, can't help but notice the magnificent mammary glands and the prominent nipples. Nonetheless he manages to say, 'I'd like to buy two tickets to Pittsburgh.'

The woman behind the counter asks, 'And how would you like your change?' He says, 'In nipples and dimes.'

The old couple were on a car trip. They stopped at a roadhouse for lunch and the old woman left her glasses on the table. She didn't miss them until they'd been driving for half an hour. The old man complained all the way back to the restaurant. When they finally arrived, as she was climbing out of the car to retrieve her specs, the old man said, 'While you're in there, you may as well get my hat, too.'

The new bride was a bit embarrassed to be identified as a honeymooner. So when she and her new husband pulled up at the motel, she asked him if there was any way they could make it appear they'd been married a long time. 'Sure,' he said, 'you carry the suitcases.'

She left him in bed when the phone rang, and was back in a few seconds. 'Who was it?' he asked.

'My husband,' she replied.

'I better get going,' he said, 'where was he?'

'Relax. He said he was downtown playing poker with you.'

PURSER: I'm sorry Mr Jones, but we left your wife behind in New York.

MR JONES: Thank goodness, I thought I was going deaf.

A young man said to his girlfriend's father, 'I realise this is only a formality, but would you mind if I married your daughter?'

'Who says it's only a formality?' asked the father angrily.

'Her obstetrician,' replied the young man.

A hubby comes home early and finds his wife in bed with another man. 'Who the hell is this?' he demands.

'Good question,' answers the wife. 'Say, fella, what's your name?'

Marriage teaches you loyalty, patience, understanding, perserverence and a lot of other things you wouldn't need if you'd stayed single.

A woman had an artist paint a portrait of her dripping with jewels. 'If I die and my husband remarries,' she explained, 'I want his next wife to go crazy looking for the diamonds.'

A husband and wife go to the fairground. She wants to go on the ferris-wheel but he's too scared, so she goes on it by herself. The wheel goes round and round and suddenly the woman is thrown out and lands in a heap at her husband's feet. 'Are you hurt?' he asks.

'Of course I'm hurt. Three times round and you didn't wave once!'

One evening a husband comes home to his apartment very roughed up. When his wife sees him she asks, 'What happened to you?'

'I got into a fight with the apartment manager.'

'Whatever for?'

'He said he had slept with every woman in the complex except one!'

'Hmmm. I bet it's that snooty Mrs Green on the third floor.'

A businessman called home at noon one day, but the maid answered. When the man asked to speak to his wife, the maid replied, 'She's upstairs in the bedroom entertaining her boyfriend.' After sputtering and fuming for a minute, the businessman asked the maid if she would like to make $100 000 for a few minutes' work. She said, 'Of course. What do I have to do?' He answered, 'Take my shotgun from the closet and shoot the both of them.'

The maid put the phone down. He heard footsteps proceeding upstairs, then two shots rang out. The maid picked up the phone and said, 'Okay, it's done. What shall I do with the bodies?'

The man said, 'Take them out back and throw them into the pool.'

'What pool?' the maid asked.

After a moment of silence, the man said, 'Is this 555 3724?'

MAN A: So, how was your honeymoon?

MAN B: Very good until the morning after waking up. I forgot and said to my wife, 'You are wonderful. Here's $100.'

MAN A: It's not that bad, she might not know that you thought of her as a hooker.

MAN B: I know, but my wife then gave me back $50 and said, 'Here's your change.'

HE: Your birthday is coming up, so I'd like some idea of what you'd like.

SHE: I want a divorce!

HE: I'm really sorry, but I hadn't planned to spend that much.

A young bloke goes on a date with his girlfriend. After some heavy petting in the back of the car, he asks her for oral sex. 'No,' she says, 'you won't respect me.'

After a few months, the young man asks again. Again she says, 'No, you won't respect me.'

Eventually the two get married and the husband says to his bride, 'Okay, we're married now. You know I love you. You know I respect you. Now, please, can I have oral sex?'

'No,' she says, 'I just know that if I do, you won't respect me.'

So he waits and waits and waits. Until, after 30 years of marriage, he says, 'Honey, we've been together for decades. We've raised three fine children. You know that I respect you utterly and completely. So please, please, PLEASE, how about oral sex? Just once.' And she finally gives in.

Afterwards they're lying in bed when the telephone rings. The husband turns to his wife and says, 'Answer that, you cocksucker.'

A bloke gets a rise and decides to buy a new scope for his rifle. He goes to the gun dealer and asks the assistant to show him one. The assistant says, 'This scope is so good that you can see my condo all the way up on that hill.' The man takes a look through the scope and starts laughing.

'What's so funny?' asks the assistant.

'Well, I see a naked man and a naked woman running around the bedroom.'

The assistant grabs the scope from the man and looks through it. Then he hands the customer two bullets and says, 'I'll give you the scope for nothing if you can take these two bullets, shoot my wife's head off and shoot the guy's dick off.'

The customer takes another look through the scope and says, 'You know what? I think I can do that with one shot.'

Two women were walking down the street. One said to the other, 'There's my husband coming out of the florist with a dozen roses. Damn! That means I'm going to have to keep my legs up in the air for three days.'

'Well, why don't you get a vase?'

A husband and wife with small children employed a coding system when discussing sex. The term for intercourse was 'washing machine'.

They were lying in bed one night when the husband turned to his wife and said, as seductively as he could manage, 'Washing machine.' She, being a working parent, was tired and murmured, 'Not tonight, dear.' He rolled away.

Five minutes later he rolled back and murmured, 'Darling, washing machine ... washing machine.' She said, 'I've got a headache.' He rolled away again.

Ten minutes later the wife, feeling guilty, turned to her husband and said, 'Okay, washing machine.'

'That's okay,' he replied, 'it was a small load and I did it by hand.'

Why do men like love at first sight?
It saves them time.

What do you give to a man who has everything?
A woman to show him how to work it.

Why don't men have mid-life crises?
They stay stuck in adolescence.

How does a man show he's planning for the future?
He buys two cases of beer instead of one.

 What makes men chase women they have no intention of marrying?

The same urge that makes dogs chase cars they have no intention of driving.

What do you do with a bachelor who thinks he's God's gift?
Exchange him.

Why are husbands like lawnmowers?
They're hard to get started, emit foul odours, and don't work half the time.

What's the difference between a new husband and a new dog?
After a year, the dog is still excited to see you.

What is the thinnest book in the world?
What men know about women.

How many does it take to screw in a light bulb?
One. Men will screw anything.

What's a man's idea of foreplay?
A half-hour of begging.

How can you tell if a man is sexually excited?
He's breathing.

What's the difference between men and government bonds?
Bonds mature.

How do you save a man from drowning?
Take your foot off his head.

What do men and beer bottles have in common?
They're both empty from the neck up.

How many men does it take to change a roll of toilet paper?
We don't know. It's never happened.

The three stages of sex life of a man:
Tri-weekly. Try-weekly. Try-weakly.

The TV is on the blink, so a woman calls a repairman. Just as he's finished, the woman hears her husband's key in the lock. 'Sorry,' she says to the repairman, 'but you'll have to hide. It's my husband and he's insanely jealous.'

The repairman hides inside the TV console. The husband plops down in his favourite chair to watch some football. Inside the TV, the repairman is all squished up and getting hotter and hotter. Finally, on the verge of suffocation, he climbs out, marches across the room and out the front door.

The husband looks at the TV set, looks at his wife, looks back at the set again and says, 'I didn't see the referee send that guy off the field, did you?'

A man returns early from a business trip to find his wife making passionate love to a total stranger in their bedroom.

Goggle-eyed, he asks, 'What on earth are you doing?'

The wife turns to the other man and says, 'See, I told you he was as dumb as a post.'

God created man before creating woman, because you need a rough draft before you create a masterpiece.

Man says to God, 'God, why did you make woman so beautiful?'

God says, 'So you would love her.'

'But God,' the man says, 'why did you make us so dumb?'

God replies, 'So she would love you.'

A woman was chatting with her neighbour. 'I feel really great today. You see, I started out this morning with an act of unselfish generosity. I gave a $5 bill to a bum.'

'You gave a bum $5? That's a lot of money to give away like that. What did your husband say about that?'

'Thanks.'

'I heard you just got married again.'

'Yes, for the fourth time.'

'What happened to your first three wives?'

'They all died.'

'How did that happen?'

'My first wife ate poison mushrooms.'

'How awful! And your second?'

'She ate poison mushrooms.'

'And your third? She ate poison mushrooms, too?'

'No, she died of a broken neck.'

'An accident?'

'Not exactly. She wouldn't eat her mushrooms.'

A semi-trailer driver stops to pick up a woman hitchhiking. The driver opens the door and says, 'Climb in. I'm not like the other truckies that only let the good-looking girls have a ride.'

'My boyfriend and I aren't compatible. I'm a Virgo and he's an arsehole.'

A man parked his car in a supermarket carpark and was walking past an empty cart when he heard a woman ask, 'Mister, are you using that cart?'

'No,' he answered, 'I'm only after one thing.'

As he walked towards the store, she murmured, 'Typical male.'

A priest and a nun were returning from the church convention when their car broke down.

They had it towed to a garage and faced the fact that they'd have to spend the night in a motel. There was only one motel in town and it only had one room available. So they had a problem.

'Sister,' said the priest, 'I don't think the Lord would mind, under the circumstances, if we spent the night together in this one room. I'll sleep on the couch and you take the bed.'

'I think that would be okay,' said the nun.

They prepared for bed and each one took their agreed place. Ten minutes later the sister said, 'Father, I'm terribly cold.'

'Okay,' said the priest, 'I'll get up and get you a blanket from the closet.'

Ten minutes later the nun said, 'Father, I'm still terribly cold.'

'Okay, Sister,' said the priest, 'I'll get up and get you another blanket.'

Ten minutes later, the nun said, 'Father, I'm still terribly cold. I don't think the Lord would mind if we acted as man and wife for just this one night.'

'You're probably right,' said the priest. 'Get up and get your own damn blanket.'

A bloke was walking his pet duck when he decided to go and see a new Bruce Willis movie. But the lady at the box office said that he couldn't take the duck inside, so he walked around the corner and put the duck inside his raincoat. Safely inside, he squeezed into the only vacant seat, beside a married couple. About half an hour later the wife whispered to her husband, 'Funny, this guy next to me ... his fly's open.'

Her husband replied, 'Well, is that the first time you've seen a man's pants unzipped?'

'No, honey, but ... his thing is sticking out!'

Her husband said, 'Well, is that the first time you saw a man's penis?'

'No,' she screamed, 'but it's the first one I ever saw eating popcorn.'

A woman is in bed with her boyfriend while her husband's at work. Suddenly she hears his car in the driveway. She yells at the boyfriend, 'Quick! Grab your clothes and jump out the window.'

The boyfriend looks out the window and says, 'I can't jump out the window! It's raining like hell!'

She says, 'If my husband catches us in here, he'll kill both of us.'

So the boyfriend grabs his clobber, jumps out the window and finds himself in the middle of a charity marathon. He starts running alongside the others, in the nude, carrying his clothes on his arm. One of the runners asks him, 'Do you always run in the nude?'

He answers, 'Oh yes, it feels so free having the air blow over your skin.'

Another runner then asks the nude man, 'Do you always run carrying your clothes on your arm?'

The nuddy answers breathlessly, 'Oh yes, that way I can get dressed at the end of the run, climb in my car and go home.'

A third runner then asks, 'Do you always wear a condom when you're running?'

The nuddy answers, 'Only if it's raining.'

An old bloke is interested in joining a nudists' colony and gets permission to just wander around the grounds to decide if it's right for him. So he strips and goes for a walk. After a while he gets tired and decides to relax on a bench. A beautiful woman walks by and the sight of her causes him to become excited. The woman, noticing his erection, goes over and performs oral sex. The man is thrilled. He hurries back to the office and says he wants to join immediately and pays the first year's dues. He then lights up a cigar and goes out for another walk. While walking, he drops his cigar, bends over to pick it up and a young man runs up and performs anal sex. The old bloke immediately returns to the office and cancels his membership. 'But why?' asks the reception. 'You just said this was one of the greatest places you'd ever visited.'

'Yes,' says the old bloke, 'but at my age I only get excited once every three months, and I'm always dropping my cigar.'

The French Health Ministry invested a million francs in a research project to find out why the male penis has a head on it. They concluded that it gives the woman more pleasure.

The Germans, not to be outdone, spent five million deutschmarks on their own research. They concluded that the shape is intended to give the man more pleasure.

The Americans decided to lay the issue to rest. They spent ten dollars and concluded that the head is there to keep your hand from sliding off.

A bloke walks into a doctor's office complaining about a little bump on his forehead. It started small but it's getting bigger by the day. 'I don't know what it is, we'll scan it and in two weeks you can phone me for the results,' says the doctor.

He phones the doctor two weeks later, who tells him that he'd better come into the office because the prognosis isn't great. The man drags himself there with shoes of lead and asks the doctor to give it to him straight.

'You're growing a dick on your forehead.'

The man asks the doctor if it can do any harm.

'No,' the doctor continues, 'of course it's not cosmetically attractive but don't worry. In eight weeks you won't be able to see it any more.'

'Do you mean it will fall off by then?'

'No, it won't fall off. But by then your scrotum will be hanging over your eyes.'

A young man went into a drug store to buy a condom. The pharmacist told him that condoms come in packs of three, nine or 12 and asks which the young man wants. 'Well,' he said, 'I've been seeing this girl for a while and she's really hot. I want the condoms because I think tonight's the night. We've having dinner with her parents and then we're going out. And I've got a feeling I'm going to get lucky. So you better give me the 12-pack.'

The young man paid for his purchase and left. Later that evening he sat down to dinner with his girlfriend and her parents. He asked if he might give the blessing, and they agreed. He began the prayer and continued praying for about ten minutes. The girl lent over and said, 'You never told me you were such a religious person.' He lent over to her and said, 'And you never told me that your father was a pharmacist.'

A golfer encountered a genie and was granted a wish. He thought a while and said, 'Well, I've always been embarrassed by being rather small, if you know what I mean. Could you make me large?'

'Done,' said the genie, and disappeared.

Continuing his game, the man noticed an immediate change in his generative member. Within several holes, it was down to his knee, and by the 18th, it had crept into his sock. After holing his final putt, the man hurriedly returned to where he'd met the genie.

'Problem?' enquired the genie.

'Yes. Do you think I could trouble you for one more wish?'

'And what might that be?' asked the genie.
'Could you make my legs longer?'

After three months in the Far East, a businessman arrives home to discover that he's contracted a strange disease in the genital region. The doctor gives him the news that his penis will have to be amputated.

'I demand a second opinion,' the businessman says. So he sees numerous doctors all over Europe and North America but all advocate the same form of surgical intervention. Despairing of western medicine, the businessman decides to consult an Oriental doctor. After all, it seems that he's contracted an Oriental disease. The doctor, whose office is full of snakes in bottles and strange herbal remedies, gives the man and his member an examination. 'No, amputation isn't necessary.' The patient is elated.

'Brilliant! I saw so many western doctors and they all said amputation was the only way.'

'Western doctors!' snorts the Chinese gentleman. 'What do they know? Any Oriental herbalist or acupuncturist could tell you that it'll drop off by itself in four to six weeks.'

What's 12 inches long and white?
Nothing.

Johnny and Jim are walking through the desert. Suddenly, a snake bites Jim's prick.

Jim panics and Johnny panics. 'What can we do? We should call for a doctor,' screams Jim.

WHAM! Suddenly, in the middle of the desert, there's a telephone box. Johnny goes in, calls a doctor.

Johnny: My friend has been bitten by a snake. What do I do?

Doctor: What kind of snake?

Johnny: A one-metre, green and yellow one.

Doctor: Aye, aye. They're very dangerous.

Johnny: What can we do?

Doctor: The only thing you can do is suck the poison out. Otherwise your friend will be dead within half an hour.

Johnny hangs up. Jim, looking pale, asks what the doctor said.

'He said you'll be dead within half an hour.'

A man is driving his Porsche along Hollywood Boulevard when he's flagged down by an attractive hooker. She says, 'I'll do whatever you tell me to for $100.'

'Okay,' says the bloke as he hands over the money, 'paint my apartment.'

Homer hired a hooker and they met in his hotel room. 'I've got a little ... little tiny favour to ask.'

'Okay, but you'll have to pay extra,' said the prostitute. Homer took all his clothes off, went into the shower and said, 'Now, take the hairdryer, turn it on and blink the lights.' The prostitute turned the hairdryer on and when she started blinking the lights, Homer moaned with pleasure. 'Ooo, oooh, man this is great!'

'Now, I'm standing in the middle of a forest, it's raining cats and dogs and lightning's lit up the sky. The wind is blowing and in the distance you can hear thunder.'

'Okay, okay,' said the prostitute, 'isn't it time to make love now?'

'Are you crazy?' said Homer. 'In this weather?'

A man at a bar, deep in private thoughts, turned to a woman just passing by and said, 'Pardon me, Miss, do you happen to have the time?'

The woman screamed, 'How dare you make such a filthy, lewd, disgusting proposition to me.'

The man snapped to attention in surprise and was uncomfortably aware that every pair of eyes in the bar had turned in their direction. 'I was just asking for the time, Miss,' he mumbled, terrified. Whereupon the woman shrieked, 'I'll call the police if you say another word!'

Grabbing his drink, and feeling terribly embarrassed, the man crept to the far end of the room and huddled at a table, holding his breath and wondering how soon he could sneak out the door. A few moments later, the woman joined him. In a

79

very quiet whisper she said, 'Sir, I'm terribly sorry to have embarrassed you, but I'm a psychologist and am studying the reaction of human beings to shocking statements.'

The man stared at her for five seconds, and then leaned back and bellowed, 'You'd do all that for me for just $2? And you'd do it to every other guy in the bar for another ten?'

A slightly drunk man walked into a bar, went up to the bartender and said, 'I'll bet you $50 I can bite my right eye!' Noticing the man had had a few to drink, the bartender took him up on it. The drunk then proceeded to pop out a glass eyeball and bite it. The bartender paid, and the man left.

The next day the man returned, a little drunker than the previous day, and he said to the bartender, 'I'll bet you $50 I can bite my left eye!' Knowing that the man couldn't have two glass eyes, the bartender again took him up on it. This time the man pulled out his false teeth and 'bit' his eye. The bartender paid up.

The next day, the man came in stone drunk. He went to the bartender and said, 'I'll give you a chance to get your money back. I'll bet you $100 that you can put a shot glass on the other end of the bar, and I can stand on this end and piss in it without getting a single drop outside the glass.'

The bartender just couldn't pass up the chance to get his $100 back, and the guy was very drunk, so he took the drunk up on his bet. He put the shot glass on the other end of the bar, and the drunk simply pissed all over the bar. The bartender smiled and said, 'You lost!' The drunk just smiled and gave him the $100.

The bartender said, 'You're not too unhappy about losing all your money. Why not?' The drunk explained, 'Because I just bet this guy $2000 that I could piss all over your bar and you wouldn't care!'

How do you make a hormone?
Don't pay her.

What's the definition of an orgy?
A party where everyone comes.

What does a man with a 10-inch dick have for breakfast?
Well, this morning I had bacon, eggs, juice ...

What do you get when you cross PMS with ESP?
A bitch who thinks she knows everything.

What are the three words you don't want to hear while making love?

Honey, I'm home.

The scene was the Garden of Eden. God called Adam to him and said, 'Now I will teach you how to kiss.'

'Lord, what is kiss?' asked Adam.

'I will show you,' said God, and taught Adam everything he needed to know about kissing. Whereupon Adam went to Eve and kissed her for a while.

Then God called Adam back and said, 'Now I will teach you how to make love.'

'Lord, what is make love?'

'I will show you,' said God, and he taught Adam everything about making love. Adam went to Eve but came back almost immediately.

'Lord,' he asked, 'what is a headache?'

Soon after a girl started working at the local bank she noticed a very handsome man walking by her office. A co-worker told her that he was the bank's president and that he made a great deal of money. She was determined to get to know him but wasn't quite sure how to go about it.

She sought the advice of her analyst. While she was around this man, he suggested, she should pretend she had a string attached to the top of her head and that it hung down her left side to her waist. She should pretend that a penny was attached to the end of the string. Then, when walking near the president, she should pretend to hit the penny with her left hip. This, stated the analyst, would provoke his interest.

Next day, she passed the man in the hall and began moving her left hip whilst in her head she was thinking, Hit the penny, hit the penny, hit the penny. And, as predicted, the man noticed her and stopped to chat.

A few days later, the man still hadn't asked her out. She went to the analyst again and this time he told her to pretend she had another string attached to the top of her head, that it hung down to her right hip. And attached to this string was a nickel. As she walked near the man, she was now to use her hips to hit first the penny and then the nickel.

The next day, she approached the man and began moving her hips according to the analyst's directions. In her head she was thinking, Hit the penny, hit the nickel, hit the penny, hit the nickel. And this time the man stopped and asked her out.

After a few weeks and many dates the girl decided she wanted to marry him. She talked to her analyst, who suggested that she pretend she had yet another string attached to the top of her head, and that it hung down her back to her bottom. Attached to this string was a dime. She was now to use her hips to hit all of these imaginary coins.

On her next date, she began moving her hips according to instructions. And in her head she was thinking, Hit the penny, hit the nickel, hit the dime, hit the penny, hit the nickel, hit the dime. And that night, just as the analyst promised, the man asked her to marry him, whereupon she began making wedding plans.

Being a virgin, she was worried about the honeymoon. She told her analyst that she was unversed in the art of making love, and he told her to pretend that one more string was attached to the top of her head, and that it hung down in front of her to her private parts. And attached to this string was a quarter. He told her that everything would be all right on the honeymoon if she hit the coins while making love.

Finally, the wedding day arrived and after the ceremony the couple went off on their honeymoon. That night, in the bathroom of her hotel, she practised moving her hips. Hit the penny, hit the nickel, hit the dime, hit the quarter. Hit the penny, hit the nickel, hit the dime, hit the quarter. Soon they were in bed and began making love for the first time. She started moving her hips. In her head she was thinking, Hit the penny, hit the nickel, hit the dime, hit the quarter. Hit the penny, hit the nickel, hit the dime, hit the quarter. Oh fuck the small change. Hit the quarter, hit the quarter.

The six most important men in a woman's life

1. The doctor, because he says, 'Take your clothes off.'
2. The dentist, because he says, 'Open wide.'
3. The hairdresser, because he says, 'Do you want it teased or blown?'
4. The milkman, because he says, 'Do you want it in the front or back?'
5. The interior decorator, because he says, 'Once it's in you'll love it.'
6. The banker, because he says, 'If you take it out too soon you'll lose interest.'

What is worse than being raped by Jack the Ripper?

Being fingered by Captain Hook.

Two gay men are walking by a morgue on a very hot day. One of them turns to the other and says, 'Want to stop in and suck down a cold one?'

A woman is talking to her best friend about getting a tattoo done for her husband's birthday. The friend recommends a popular tattoo artist who can tattoo just about anything. The woman visits the tattoo parlour the next day and asks for two butterflies to be tattooed on her butt. She wants the butterflies because her husband calls her his 'little butterfly'. The tattoo artist says he can't do such a large tattoo in such a short time and suggests that he puts two bees on her butt instead. The woman's a little disappointed, but agrees.

The next day she invites her husband into the bedroom and says, 'Sweetie, your birthday present is under my housecoat.'

He proceeds to undress his wife, lifting up her bottom so that he can have a good look.

'And who the hell is Bob?'

A young man joins the Foreign Legion, and is sent to live deep in the heart of Africa, surrounded by desert. After a few months with no female contact, he visits his commander. 'I haven't had sex for ages. Can you help me?'

'Well,' says the commander, 'you can borrow my camel any time you like.' The man declines, not wishing to seem that desperate. Six months later, feeling increasingly frustrated, he goes to the commander again, who says, 'The offer of my camel is still there.'

A year goes by and the poor man can stand it no longer. He goes to the commander one more time, his hands shaking. 'It's no use – I haven't had sex for a year. I must use your camel.' The commander agrees, the man takes the animal around the back of the compound and relieves his frustrations.

On returning, the man thanks the commander who says, 'Any time, young man. It's much quicker to the local brothel by camel, isn't it?'

One day a little boy went to his mother and asked, 'Mummy, what's a pussy?' A little shocked, his mother remained composed, went to the encyclopaedia, opened to the Cs and showed her son a picture of a cat. 'That is a pussy.'

'Oh,' replied the boy. 'Well, Mum, what's a bitch?' Again the mother went to the encyclopaedia, opened to the Ds and showed her son a picture of a dog. 'Son, this is a dog. A female dog is called a bitch.'

The little boy sought confirmation from his father. 'Dad, what's a pussy?' His father went to the dresser drawer, pulled out an issue of *Penthouse* and drew a circle. 'Son, that is a pussy.'

'Oh,' replied the boy. 'Well, what's a bitch?'

'Everything outside of the circle,' replied his father.

Two businessmen working in New York decided to get themselves a mistress. They set her up in her own apartment and agreed to split all expenses 50/50. The men alternated evenings with her, and things went fine for a few months.

One day the mistress announced to the two men that she was pregnant. They decided to do the right thing, and split all expenses 50/50.

When the mistress went into labour, one of the men was out of town on a business trip, so the other man went to the hospital with her. When the traveller returned, he headed for the hospital and saw his friend looking very glum outside the maternity ward.

'Is she all right? Were there problems with the birth?' he asked his friend.

'Oh, she's fine, but I've got some bad news for you. She had twins, and mine died.'

A man and a woman lived in a nursing home and over a period of years became best friends. They did everything together – they ate together, played chess together, went for walks together. One night after dinner the gentleman leaned over the table and said, 'Let's have sex together.' The woman protested that it had been 15 years since her last attempt. She wasn't sure if she could. But after further consideration, she decided that you only live once. 'What the heck,' she told him. 'Meet me at my room at 9 tonight.'

Arriving all excited, he began to undress, but the woman said there was something she had to say. 'I've lived a full life and have no complaints. Please don't let what I'm about to say make you think I don't want to do this, but I feel I have to tell you this. I have acute Angina.'

The old man reflected for a while, then continued to undress himself. 'Well, that's good, because the rest of you ain't so hot.'

A couple from Fresno, a real hick town, were on their honeymoon in a hotel. They were getting ready to get to know each other in the biblical sense when the wife looked over at her new husband and said, 'I've never done this before. So please be gentle.'

The husband got a scared look on his face and said, 'Wait a minute.' He ran outside to a phone booth where he called his father. 'Dad, she's a virgin. What'll I do?'

'Come home, son. If she's not good enough for her family, she's not good enough for our family.'

A very, very old man was staying at an expensive hotel. As he walked through the lobby he saw a most attractive older woman. Knowing that his life was short, he decided to take a chance and proposition her. He walked over and said, 'I have never done this before, but I find you very attractive, and wonder if I paid you $1000 would you come up to my room and have sex with me?' The woman was surprised, but considering the man's age, she figured that he'd be quite harmless and unable to perform. So she agreed. To her astonishment, the old man's performance truly amazed her. He put everything he had into it.

As he paid her the $1000 he said, 'Had I known you were a virgin, I would never have propositioned you. Or I would have offered you more money.'

The woman replied, 'That's okay. Had I known you were able to get it up, I would have pulled my pantyhose down.'

A marine, long stationed overseas, was contemplating his return home. He sent his wife an e-mail message. 'When I get home, there's going to be a lot of lovemaking going on. If you want in on it, you better meet me at the gang plank.'

She e-mailed back. 'You're so right. And if you want in on it, you'd better be the first guy down the gang plank.'

A guy goes to the doctor and discovers he has only one night to live. He tells his wife and they decide to get into some serious sex. After about an hour, they both fall asleep, but soon the guy awakes and decides he hasn't got much time left, so he tries some more foreplay.

After a while, she begins to respond and soon they're going at it like wild animals. Again they fall asleep. But, shortly, the husband wakes up and thinks he could do with one final round. He grabs his wife but she just ignores him.

He tries everything to get her excited, but she just gets pissed off, saying, 'That's enough. I know you want to do it again, but you don't have to get up in the morning.'

Abe, an 84-year-old New Yorker, is complaining to his old friend Sam that his sex life 'ain't so good any more'. Sam suggests that Abe goes to see a porno movie – that way he'll learn all the new techniques and enhance his sex life. Abe goes to Times Square and watches *Deep Throat* and *Debbie Does Dallas*. When he gets home, his wife, Golda, also in her 80s, asks where he's been and he tells her.

'You went to a porno movie, for heaven's sake why?' she asks.

'So I could learn the new ways and improve our sex life.'

'And did you learn anything useful?'

'Yes, I learnt that you should moan during sex. They moan a lot when they do it nowadays.'

'You want me to moan?' Golda asks.

'That's right, I want you should moan when we do it.'

That night they begin making love and Golda asks, 'Now you want I should moan, Abe?'

'Not yet Golda.'

Fifteen minutes she asks again if she should start moaning, and he again replies, 'Not yet.'

A half hour passes and the lovemaking is now really intense. 'You want I should moan now Abe?'

He pants, 'Yes, yes, now!'

'Oiyev, the crowds at Macy's today. I couldn't stand it ... and the prices at the market ... terrible. And the subway was stuck for 15 minutes ... and ... '

A woman walked into the drug store and said, 'I want to buy a vibrator.' The druggist waggled a finger and said, 'Come this way.'

The woman replied, 'If I could come that way, I wouldn't need a vibrator.'

Two sailors are on shore leave. They're walking down a busy street when one sees a beautiful blonde. He asks his buddy if he's ever slept with a blonde. 'Yeah, I've slept with a blonde before,' replies his friend.

They continue walking on down the street, taking in the sights, when the sailor sees a gorgeous brunette. 'Oh, what a babe!' he exclaims. 'Have you ever slept with a brunette?'

'Sure,' replies his buddy, 'I've slept with brunettes several times.'

They continue along and after a while the first sailor sees a beautiful redhead. He can't get over how lovely she is. 'How about a redhead?' he asks his buddy. 'Have you ever slept with a redhead?'

'Not a wink!'

As a truck driver came flying over the top of a steep hill, he spotted two figures in his path rolling around in the middle of the road. The driver blew his horn and braked frantically, but the couple continued their lovemaking in spite of his warnings.

The truck finally slid to a halt barely three inches

from the pair. 'Are you crazy?' the driver shouted at them. 'You could have been killed!'

The man stood up and faced the driver. 'Well, I was coming, she was coming and you were coming,' he panted, 'and you were the only one with brakes.'

Back in the good old days when Dudley Fuzz was in the habit of whooping it up, he was standing at a bar when a lady of enticing appearance approached him and suggested that they have a drink. Dudley said, 'Well, I'm no John D. Rockefeller, but I'll buy.'

After developing a slight buzz, she suggested a dance. Dudley smiled and said, 'I'm no Fred Astaire, but I'll give it a whirl.'

Later, she suggested that they go up to her room. 'I'm no Cary Grant,' he replied, 'but I'll follow you up there.'

They then went to the lady's apartment, where they had another drink, then did what had been on their minds all evening, anyway. Afterwards, the lady said, 'What about some money?'

Dudley shot back, 'Well, I'm no gigolo, but I'll take it.'

'Sangfroid' is when you find your lover in bed with someone else and you shoot them both in cold blood. 'Savoire faire' is when you find your lover in bed with someone else but you laugh because today's your turn with the hamster.

Three married couples want to join a new movement – the Orthodox Church of Sexual Repression. The first couple are in their 20s, the second in their 30s, the third in their 40s. Near the end of the introductory interview the priest tells them that they have to pass one small test, which entails abstaining from sex for a month. The three couples agree to try.

A month later they're having their final interview. The cleric asks the 40-year-old couple whether they'd managed to abstain. 'Well, it wasn't too difficult,' says the man, 'I spent hour after hour in my workshop and she loves gardening, so we had plenty of distractions. We did okay.'

'Very good, my children, you are welcome in our anti-fornicative faith. And how well did you manage?' he asks the 30-year-olds. 'Frankly, it was very difficult,' the husband says. 'We thought about sex all the time and we had to sleep in different rooms. And we prayed and prayed and prayed. However, we have been celibate for the entire month.'

'Very good, my children, you are welcome amongst the ranks of the spiritual and celibate. And how about you?' he asks the 20-year-old couple. 'Father, not too good at all. Oh, we did fine for the first week. But by the second week we were going crazy with desire. Then, one day during the third week, my wife dropped a head of lettuce, and when she bent over to pick it up, I weakened and took her right then and there.'

'Verily I say unto you, my son, you are not welcome in our church.'

'Yeah? Well, we're not too welcome at the greengrocer's either.'

What's the difference between hard and light?
You can get to sleep with a light on.

King Arthur was heading off for the Crusades when he called one of his squires and said, 'Here is the key to Guinevere's chastity belt. If in ten years I haven't returned you may use the key.'

His Majesty crossed the drawbridge and set off along a long dusty road. He stopped, turned his horse and took one last look at his castle. Whereupon the squire rushed towards him yelling, 'Stop! Your majesty! Thank goodness I was able to catch you. This is the wrong key!'

Mrs Jones woke up one night to discover her drunk husband trying to fill her mouth with aspirin.

She screamed, 'What in hell do you think you're doing?'

'Don't you have a headache?' he asked.

'No, I bloody well don't.'
'Great, let's fuck.'

A man picks up a girl in a bar and convinces her to come back to his hotel room. When they're relaxing afterwards he asks, 'Am I the first man you ever made love to?'

She looks at him thoughtfully. 'You might be,' she says, 'your face looks familiar.'

Two fellows were sitting in a coffee shop when the town's fire alarm went off. One jumped up and headed for the door. His friend shouted, 'Tom, I didn't know you were a fireman.'

'I'm not,' said Tom, 'but my mistress's husband is.'

A reverend gentleman decided it was time to tell his triplet daughters about the birds and the bees. At the same time he would test their innocence. Thus, he approached his first daughter, dropped his trousers and pointed to his generative member. 'Do you know what this is?'

'That's your cock,' she replied.

'You foul-mouthed hussy. Go and rinse your mouth out with soap,' he ranted.

Still fuming, he approached his second daughter,

pointed to his generative member and asked if she knew what it was.

'That's your dick.'

'Be gone, you daughter of Jezebel. Ye scarlet woman. Go and stick your tongue in boiling vinegar.'

Finally, he sought his third daughter and, dropping his trousers, pointed to his manhood and asked if she knew what it was. 'I've no idea,' she replied.

'Oh my chaste darling,' he said, 'that is my penis.'

To which she responded, 'You call that a penis?'

A tired traveller pulled into a three-star hotel around midnight and asked reception for a single room. As the clerk filled out the paperwork the traveller looked around and saw a gorgeous blonde sitting in the lobby. Asking the clerk to wait, he went over and talked to her. A few minutes later he came back with the girl on his arm and said, 'Fancy meeting my wife here! Guess I'll need a double room.'

Next morning, he came to settle his bill. Handing over his Amex card, he was appalled to be confronted with an account for $3000. 'What's the meaning of this?' he yelled at the clerk, 'I've only been here one night.'

'Yes,' said the clerk, 'but your wife has been here for three weeks.'

Have you heard Hugh Grant's next movie is called *Nine Months, Four Weddings and a Blow Job*?

Nine Months had a great opening weekend. Took $13 million at the box office. Pretty good, given that Hugh spent just $60 on the advertising.

What's pink and hard in the morning?

The *Finance Times* crossword.

What's pink, wrinkled and hangs out your trousers?

Your gran.

A bunch of guys are hanging out in their usual bar after work one day when a very attractive woman walks in and sits down right in the midst of them. After about two minutes of amazed looks, one of the men manages to ask the woman her name.

'Don't you recognise me, guys? It's me, Bernie. I had a sex change!'

Well, the men are all amazed at how their old drinking buddy, Bernie, looks with all his new equipment. So they buy some more drinks and get to talking about old times with Bernie/Bernice. After a few hours, the conversation rolls around to the subject of Bernice's operation. One of the guys says,

'Tell me, Bernice, what was the most painful thing about the operation? Was it when they cut your dick off?'

'No. That was painful, but that wasn't the most painful thing.'

Another man pipes up, 'I bet I know! I'll bet the worst part was when they cut your balls off, right?'

'No,' Bernice says, 'that really hurt, too, but that wasn't the worst part either.'

Finally, one of the men asks, 'Well, just what was the worst, most painful part of the operation?'

'When they cut my skull open and removed half my brain.'

A Freudian critique of Dr Seuss's *The Cat in the Hat*:

The Cat in the Hat is a hard-hitting novel of prose and poetry in which the author re-examines the dynamic rhyming schemes and bold imagery of some of his earlier works, most notably *Green Eggs and Ham*, *If I Ran the Zoo*, and *Why Can't I Shower with Mommy?* In this novel, Theodore Geisel, writing under the pseudonym Dr Seuss, plays homage to the great Dr Sigmund Freud in a nightmarish fantasy of a renegade feline helping two young children understand their own frustrated sexuality.

The story opens with two youngsters, a brother and a sister, abandoned by their mother, staring mournfully through the window of their single family dwelling. In the foreground, a large tree/phallic symbol dances wildly in the wind, taunting the children and encouraging them to succumb to the sexual yearnings they undoubtedly feel for each other. Even to the most unlearned reader, the blatant references to the incestuous relationship the two share set the tone for Seuss's probing examination of the satisfaction of primitive needs. The cat proceeds to charm the wary youths into engaging in what he so innocently refers to as 'tricks'. At this point, the fish, an obvious Christ figure who represents the prevailing Christian morality, attempts to warn the children, and thus, in effect, warns all of humanity of the dangers associated with the unleashing of the primal urges. In response to this, the cat proceeds to balance the aquatic naysayer on the end of his umbrella, essentially saying, 'Down with morality; down with God.'

After pooh-poohing the righteous rantings of the waterlogged Christ figure, the cat begins to juggle several icons of western culture, most notably two books, representing the Old and New Testaments, and a saucer of lacteal fluid, an ironic reference to maternal loss the two children experienced when their mother abandoned them 'for the afternoon'. Our heroic Id adds to this bold gesture a rake and a toy man, and thus completes the Oedipal triangle.

Later in the novel, Seuss introduces the proverbial Pandora's box, a large red crate out of which the Id releases Thing One, or Freud's concept of Ego, the division of the psyche that serves as the conscious mediator between the person and reality, and Thing Two, the Super-ego which functions to reward and punish through a system of moral attitudes, conscience, and guilt. Referring to this box, the cat says, 'Now look at this trick. Take a look!' In this, Dr Seuss uses the children as a brilliant metaphor for the reader, and asks the reader to re-examine his own inner self.

The children, unable to control the Id, Ego and Super-ego, allow these creatures to run free and mess up the house, or more symbolically, control their lives. This rampage continues until the fish, or Christ symbol, warns that the mother is returning to reinstate the Oedipal triangle that existed before her abandonment of the children. At this point, Seuss introduces a many-armed cleaning device which represents the psychoanalytic couch, and proceeds to put the two youngsters' lives back in order.

With powerful simplicity, clarity, and drama, Seuss reduces Freud's concepts on the dynamics of the human psyche to an easily understood gesture. Seuss's poetry and choice of words is equally impressive and serves as a splendid counterpart to his bold symbolism. In all, his writing style is quick and fluid, making *The Cat in the Hat* impossible to put down. While this novel is 61 pages in length, and one can read it in five minutes or less, it is not until after multiple readings that the genius of this modern-day master becomes apparent.

One sunny afternoon Superman was out flying around. Crime was slow that day so he decided to go over to Spiderman's house.

'Hey Spidey,' said Superman, 'let's go get a burger and a beer.'

'No can do,' said Spiderman. 'I've got a problem with my web-shooter. Can't fight crime tomorrow without it.'

So Superman went over to the Batcave. 'Hey Batman,' said Superman, 'let's go get a burger and beer.'

'Not today, Supe,' said Batman. 'My Batmobile has a flat tyre and I've got to fix it today. Can't fight crime tomorrow without it.'

A somewhat disgruntled Superman took to the air, cruised around the skies and found himself over a penthouse apartment. And what did his super vision see? None other than Wonder Woman, lying on the deck, spread-eagled, stark-naked.

Superman had a brilliant idea. 'They've always said I'm faster than a speeding bullet. And I've always wondered what she'd be like.' He zoomed down, did the deed, and flew off in a flash.

All of a sudden Wonder Woman sat up and said, 'What the hell was that?' and the Invisible Man climbed off her replying, 'I don't know, but it hurt like hell.'

GOD, I DON'T KNOW

Why God never received tenure at any university:

1. He had only one major publication.
2. It was in Hebrew.
3. It had no references.
4. It wasn't published in a referee journal.
5. Some even doubt he wrote it himself.
6. It may be true that he created the world, but what has he done since then?
7. His co-operative efforts have been quite limited.
8. The scientific community has had a hard time replicating his results.
9. He never applied to the Ethics Board for permission to use human subjects.
10. When one experiment went awry he tried to cover it up by drowning the subjects.
11. When subjects didn't behave as predicted he deleted them from the sample.
12. He rarely came to class, just told students to read the Book.

13. Some say he had his son teach the class.
14. He expelled his first two students for learning.
15. Although there are only ten requirements, most students failed his test.
16. His office hours were infrequent and usually held on a mountain top.

What do you get when you cross a nun with a PC?

A computer that will never go down on you.

An electrical engineer, a mechanical engineer and a civil engineer were having a discussion about what kind of engineer God was. The electrical engineer insisted God was an electrical engineer because the brain, the most important part of the body, employs electrical impulses.

The mechanical engineer insisted that God was a mechanical engineer because of the design of the world's best pump, the heart.

The civil engineer just laughed and said that she knew for a fact that God was a civil engineer. 'After all,' she said whilst pointing to their private parts, 'who else but a civil engineer would put a waste-water system through a recreation zone?'

A Catholic, a Baptist and a Mormon were sitting together one Sunday bragging about the size of their respective families.

The Catholic said, 'I've got a pretty big family. In fact I've now got four kids, all boys. One more and I could have a basketball team.'

The Baptist said, 'That's nothing. I've got eight boys, one more and I could have a baseball team!'

The two looked at the Mormon. After a moment of contemplation, he said, 'Well guys, I now have 17 wives. One more and I could have a golf course.'

ı ı doctor, an architect and a computer scientist were arguing about whose profession was the oldest. In the course of their arguments, they got back to the Old Testament. The doctor said, 'The medical profession is clearly the oldest, because Eve was made from Adam's rib, and that was a simply incredible surgical feat.'

The architect didn't agree. 'In the beginning there was chaos and a void, and out of that the garden and the world were created. So God must have been an architect.'

The computer scientist said, 'Yes, but where do you think the chaos came from?'

ı ı man walks along a lonely beach. Suddenly he hears a deep voice shout, 'DIG!' He looks around, but nobody's there. I am having hallucinations, he thinks.

Then he hears the voice again. 'I SAID DIG!' So he starts to dig in the sand with his bare hands and, after some time, he finds a small chest with a rusty lock. The deep voice says, 'OPEN!' So the man opens it and he sees lots of gold coins.

The deep voice says, 'TO THE CASINO!' The man takes the chest to the casino and the deep voice says, 'ROULETTE!' So he changes all the gold into a huge pile of roulette tokens and goes to one of the tables, where the players gaze at him with disbelief. The deep voice says, '27!' He takes the whole pile and drops it at 27. The table nearly bursts. Everybody is quiet when the croupier throws the ball. The ball stays at 26. The deep voice says, 'SHIT!'

Jesus and Moses are bored stiff in Heaven. 'Hey Moses,' says Jesus, 'why don't we disguise ourselves, go down to Earth and play 18 holes?' Moses agrees. So after donning appropriate clobber and renting clubs and carts, they arrive on the tee of the first hole. A long par-four with trouble down both sides.

They flip a coin and Moses wins the honour. He gets up over the ball and takes a mighty swing. The ball sails 300 metres down the middle of the fairway, coming to rest in a perfect position. 'Nice shot,' says Jesus grudgingly.

Jesus tees up a ball and hits a hard duck hook, which ends up on the side of a hill, not 100 metres away.

A squirrel spots the ball, picks it up in his mouth

and takes off running. A snake curled up on the rocks strikes at the squirrel and swallows it, ball and all. An eagle spots the snake, swoops down and carries it away in its talons. As it flies over the first green, a bolt of lightning flashes from the sky and hits the eagle. The eagle drops the snake, the snake regurgitates the squirrel, the squirrel lets the ball drop from its mouth, the ball rolls five metres across the green and into the hole. Moses lifts an eyebrow and asks Jesus, 'Are we going to play golf, or just screw around?'

Jesus and Moses were sitting up in Heaven, talking about Earth and some of the things they never got to do there. Jesus said to Moses, 'Man, I really want to go and play just one game of golf. Maybe God will let me go and play a game.' So Jesus went and asked God if he could play a game of golf. 'Well, I suppose,' said God, 'but Moses has to go with you as your caddy.' Jesus and Moses agreed, and soon found themselves at Pebble Beach, with golf shoes, and a bag of clubs, and one ball.

Jesus had been playing a good game, when he came to the ninth hole and saw a plaque. It read: 'The only person to ever score a hole-in-one on this hole was Arnold Palmer.' 'Well,' said Jesus, 'if Palmer could do it, why can't I? I'm Jesus Christ.' Moses gave him his ball and tee, and stood back to watch. Jesus adjusted his robe and halo, fixed his stance and exhaled deeply. He shouted, 'Fore!' and whacked the ball. It sailed into the air, hooked a little to the left, and splashed nicely into the water trap.

'Oh, no!' said Jesus. 'That was my only ball! Hey Moses, could you go and get it for me?' Moses went down to the water trap, parted the water, and walked in to get the ball back. Jesus teed off. 'Fore!' It sailed down into the water trap again. 'Hey Moses ...' But Moses was already on his way to get the ball. Moses came back, but before he returned the ball he said, 'I'm tired of getting your ball. If you hit it in the water again, you can get it yourself.'

Jesus took the ball and, sure enough, hit it straight into the water. He went down to the water, looking for the ball while walking on top of the water. Some other golfers started to play through and noticed this guy walking around on the water. One of them said to Moses, 'Who's that guy think he is? Jesus Christ or something?'

'No,' replied Moses, 'Arnold Palmer.'

A man finds a corked bottle on the green. He opens it and a genie appears to grant him one wish. After thinking about it for a while, the golfer says, 'I'd like to shoot par golf regularly.'

'No problem,' says the genie, 'but understand that your sex life will be reduced as a side effect.'

'Fine by me,' the man says. And POOF, the deed's done.

A few months later the genie reappears on the same golf hole and asks the man how his golf game is going.

'Great,' says the man, 'I'm now carrying a scatch handicap.'

'And what effect has it had on your sex life?'

'I can still manage to have relations two or three times a month.'

'Two or three times a month!' the genie says. 'That's not much of a sex life.'

'Well,' the golfer responds, 'I don't think it's too bad for a middle-aged priest with a very small parish.'

Sitting on the train with a young curate, the bishop was doing *The Times* crossword. 'Three across,' he said out loud, 'exclusively female, four letters, ends in U-N-T.'

'Aunt,' suggested the curate.

'Shit,' said the bishop, 'have you got an eraser?'

The scene is the confessional. A sinner murmurs to the priest, 'Forgive me, Father, I used the f-word this week.' 'Dear oh dear. Tell me, my son, the circumstances in which you used the f-word. Perhaps you suffered extreme provocation?'

'Well, I was golfing. And I hit a beautiful shot that sailed straight as an arrow for 300 metres. But then it suddenly detoured into the woods.'

'And that is when you used the f-word? I can appreciate your frustration, my son. I am a golfer myself.'

111

'No, not at that point Father. I then hit a perfect shot out of the woods. Only to see it land in the sand trap.'

'Now, I can understand you saying the f-word at that moment.'

'No, Father, I remained calm even then. I got out my sand wedge, hit a perfect shot right at the pin. But the ball stopped an inch from the cup.'

'How frustrating. And that, of course, is when you used the f-word.'

'No, Father, I was still calm.'

'YOU MEAN YOU MISSED THE FUCKING PUTT?'

Jew dies, goes to Heaven. Meets St Peter at the Pearly Gates. Gets guided tour of Heaven. At one point they come to a huge wall. St Peter says, 'Ssshh.' The Jew asks why. St Peter says, 'On the other side of the wall are the Christians, and they think they're the only ones here.'

St Peter has a day off and Jesus is standing in for him. Whilst booking in the new arrivals, Jesus notices an old man in the queue who seems familiar. When he gets to the front of the line, Jesus asks him his name.

'Joseph.'

Jesus is now more inquisitive. 'Your occupation?'

'Carpenter.'

By now Jesus is getting quite excited. 'Did you have a little boy?'

'Yes.'

'Did he have holes in his wrists and ankles?'

'Yes.'

Jesus looks at the old man and with a tear in his eye shouts, 'Father! Father!'

The old man looks puzzled and, after a moment, replies, 'Pinocchio?'

Three men were standing in line at the Pearly Gates. It had been a pretty busy day so Peter told the first one, 'We're just about full up at the moment, so I've been asked to admit only people who've had a particularly horrible death. What's your story?'

The first replies, 'Well, I'd suspected my wife of cheating on me. So today I came home early to try to catch her. As I came into my 25th-floor apartment, I could tell something was wrong. But all my searching around didn't reveal where this other guy could have been hiding. So I went out onto the balcony and, sure enough, there was this bloke hanging off the railing. I was really mad, so I started beating him and kicking him, but he wouldn't fall off. So I went back into the apartment, got a hammer and started bashing his fingers. He let go and fell. But he fell into the bushes, stunned but okay. I was so angry I rushed into the kitchen, grabbed the fridge and threw it over the edge. It landed on him, killing him instantly. But all the stress and anger got to me, and I had a heart attack and died on the balcony.'

'That sounds like a pretty bad death to me,' said Peter, letting the man in.

'It's been a very strange day,' said the second man. 'You see, I live on the 26th floor of my apartment building and every morning I do exercises out on my balcony. Well this morning I slipped and I fell over the edge. I got lucky and caught the railing of the balcony on the floor below me. But suddenly this man burst onto the balcony and started beating me and kicking me. Then he got a hammer and started bashing at my hands. Finally I let go but again I got lucky and fell into the bushes. I was stunned but okay. Whereupon a refrigerator came falling out of the sky and crushed me. And now I'm here.'

Once again, St Peter conceded it was a pretty horrible death.

Then the third man told his story. 'Picture this,' he says, 'I'm hiding naked inside a refrigerator . . .'

A bloke applies for admission at the Pearly Gates. St Peter says that there's a test consisting of three questions.

'For the first question, tell me which two days of the week begin with the letter T.'

'That's easy,' said the bloke, 'today and tomorrow.'

'Hmm,' said St Peter. 'Okay, just. Now for the second question. Tell me how many seconds there are in a year.'

'Twelve.'

'Twelve!' exclaimed St Peter. 'How twelve?'

'There's January 2nd, February 2nd, March 2nd, etc.'

'Okay,' said St Peter, 'for the third question, tell me God's first name.'

'Andy.'

'Andy?'

'Yeah, it's there in the song. "Andy walks with me, Andy talks with me, Andy tells me I'm His own ..."'

A busload of priests have an accident and all of them are killed instantly. On arriving at the Pearly Gates, they find there's a terrible queue. St Peter is there looking at a big book, jotting down notes, mumbling occasionally. There's a person standing in front of his desk being processed. There is an enormous number of people waiting, and the wait seems to take forever.

People are arriving all the time, some in mangled states, some famished and some looking normal. Then a dishevelled man comes in, cigarette hanging from his lips like it has taken root. The stubble on his chin looks as though it could sand diamonds. He stands at the back of the queue like everyone else. St Peter spies him, stands up and goes over to him. 'Oh, come in. Come in! Welcome. No need to queue, we have you already processed. Special treatment for you.'

'Hey,' says one of the priests. 'How come he gets special treatment? We are, after all, men of God.'

'That man,' says St Peter, 'was a taxi driver. He has scared the hell out of a lot more people than any of you.'

A political activist named Colin had just arrived in Hell and was told he had to make a choice. He could go to Capitalist Hell or Communist Hell. Wanting to compare the two, he wandered over to Capitalist Hell where, outside the door, Adam Smith stood looking bored.

'What's it like in there?' asked Colin.

'Well,' replied Adam, 'in Capitalist Hell they flay you alive, boil you in oil, chain you to a rock, and let a vulture tear your liver out. Then they cut you up into small pieces with sharp knives.'

'That's awful,' said Colin, 'I'm going to check out Communist Hell.' He went over to Communist Hell, where he discovered a long line of people waiting to get in. The line went round and round seven times and then receded towards the horizon. Colin pushed his way to the head of the line where, lo and behold, Karl Marx was busily signing people in. He asked Karl what Communist Hell was like.

'In Communist Hell,' said Marx impatiently, 'they flay you alive, boil you in oil, chain you to a rock, and let vultures tear out your liver. Then they cut you up into small pieces with sharp knives.'

'But isn't that the same as Capitalist Hell?' Colin asked.

'Yes,' sighed Marx, 'but sometimes we don't have oil, sometimes we don't have knives ...'

A guy dies and goes to Hell. The Devil greets him warmly at the gates and they enter a long corridor. As they walk along the Devil explains, 'Now that you're in Hell, you must choose the manner in which you will spend all eternity. I will show you some rooms and you must choose one.'

They get to the first room. The door opens and the man peers in. An endless circle of the damned with weights strapped to their backs walk around barefoot on hot coals. 'Oh, I don't think I like that,' says the man. They continue on to the second room.

In the second room, the damned walk around listening to elevator Muzak, walking on broken glass. 'Oh, I don't think I could stand that,' says the man.

In the last room, the man is surprised to find the damned standing around up to their armpits in shit, drinking coffee. 'That doesn't look so bad!' says the man. 'I'll stay here for eternity.'

'Very well,' says the Devil, closing the door behind him.

'Hmm, this isn't so bad,' thinks the man, as a demon gives him a cup of coffee. Suddenly the room supervisor calls out on his megaphone, 'All right everybody, coffee break's over! Back on your heads!'

Jesus walks into a hotel, tosses three nails on the front desk and says, 'Hey, can you put me up for the night?'

Jesus, hanging on the cross, spots Peter in the crowd at the bottom of the hill. 'Peter,' he calls, 'Peter.' Peter hears his name and replies, 'I hear, Lord. I'm coming,' and starts up the hill towards the cross. A Roman guard blocks Peter's way and says, 'Stop, or I'll cut off your arm.' But Peter says, 'I must go on, my Lord is calling me,' and tries to pass the guard, who cuts off his arm with a sword.

Jesus calls again, 'Peter, Peter ...' Peter continues, bleeding and in terrible pain, up the hill towards the cross. Another guard blocks his way and says, 'Stop, or I'll cut off your other arm.' Peter ignores this, saying, 'I must go on, my Lord is calling me.' As Peter tries to pass, the second guard cuts off his other arm with his sword.

Jesus calls again, 'Peter ...' Peter, getting weak from the pain, continues up the hill. A third guard blocks his way and says, 'Stop, or I'll cut off your leg.' Peter says to the guard, 'I must go on, my Lord is calling me.' As Peter tries to continue up the hill, the guard cuts off his leg. Peter falls in a heap of pain and blood, but still manages to push and drag himself up the hill towards the cross with his one remaining leg.

Jesus calls again, 'Peter, Peter ...' Peter replies, 'I hear Lord, I'm coming.' Another guard steps in front of Peter and says, 'Stop, or I'll cut off your other leg.' Peter squirms to try to pass the guard, and the guard cuts off Peter's other leg. In excruciating pain, Peter uses sheer willpower to drag his mutilated body to the base of the cross. Panting, he raises his eyes towards Jesus and says, 'I am here, Lord. I have answered your call.'

Jesus looks down at Peter and says, 'Peter ... I can see your house from up here.'

W hat was the last thing Jesus said to Mary as he was hanging from the cross?
'Mary, bring me my pumps, these spikes are killing me!'

W hy doesn't Jesus eat M&Ms?
They fall through his hands.

A crowd of people has collected around a harlot, preparing to stone her. Jesus walks through the crowd, saying, 'Whosoever is without sin, let them cast the first stone.' Over the crowd comes a rock and, POW, it hits the harlot square on the head and kills her. Jesus says, 'Mother, sometimes you just piss me off!'

W hat's the difference between Jesus and a painting?
It takes only one nail to hang a painting.

A man was trapped on a desert island and it was sinking into the sea. As the water lapped round his feet a motorboat suddenly approached. 'Come on man, get in,' said the boatman.

'No,' the man said, 'I have faith in Jesus. He will save me.'

So the boat went off and the water continued to rise. When it was up to his chest another boat appeared. 'Get in the boat or you're going to drown,' said the boatman.

Again he said, 'No, I have faith in Jesus. He will save me.'

The boat went off and the water continued to rise. When it was up to his chin, a third boat appeared. 'This is your last chance, get in!'

'No, Jesus will save me.'

The boat departed, the water continued to rise and the man drowned. Arriving in Heaven he was greeted by Jesus. 'Hey Jesus, I trusted in you all my life and you let me down. You let me drown! I don't believe it.'

'*You* don't believe it!' said Jesus. 'I sent three fucking boats to save you.'

There was a wealthy Jew who owned a nail company. His only son had just graduated from college and the father wanted to get him involved in the company. So he placed his son in charge of the new advertising campaign. He told him that he would have no supervision and that any and all resources he needed would be at his disposal. The son was elated and immediately set off to make his father proud.

Four weeks later the son proudly proclaimed, 'I have finished!' He took his father out to examine the first product of the new campaign: a billboard portraying Christ on a cross with the caption, 'Even Then They Used Goldberg Nails'.

The father explained to the son that they couldn't portray Christ on a cross as it might offend their Christian clients. Dejected, the son said that he would fix the problem and report back to his father.

One week later the son took his father to see the billboard. Christ was no longer on the cross; he was lying at the base of the cross and the caption read, 'This Wouldn't Happen With Goldberg Nails'.

Have you heard of Salman Rushdie's new book? It's called *Buddha, You Fat Fuck*.

One day a nun was fishing and caught a huge fish for supper. A man was walking by and said, 'Wow, what a goddamn fish!' The sister said, 'Sir, you shouldn't talk to me like that, I'm a nun!' and the man said, 'But that's the name of it: a goddamn fish.'

So the sister took the fish back to the rectory and said, 'Mother Superior, look at the goddamn fish I caught.' The Mother Superior said, 'Sister, you shouldn't talk like that!' And the sister said, 'But Mother Superior, that's the name of it: a goddamn fish.'

The Mother Superior said, 'Well give me the goddamn fish and I'll clean it.' While she was cleaning the fish the Monsignor walked in and she said, 'Monsignor, look at the goddamn fish that Sister caught.' The Monsignor said, 'Mother Superior, you shouldn't talk like that!' and the Mother Superior said, 'But that's the name of it: a goddamn fish.' So the Monsignor said, 'Well, give me the goddamn fish and I'll cook it.'

That evening at supper there was a new priest at the table, and he said, 'Wow, what a nice fish.' The sister said, 'I caught the goddamn fish.' And Mother Superior said, 'I cleaned the goddamn fish.' And the Monsignor said, 'I cooked the goddamn fish.' And the new priest said, 'I like this fucking place already!'

Two nuns are bicycling down a cobblestone street. The first one says to the other, 'I haven't come this way before.'

The second one says, 'I know, it's the cobbles.'

How do you get rid of a nun's hiccups?
Tell her she's pregnant!

What is the definition of suspicion?
A nun doing press-ups in a cucumber field.

What is the definition of innocence?
A nun working in a condom factory thinking she's making sleeping bags for mice.

What do you call a nun who walks in her sleep?
A roaming Catholic.

How do you get a nun pregnant?
Dress her up as an altar boy.

What's black and white and red and has trouble getting through a revolving door?
A nun with a spear through her head.

Two nuns in a bath. The first one says, 'Where's the soap?'
The second one replies, 'Yes it does, doesn't it?'

'I would like to have 120 bananas for the convent,' says Mother Superior at the grocery store.

'If you buy such a large quantity, it is more economic to buy 144 of them,' says the shopkeeper.

'Oh well, we could always eat the other 24.'

MOTHER SUPERIOR: Sister Maria, if you walk through town at night and you're accosted by a man with bad intentions, what would you do?'

SISTER MARIA: I would lift my habit, Mother Superior.

MOTHER SUPERIOR (shocked): And what would you do next?'

SISTER MARIA: I would tell him to drop his pants.

MOTHER SUPERIOR (even more shocked): And what then?'

SISTER MARIA: I would run away. I can run much faster with my habit up than he can with his pants down.

A priest asks a nun if he can walk her back to the convent. She says, 'Just this once.' Upon arriving, he asks if he can kiss her. She replies, 'Well all right, as long as you don't get into the habit.'

Two nuns are walking down an alley at night. Two guys jump out and start raping them. The first nun looks to Heaven and says, 'Forgive them, Father, for they know not what they're doing.' The second nun looks up and says, 'This one does!'

It was Friday, and four nuns went to the priest at the local Catholic church to ask for the weekend off. They argued back and forth for a few minutes. Finally the priest agreed to let them leave the convent for the weekend. 'However,' he said, 'as soon as you get back Monday morning I want you to confess to me what you did over the weekend.' The four nuns agreed, and ran off.

Monday came, and the four nuns returned. The first nun said to the priest, 'Forgive me, Father, for I have sinned.' The priest asked, 'What did you do, Sister?' She replied, 'I watched an R-rated movie.' The priest looked up at Heaven for a few seconds, then replied, 'You are forgiven. Go and drink the holy water.'

The first nun left, and the fourth nun began to chuckle quietly under her breath.

The second nun said to the priest, 'Forgive me, Father, for I have sinned. I was driving my brother's car and I hit a neighbour's dog and killed it.' The priest looked up to Heaven for half a minute, then said, 'You are forgiven. Go and drink the holy water.'

By this time the fourth nun was laughing quite audibly.

125

Then the third nun said, 'Forgive me, Father, for I have sinned. Last night, I ran naked up and down Main Street.' The priest looked up at Heaven for a full five minutes before responding. 'God forgives you. Go and drink the holy water.'

The fourth nun fell on the floor, laughing so hard, tears ran down her cheeks.

The priest asked her, 'Okay, what did you do that was so bloody funny?'

The fourth nun replied, 'I peed in the holy water.'

The nuns at the local convent had their daily announcement session. The Mother Superior walked out in front of the 100 nuns with a very serious frown on her face.

MOTHER SUPERIOR: There was a sinful deed committed here yesterday.

99 NUNS: Oh, no!

ONE NUN: Hee, hee, hee.

MOTHER SUPERIOR: Today I found a pair of men's underwear.

99 NUNS: Oh, no!

ONE NUN: Hee, hee, hee.

MOTHER SUPERIOR: And I also found a condom.

99 NUNS: Oh, no!

ONE NUN: Hee, hee, hee.

MOTHER SUPERIOR: And it has been used!

99 NUNS: Oh, no!

ONE NUN: Hee, hee, hee.

MOTHER SUPERIOR: And there was a hole in it!

ONE NUN: Oh, no!
99 NUNS: Hee, hee, hee!

Four nuns were standing in line at the gates of
Heaven. Peter asks the first if she has ever sinned.
'Well, once I looked at a man's penis,' she said.
'Put some of this holy water on your eyes and
you may enter Heaven,' Peter told her.
Peter then asked the second nun if she had ever
sinned. 'Well, once I held a man's penis,' she replied.
'Put your hand in this holy water and you may
enter Heaven,' he said.
Just then the fourth nun pushed ahead of the
third nun.
Peter asked her, 'Why did you push ahead in
line?' She said, 'Because I want to gargle before she
sits in it.'

The seven dwarfs are in Rome and they go on a
tour of the city. After a while they go to the
Vatican and meet the Pope. Grumpy, for once,
seems to have a lot to say. He keeps asking the
Pontiff questions about the church and, in particular,
nuns.
'Your Holiness, do you have any really short
nuns?'
'No, my son, all our nuns are at least five feet
tall.'
'Are you sure? I mean, you wouldn't have any

nuns that are, say, about my height? Maybe a little shorter?'

'I'm afraid not. Why do you ask?'

'No reason ... you're positive? Nobody in a habit that's about three feet tall, two and a half feet tall?'

'I'm sure.'

'Okay.' Grumpy looks dejected at this news, and the Pope wonders why, so he eavesdrops on the dwarfs as they leave the building.

'What'd he say?' What'd he say?' chants the other six dwarfs.

Grumpy says, 'He said they don't have any.'

And the other six start chanting, 'Grumpy fucked a penguin! Grumpy fucked a penguin! Grumpy fucked a penguin!'

A nun is undressing for a bath when there's a knock at the door. The nun calls out, 'Who is it?' A voice answers, 'A blind man.'

The nun decides to get a thrill by having the blind man in the room while she's naked, so she lets him in. The man walks in, looks straight at the nun and says, 'Cornrr, and can I sell you a blind, dearie?'

A nun and a priest were travelling across the desert and realised halfway across that the camel they were using for transportation was about to die. They set up a makeshift camp, hoping someone would come to their rescue, but to no avail. Soon the camel died.

After several days of not being rescued, they agreed that they were not going to be rescued. They prayed a lot, and discussed their predicament in great depth.

Finally, the priest said to the nun, 'You know, Sister, I am about to die, and there's one thing I've always wanted here on Earth – to see a woman naked. Would you mind taking off your clothes so I can look at you?'

The nun thought about this request for several seconds and then agreed to take off her clothes. As she was doing so, she remarked, 'Well, Father, now that I think about it, I've never seen a man naked either. Would you mind taking off your clothes, too?' With little hesitation, the priest also stripped.

Suddenly the nun exclaimed, 'Father! What is that little thing hanging between your legs?'

The priest patiently answered, 'That, my child, is a gift from God. If I put it in you, it creates a new life.'

'Well,' responded the nun, 'forget about me. Stick it in the camel.'

Three nuns who had recently died were on their way to Heaven. At the Pearly Gates they were met by St Peter. Clustered around the gates was a collection of lights and bells.

St Peter stopped them and told them that they would each have to answer a question before they could enter.

ST PETER: What were the names of the two people in the Garden of Eden?

1ST NUN: Adam and Eve.

The lights flashed, the bells rang and in she went through the Pearly Gates.

ST PETER: What did Adam eat from the forbidden tree?

2ND NUN: An apple.

The lights flashed, the bells rang and in she went through the Pearly Gates.

And finally it came the turn of the last nun.

ST PETER: What was the first thing Eve said to Adam?

Afer a few minutes thinking she said, 'Gosh, that's a hard one!'

The lights flashed, the bells rang and in she went through the Pearly Gates!

A man is driving down a deserted stretch of highway when he notices a sign out of the corner of his eye. It says SISTERS OF MERCY HOUSE OF PROSTITUTION 10 MILES. He thinks it is just a figment of his imagination and drives on without a second thought. Soon he sees another sign which says SISTERS OF MERCY HOUSE OF PROSTITUTION 5 MILES and realises that these signs are for real.

When he drives past a third sign saying SISTERS OF MERCY HOUSE OF PROSTITUTION NEXT RIGHT his curiosity gets the best of him and he pulls into the drive.

On the far side of the parking lot stands a

sombre stone building with a small sign next to the door reading SISTERS OF MERCY. He climbs the steps and rings the bell. The door is answered by a nun in a long black habit who asks, 'What may we do for you, my son?' He answers, 'I saw your signs along the highway and was interested in possibly doing business.'

'Very well, my son. Please follow me.'

He is led through many winding passages and is soon quite disoriented. The nun stops at a closed door, and tells the man, 'Please knock on this door.' He does as he is told and the door is answered by another nun, holding a tin cup.

'Please place $50 in the cup, then go through the large wooden door at the end of this hallway,' she says. He gets $50 out of his wallet and places it in the second nun's cup. He trots eagerly down the hall and slips through the door, pulling it shut behind him. As the door locks behind him, he finds himself back in the parking lot, facing another small sign: GO IN PEACE. YOU HAVE JUST BEEN SCREWED BY THE SISTERS OF MERCY.

Sister Catherine is asking all the Catholic school children in fourth grade what they want to be when they grow up.

Little Sheila says, 'When I grow up, I want to be a prostitute!'

Sister Catherine's eyes grow wide and she barks, 'What did you say?'

'A prostitute!' Sheila repeats.

Sister Catherine breathes a sigh of relief and says, 'Thank God! I thought you said a Protestant.'

A nun gets on a bus and sits behind the driver. She tells the bus driver that she is very ill and wants to experience sex before she dies. The bus driver agrees to accommodate her, but the nun explains that she can't have sex with anyone who is married, as that would be a sin. The bus driver says he's not married. The nun says she also has to die a virgin, so she will have to take it in the arse.

Being the only two on the bus, they go to the back and take care of business. When they are done, and he has resumed driving, he says, 'Sister, I have a confession to make. I am married and have three children.'

The nun replies, 'That's okay. I have a confession, too. My name is Dave, and I'm on my way to a costume party.'

An old nun is walking home from the convent one day, when a man jumps out from the bushes and has his way. Then the man says, 'What will you tell the Holy Father now, Sister?'

She says, 'I must tell the truth! I will say I was walking home from the convent when a man jumped out from the bushes and raped me twice, unless you're tired!'

Did you hear the one about the man who opened a dry cleaning business next door to the convent?

He knocked on the door and asked the Mother Superior if she had any dirty habits.

Three nuns are walking down the street, when a man jumps out and flashes at them. The first nun has a stroke, the second nun has a stroke, but the third one doesn't touch him.

There was an Irish nun sitting on the curb, sipping a bottle of stout, and obviously drunk out of her mind. The town constable walked up to her and said, 'Sure now, Sister Colleen, and why'd ya be doing a thing like this?'

The sister replied, 'Oh now, it's not fer meself I done it, sir. I done it fer the Mother Superior, to cure her constipation.'

The perplexed policeman looked askance at this and asked, 'And how might it be that yer present state could have anything to do with the Mother Superior's constipation?'

To which Sister Colleen said, 'When she sees me this way, she'll be shittin' a brick.'

A priest decides to pay a visit to a nearby convent which is in a rundown neighbourhood. As he walks down the street, several prostitutes approach and proposition him.

'Twenty bucks a trick!'

These solicitations embarrass the priest, who lowers his head and hurries on until he gets to the convent. Once inside he displays his naivety by asking the Mother Superior, 'What's a trick?'

She answers, 'Twenty bucks — just like on the outside!'

A nun is driving through some very lonely countryside. The car stops and she notices there is no petrol left, so she walks to the nearest filling station. But, of course, being a nun, she is a little unworldly, and she forgets to take along a jerrycan for the petrol. The nice guy at the filling station doesn't have one either. He thinks for a while, then hands her a chamberpot full of petrol. The nun walks back to her car and starts pouring the petrol into the tank. A bypassing car stops, and the driver looks out and says, 'Sister, how I would like to have as much faith as you!'

A guy gets on a bus and sees a nun sitting in the corner. Under her wimple he spots a glimmer of her face, which is remarkably beautiful. When she moves, her vestment cannot hide the fact that she has a gorgeous figure. He gets more and more excited until, finally, he approaches her and says, 'Sister, I don't normally do this sort of thing, but I think I love you. Can we get together some time?' Enraged, the nun gets off the bus.

The bus driver asks him why he was bothering the nun. The guy apologises, insisting that he has never done this sort of thing before. But the bus driver says, 'Don't apologise, I was checking her out myself. In fact, let me do you a favour. Did you see where she got off? There's a little park there, and every day she goes to pray, at the same time. If you go there tomorrow, maybe you'll get lucky.' The guy thanks him and leaves.

Next day, he goes to the park and there is the nun in a secluded spot by some trees. So he walks off into the bushes and comes back a few minutes later dressed in a long white robe, with a long blonde wig, a blonde beard and a crown of thorns. The nun is overwhelmed. She asks what he wants her to do. He explains that every few thousand years he likes to come to Earth and get laid. Blushing, the nun says it would be an honour, but insists on turning her back on him.

Afterwards, he is suddenly overcome with a blast of guilt and says, still panting, 'Sister, I have to confess. I'm not really Jesus. I'm actually the guy who was annoying you on the bus yesterday.'

The nun says, 'That's okay. In fact, I'm not really a nun. I'm actually the bus driver.'

A pale-faced nun, still in shock, enters the office of the Mother Superior and reports, with a profound blush, 'Mother Superior, we've discovered a case of syphilis.'

'Wonderful!' says the old nun. 'I was getting sick of the Chablis.'

The Mother Superior is praying in the chapel when she hears an inordinate amount of laughing and giggling outside. Looking through a chink in the stained glass, she sees all the sisters riding around on their new bikes, and having a great deal of fun. However, they're making so much noise, she can't concentrate on her praying. So she goes out and says, 'Sisters, please! A bit more quiet or you'll all have to put the saddles back.'

During his visit to the US, Pope John II had a meeting with a senator. The senator asked the Pope, 'Your Holiness, how do you find our country?'

The Pope replied, 'I love it! It's a wonderful country! Friendly people, blessed with an abundance of natural resources ...' and so on and so forth. The senator asked, 'Is there anything about our country that you don't like? I am, after all, a United States senator, and maybe I could change some things.'

The Pope thought a while and said, 'Now that

you mention it, there are two things about your country that I do not like.' The senator asked, 'What are they? Maybe I can help.'

'The first thing I don't like about your country is the large number of Polish jokes told. They make my countrymen out to be a bunch of idiots!'

The senator said, 'I have a solution for that! When I get back to Washington, I'll get together with some of my Senate colleagues and we'll pass a bill, which I'm sure will become law, that will make it a federal crime to tell a Polish joke, and anyone caught telling a Polish joke will be fined $50. How do you like that?'

The Pope replied, 'Great idea! I love it!'

The senator asked, 'Now, why don't you tell me the second thing you don't like about the US? Maybe I can do something about it as well.' The Pope answered, 'M&Ms.'

The senator, a bit confused, asked, 'M&Ms? What's not to like about M&Ms?'

The Pope replied, 'They're hard to peel.'

The Pope died. Like all good Christians he went to Heaven and knocked on the door. Peter opened the door and lifted an enquiring eyebrow. The Pope said, 'I'm the Pope.' Peter picked up the phone and rang Jesus. 'I have someone here who says he's the Pope. Do you know him?'

'No, never heard of him. Send him to Hell,' Jesus answered.

'That can't be true. Ring God himself,' the Pope

said. So Peter rang God and said, 'We've got someone who says he's the Pope. Do you know him?' God answered, 'No, never heard of him, send him to Hell.'

'The last chance I have is the Holy Spirit,' the Pope said. Peter rang him and said, 'I have someone here who says he's the Pope. Do you know him?'

'Yes,' he said, 'I know him. He's the one who told everyone I got Maria pregnant. Send him to Hell.'

A rich American tourist holidaying in Rome was intent on seeing the Pope. He waited in a long queue, wearing a rather expensive suit and hoping the Pope would notice how smart he was and perhaps exchange a few words with him.

As the Pope made his way slowly down the queue, he walked right passed the American without noticing him. The Pope then stopped next to a tramp, leaned over and whispered something in his ear, and made his way on again.

This pissed off the American, so he agreed to pay $1000 to the tramp for his suit in the hope that the Pope would speak to him the next day.

The next morning, the Pope made his way slowly up to the American. When he finally reached him, the Pope leaned over and spoke softly in his ear, 'I thought I told you to fuck off!'

What happened to the Pope when he went to Mount Olive?

Popeye beat the shit out of him.

The Pope is on his 1988 tour of America, in the middle of a three-day bash in New York. On the second day, he is driving back to his motel after a heavy day's bible bashing. It suddenly occurs to him that he is a little peckish and so he decides to go for something to eat. Out of the corner of his eye he notices Mel's Diner and immediately pulls over.

He hops out, kisses the ground a couple of times and then goes in and sits down. A sleazy waitress wanders over, notices who he is and then straightens herself up. 'Yes, your Holiness, what would you like?' The Pope thinks for a while. 'Well, daughter, I have this terrible craving for a nice steak.'

'Sure Mac, er, I mean your Holiness. Would you like it well done, medium or rare?'

'Oh, I think I'd like a very rare one please.' The waitress raises her arm. 'One bloody steak, Mel!' she shouts. The Pope is horrified. 'Oh no, my daughter, you mustn't swear. There's no call for that!'

'But you don't understand – "bloody" describes how the steak is cooked. Very rare.' The Pope smiles. 'I understand, how stupid of me.

A little later, the Pope's steak arrives and he gets stuck in. It's delicious, and he goes to bed that night feeling satisfied. The next day, the Pope has an even bigger God-squadding session, in which he is assisted by 31 of his cardinals. Afterwards he calls his cardinals together. 'Right lads, as you've done a really good job today, I'll treat you to a bit of nosh at this place I know. You'll like it, I'm sure.'

So the Pope takes his cardinals to the diner and calls to the waitress, 'Can I have 32 bloody steaks please?'

Immediately, one of the cardinals slaps his knee. 'Hey, yeah! And plenty of fucking chips, okay?'

The Pope is travelling along in the Popemobile, beside a large river in South Africa. He catches sight of a black man struggling and screaming in the river as he tries in vain to fight off a huge crocodile. Suddenly, two white men leap into the water, drag the man and the croc to land, and then beat the crocodile to death with sticks.

The Pope is really impressed by this. He goes over to where the two men are standing next to the bleeding and unconscious black man and says, 'Congratulations. That was the most wonderful thing to do, and I can see that it is men like you who will rebuild this country as an example of racial harmony.'

The Pope then goes on his way. One of the white men says, 'Who was that?' and the other replies, 'That was the Pope, he is in direct communication with God. He knows everything.'

The first man says, 'Maybe, but he knows fuck all about crocodile fishing.'

A fellow was visiting the Vatican and became separated from his tour group. Desperately needing a pee, he found a bathroom and walked in and, to his horror, discovered the Pope sitting on the toilet, masturbating. He promptly snapped a couple of pictures. The Pope, recovering his composure, offered the photographer ten million lira for his camera, which the fellow accepted.

After disposing of the film, his Holiness decided he'd take the camera on his travels. One day, whilst visiting the US, a bishop was admiring his Holiness's camera. 'How much did you pay for it?'

'$10 000.'

'Wow! The guy that sold you that must have seen you coming!'

One day, a young priest is instructed by his elders that he must hear confessions. He has never done this before, and so he is given a list of what to give out as penance.

A woman comes into the confessional and begins. 'Forgive me Father, for I have sinned.' The priest replies, 'What is your sin, my child?'

'I have told lies,' she says. The priest consults his list and sees that the required penance is two Hail Marys.

'Anything else, my child?' he asks. 'Father, I've committed fellatio,' she replies. The priest scans the list and panics because he cannot find fellatio! He sticks his head out of the door of the confessional and sees an altar boy passing by. 'Quick, what does

Father Brown give for fellatio?' he asks. 'Ten dollars' the boy replies.

One day, the old man in charge of ringing matins at the local monastery died, so the abbot decided to advertise for a new bellringer. After running an ad for several days in the local newspaper, an applicant finally showed up. Much to the abbot's dismay, this man had no arms.

'I'm afraid,' said the abbot, 'that you don't have much of a career as a bellringer ahead of you.'

'Nonsense,' said the man, 'let me show you what I can do.'

They climbed up the bell tower, and the man proceeded to run full-speed across the tower, throwing himself face-first into the bells. A lovely pealing sound resulted, and the abbot decided then and there to hire the man.

The man acted as the monastery's bellringer for several months until, while ringing the evening meal, he missed the bells and plummeted from the tower, killing himself. In the resulting investigation, the chief of police called over the abbot and pointed out the dead man. 'Do you recognise this man?' asked the police chief.

'Hmmm,' said the abbot, 'I don't recall his name, but his face rings a bell.'

What is red and full of feathers?
A fallen angel.

What's an atheist's favourite Christmas movie?
Coincidence on 34th Street.

An old man was unhappy because he'd lost his favourite hat. Instead of buying a new one, he decided to go to the local church and pinch one out of the vestibule. But when he tried, an usher saw him and forced him to sit in the pew and listen to the entire sermon on the Ten Commandments.

After church, the old man went to the preacher, shook his hand and said, 'I want to thank you for saving my soul today. I came to church to steal a hat and after hearing your sermon on the Ten Commandments, I decided against it.'

'You mean the Commandment "Thou shalt not steal" changed your mind?' asked the preacher.

'No,' said the old man. 'The one about adultery did. As soon as you mentioned it, I remembered where I'd left my hat.'

Two clergymen were discussing the present sad state of sexual morality. 'I didn't sleep with my wife before we were married,' one clergyman said self-righteously. 'Did you?'

'I'm not sure,' said the other, 'what was her maiden name?'

A preacher is buying a parrot. 'Are you absolutely certain it doesn't swear?' asked the preacher. 'Oh absolutely. It is a very religious parrot,' the storekeeper assured him. 'Do you see those strings on his legs? If you pull the right one he'll recite the Lord's Prayer. And if you pull the left one, he'll recite the 23rd Psalm.'

'That's wonderful,' said the preacher. 'But what happens if you pull both strings?'

'I fall off my fuckin' perch, you goddamn shit-for-brains,' screeched the parrot.

A monastery was perched high on a cliff and the only way to reach it was to ride in a basket which was hauled to the top by several monks. Obviously, the ride up the steep cliff in the basket was terrifying. One visitor got exceedingly nervous. About halfway up he noticed that the rope by which he was suspended was old and fraying. With a trembling voice, he asked the monk who was riding with him how often they changed the rope. The monk thought for a moment and answered, 'Whenever it breaks.'

A drunk gets on a bus, staggers up the aisle and sits next to an old lady, breathing fumes all over her. She looks at him with withering contempt and says, 'I've got news for you. You're going straight to Hell.' The drunk jumps out of his seat and shouts, 'Christ! I'm on the wrong bus!'

An Irish priest and a rabbi found themselves sharing a compartment on a train. After a while, the priest opened a conversation by saying, 'I know that in your religion, you're not supposed to eat pork. Have you actually ever tasted it?'

The rabbi said, 'I must tell the truth. Yes, I have, on the odd occasion.'

Then the rabbi had his turn of interrogation. He asked, 'Your religion, too. I know you're supposed to be celibate. But ...'

The priest replied, 'Yes, I know what you're going to ask. I have succumbed once or twice.'

There was silence for a while. Then the rabbi peeped around the newspaper he was reading and said, 'Better than pork, isn't it?'

Above a monastery on Mount Athos, there's a cave that particularly spiritual monks choose to spend some years sitting inside. It's very difficult to get up there. Very dangerous.

A monk was told that once he had entered the cave, his only contact with the world would come every six years, when he'd be allowed to speak just two words. Six years later the head monk asked the novice what his two words were. 'More food,' said the novice. 'Okay,' the head monk said, 'I'll leave you a couple of extra loaves of bread.'

Six years later the head monk asked again. 'I'm cold,' said the novice. 'No problem,' said the head monk, 'I'll leave you this blanket.'

Six years later the head monk inquired of the

145

novice if there was anything else he wanted to say. 'I quit,' said the novice. To which the head monk testily responded, 'Fine by me. Good riddance. All you've ever done since you got here is complain.'

One day a mum and her eight-year-old daughter were walking along the beach, just at the water's edge, when a huge wave crashed on the beach, sweeping the child out to sea. 'Oh God,' lamented the mother, looking up at the heavens and shaking her fist. 'She was my only child. I can't have more. She was the love and joy of my life and I've cherished every moment she's been with me. Give her back to me and I'll be in church every day. Forever!'

Suddenly an even bigger wave deposited the girl back on the sand. The mother looked up to Heaven and said, 'She was wearing a hat!'

In the beginning was the Plan.

And then came the Assumptions.

And the Assumptions were without form.

And the Plan was without substance.

And darkness was upon the face of the Workers.

And they spoke amongst themselves, saying, 'It is a crock of shit, and it stinketh.'

And the Workers went unto their Supervisors and said, 'It is a pail of dung, and none may abide the odour thereof.'

And the Supervisors went unto their Managers,
saying, 'It is a container of excrement, and it
is very strong, such that none may abide
by it.'

And the Managers went unto their Directors,
saying, 'It is a vessel of fertilizer, and none may
abide its strength.'

And the Directors spoke amongst themselves,
saying to one another, 'It contains that which aids
plant growth, and it is very powerful.'

And the Vice Presidents went unto the President,
saying unto him, 'This new plan will actively
promote the growth and vigor of the company,
with powerful effects.'

And the President looked upon the Plan, and saw
that it was good.

And the Plan became Policy.

This is how Shit happens.

Why did Jesus cross the road?
He was nailed to the chicken.

Deciding that the time had come, God calls Boris
Yeltsin, Bill Clinton and Bill Gates into his office and
says, 'The world will end in 30 days, go back and
tell your people.'

So Bill Clinton goes on TV and tells the
American people, 'I have good news and I have bad
news. The good news is that the basic family values

147

upon which we have based our lives are right. Yes, there is a god. The bad news is that the world will end in 30 days.'

Boris Yeltsin goes to the Russian people and says, 'I have bad news and I have worse news. The bad news is that we were wrong. There is a god. The worse news is that the world will end in 30 days.'

Bill Gates goes to his executive committee and says, 'I've great news and I've got fabulous news. The great news is that God thinks I'm important. The fabulous news is that we don't have to ship Windows 95 after all.'

What's the difference between *Jurassic Park* and IBM?

One is a high-tech theme park dominated by dinosaurs. The other is a Steven Spielberg film.

SHAGGY DOGS

A farmer purchased 20 pigs. On arriving back at the farm, he found he'd bought all females. He asked his neighbour if he could bring them over to mate with his boars and the neighbour was willing to oblige.

So he took his female pigs next door to frolic all day with the males. When he came to take them home, he asked, 'How will I know if they're pregnant?' The neighbour answered, 'Tomorrow morning. If they're agrazin', they're pregnant.'

The next morning the pigs weren't agrazin', so the farmer loaded them back on his truck and took them to the neighbour. He didn't mind, and the male pigs didn't. They were waiting by the gate when they heard the truck coming.

The next day, same thing. So he put them on the truck and took them back to the neighbour.

On the fourth day the farmer was feeling discouraged, and tired of loading all the pigs and driving to the neighbour's with them. So he said to his wife, 'Honey, I just can't bear it. Would you look at the pigs and tell me if they're agrazin'.' She looked out, smiled, turned to him and said, 'Honey, they're not agrazin', but they're all lined up at the truck, and one's up on the front seat, honkin' the horn.'

Tonto and the Lone Ranger were lost on the prairie one day. The Lone Ranger says to Tonto, 'Use your Indian instincts and get us out of this mess.'

Tonto bends down and puts his ear to the ground. He turns and says to the Lone Ranger, 'Buffalo come.' The Lone Ranger says to Tonto, 'How do you know?'

Tonto says, 'Ear sticky.'

A cowboy rides into town, hitches up his horse and walks into a bar. He gets a beer, drinks it, and walks out. Half a second passes and he bursts back into the bar and says, 'ALL RIGHT, WHICH ONE OF YOU MOTHERS PAINTED MY HORSE'S FACE YELLOW?' A huge man-mountain stands up, looks down at the cowboy and says, 'I did.' The cowboy looks up at him and whispers, 'The first coat's dry.'

A cowboy goes into a bar, has a beer, walks outside and finds his horse has been stolen. He walks back into the bar, and fires his gun through the ceiling. 'WHICH ONE OF YOU MOTHERS STOLE MY HOSS?' he yells. No one answers. 'ALL RIGHT, I'M GONNA HAVE ANOTHA BEER, AND IF MY HOSS AIN'T OUTSIDE BY THE TIME I FINISH, I'M GONNA DO WHAT I DUN IN TEXAS.'

He gets another beer, walks outside, and his horse is back. So he gets on it and makes to ride out of town. The bartender wanders out of the bar and asks, 'Say pardner, what happened in Texas?'

The cowboy turns to him and says, 'I had to bloody walk home.'

It was a boring Sunday afternoon in the jungle so the elephants decided to challenge the ants to a game of soccer. The game was going well, with the elephants beating the ants ten goals to nil, when the ants gained possession.

The ants' star player was dribbling the ball towards the elephants' goal when the elephants' left-back came lumbering towards him. The elephant trod on the little ant, killing him instantly.

The referee stopped the game. 'What the hell do you think you're doing? Do you call that sportsmanship, killing another player?'

The elephant replied, 'Well I didn't meant to kill him – I was just trying to trip him up.'

153

A man went to a doctor to have his penis enlarged. This particular procedure involved splicing a baby elephant's trunk onto the man's penis.

Overjoyed, the man went out with his girlfriend to a very fancy restaurant. After cocktails, the man's penis crept out of his pants, felt around the table, grabbed a roll and quickly disappeared under the tablecloth. The girl was startled and exclaimed, 'What was that?'

Suddenly the penis came back, took another roll and just as quickly disappeared. The girl was silent for a moment, then finally said, 'I don't believe I saw what I think I just saw. Can you do that again?'

With a bit of an uncomfortable smile, the man replied, 'Honey, I'd like to, but I don't think my ass can take another roll.'

An elephant is walking through the jungle when she gets a thorn in her foot. She is in absolute agony until an ant strolls by. So the elephant says, 'Help me, help me.'

But the ant refuses unless the elephant agrees to let the ant have his wicked way with her. Replies the elephant, 'Anything! Anything!' So, out comes the thorn and up gets the ant and proceeds to enjoy himself.

Meanwhile, in a tree directly above them, a monkey who is witnessing the whole episode is in knots of laughter. Consequently he falls out of the tree on top of the elephant.

Says the elephant, 'Ouch!'

Says the ant, in his own little frenzy, 'Suffer bitch, *suffer!*'

An elephant is walking through the jungle. All of a sudden he falls into a pit and starts screaming. By chance a chicken hears the screaming and decides to investigate. He sees the elephant in the pit and shouts, 'Don't worry, I am going to save you.' The chicken then calls on the King of the Jungle.

The King of the Jungle promptly arrives in his red Porsche. He throws a rope from the Porsche into the pit, the elephant ties it around himself and the King of the Jungle pulls him out of the pit. The elephant is saved.

So grateful is the elephant to the chicken that he promises him he will one day do the same for him.

As chance would have it, the next week the elephant is walking through the jungle and hears the screaming of a chicken. He wanders over and sees that his friend the chicken is stuck in a pit. The elephant shouts, 'Don't 'worry, chicken. I will save you.'

So the elephant throws his tail into the pit. However the tail is too small and the chicken cannot reach it. Undeterred by this, the elephant throws in his trunk but, alas, this also is too small. As a last desperate effort the elephant throws in his penis.

Success! The chicken grabs the elephant's enormous penis and climbs out to safety.

Moral of the story: if you have a big dick you don't need a red Porsche to pull a chick.

Father, mother and son decide to go to the zoo. At the elephant enclosure the boy looks at the elephant, sees its willy, points to it and says, 'Mummy, what is that long thing?' His mother replies, 'That, son, is the elephant's trunk.'

'No, at the other end.'

'That, son, is the tail.'

'No, Mummy, the thing under the elephant.'

A short embarrassed silence after which she replies, 'That's nothing.'

The mother goes to buy some ice-cream and the boy, not being satisfied with her answer, asks his father the same question. 'Daddy, what is that long thing?'

'That's the trunk, son,' replies the father.

'No, at the other end.'

'Oh, that's the tail.'

'No, no Daddy, the thing below,' asks the son in desperation.

'That is the elephant's penis. Why do you ask, son?'

'Well, Mummy said it was nothing,' says the boy.

Replies the father, 'I tell you, I spoil that woman.'

How do you get four elephants into a Volkswagen?

Two in the front and two in the back.

What do you get when you cross an elephant with a kangaroo?

Bloody great holes all over Australia.

How do you know if there is an elephant under the bed?

Your nose is touching the ceiling.

Why do elephants paint the soles of their feet yellow?

So that they can hide upside down in bowls of custard.

Did you ever find an elephant in your custard?

No? Well, it must work.

What do elephants use for tampons?

Sheep.

How do you stop an elephant from charging?

Take away his credit card.

Have you heard about Hannibal crossing the Alps with elephants?

None of the offspring survived.

What do you do if an elephant comes through your window?
  Swim for your life!

Why are elephants wrinkled?
  Have you ever tried to iron one?

Why does a duck have flat feet?
  To stamp out fires in the woods.

Why does an elephant have flat feet?
  To stamp out burning ducks.

After the flood when the ark came to rest on Ararat, Noah released all the animals, and held a meeting and explained to them that the Lord wanted them to be fruitful and multiply and repopulate the Earth.

  In a week he went around to check on things. The place was humming with activity: the insects had all reproduced and there were flies, mosquitoes, bees, and so on; the mice and hamsters were pregnant, the birds were building nests, and the other animals were going about the courting process. All except two snakes down by a stream in a swampy bit that no one else wanted. They were just lying there, curled up on rocks in the sun. 'Hey, be fruitful and multiply!' Noah told them.

The male snake raised his head and said, 'Don't sweat it!' So Noah went back to his business.

A couple of weeks later Noah made another trip around. The insects were into the third generation already, and the place was fairly hopping with baby hamsters, mice, bunnies, and so on. The cat and the dog were both pregnant, and the birds were all sitting on eggs. Even some of the larger animals were showing signs of mating. All but the snakes. The only sign of activity was that the two had changed rocks. Noah again enjoined them to get with it. 'We're cool!' the male snake assured him.

A few weeks later, Noah again made the rounds. Almost all the large animals were pregnant by now, and many birds had hatched. There was a litter of kittens, and the dog was expecting her litter any minute. Noah hurried down to the stream to see the snakes. He found them chopping down trees, sawing the wood into logs and building furniture!

'Will you two get with it!' he said. 'Don't sweat it, everything is under control!' the male snake replied.

Well, a few weeks later Noah again took a look around. By now even the elephant was pregnant, and the place was alive with baby animals. And when Noah hurried down to check on those snakes, the area around the stream was positively wriggling with baby snakes. Which, of course, proves that anybody can multiply with log tables!

Once there was a marine biologist who loved dolphins. He spent his time trying to feed and protect his beloved creatures of the sea. One day, in a fit of inventive genius, he came up with a serum that would make dolphins live forever. Of course, he was ecstatic. But he soon realised that in order to mass produce this serum he would need large amounts of a certain compound that was only found in nature, in the metabolism of a rare South American bird.

Carried away by his love for dolphins, he resolved that he would go to the zoo and steal one of these birds. Unbeknown to him, as he was arriving at the zoo an elderly lion was escaping from its cage. The zookeepers were alarmed and immediately began combing the zoo for the escaped animal, unaware that it had simply lain down on the sidewalk and gone to sleep.

Meanwhile, the marine biologist arrived at the zoo and procured his bird. He was so excited by the prospect of helping his dolphins that he stepped absentmindedly over the sleeping lion on his way back to his car.

Immediately, 1500 policemen converged on him and arrested him for transporting a myrna across a staid lion for immortal porpoises.

One afternoon there was a good witch who was flying along, when all of a sudden she heard a soft crying from down below. When she landed, she saw a yellow frog. Touched by his sadness, the witch asked why he was crying. 'None of the other frogs will let me join in all their frog games. Boo hoo.'

'Don't cry, little one,' replied the witch, and with a wave of her magic wand, the frog turned green. All happy now, the frog was checking himself over when he noticed that his penis was still yellow. He asked the embarrassed witch about this, and she told him there were some things that she just couldn't do. But if he saw the wizard, he'd fix things up for him. So, happily, the little green frog hopped along his merry way.

Feeling quite happy about herself, the witch once more took to the skies. And once more she heard crying. But this time of a thunderous sort. So down to the ground she flew, only to discover a pink elephant. The witch asked him why he was crying. 'None of the other elephants will let me join in their elephant games. Boo hoo.'

Now, if you have ever seen an elephant cry, you know it's a pathetic looking sight, but a pink elephant crying is just downright heart-breaking. So once again the witch waved her magic wand and POOF, the elephant was grey.

All happy now, the elephant was checking himself all over when he noticed that his penis was still pink. He asked an embarrassed witch about this, and she told him that there were some things that she just couldn't do. But if he saw the wizard he would fix things up for him.

At this point the elephant started wailing. 'I don't know where the wizard is,' he sobbed.

'Just follow the yellow prick toad.'

Bilbo Backens was sitting in his hobbit hole one day when a group of young hobbits known for causing trouble in the village began harassing young Frodo, calling him names. Bilbo, sick and tired of these young ruffians and their untame ways, began throwing bricks at them from his window. However, try as hé might, he couldn't seem to hit a single one. Why? Because, of course, everyone knows bad hobbits are hard to brick!

Hank had a problem with flatulence. No matter what he ate, he farted. So he dreaded his new girlfriend's invitation to have dinner with her parents.

It was a very formal occasion and after he'd been sitting at the table for a while, he felt an incredible pain in his stomach and just had to fart. Just then, the family's dog Fido, which was sitting under the table, let out a growl. His girlfriend's mother yelled, 'Fido!' Hank was relieved. It didn't matter if he farted, they'd blame the dog.

So he let go a bigger fart and, sure enough, the father yelled at the dog. 'Fido!' But the pressure was still building up so Hank lets out a huge, ripping fart and the mother yelled at the dog again. 'Fido, get out from under the table before he shits all over you!'

Dave, out caught in the rain, ducked into a pub. There he met some old friends, had a few drinks and a few more, and at midnight started to stagger home through the rain. Feeling cold, he decided to get himself an Indian curry, so he headed for his local Taj Mahal take-away and ordered an extra hot vindaloo.

Arriving home, he placed the curry on the table and went upstairs for a pee. Whereupon the cat approached the curry and, feeling neglected and hungry, decided to have a go at it. Nibble nibble, chomp chomp, lick lick. The vindaloo vanished.

Dave returned and was appalled to discover the cat licking the plate. He grabbed it by the neck and dragged it outside. 'You dreadful little moggie. I hate you. You're dead,' he ranted. Filling a dustbin with water, he threw the hissing cat into it and slammed the lid down. He then put a few bricks on top, just to be on the safe side.

Dave returned to his sitting room feeling very sorry for himself. A few minutes later he heard a knock on the window and, lo and behold, there was the cat. The cat looked at him and said, 'You wouldn't happen to have any more water, would you?'

A woman buys a parrot only to find that it says nothing but, 'My name is Mary and I'm a whore.' She tries to teach the bird more acceptable phrases but, after weeks, has failed utterly. 'My name is Mary and I'm a whore,' it says over and over again, often at the most inopportune moments and much to the lady's embarrassment.

One day her parish priest dropped by and, sure enough, the parrot squawked out the only words it would say. She apologised to the priest, explaining that the bird resisted all efforts at reform. The priest offered to take the bird to visit the two birds he had, as all his birds would say were Hail Marys while clutching rosaries in their talons. Perhaps they'd have a good influence on the lady's parrot.

So he took her parrot to his house and put it in the cage with his parrots. 'My name is Mary and I'm a whore,' said the lady's parrot. Whereupon one of the priest's birds said to the other, 'Throw that damn rosary away, our prayers have been answered.'

In Africa a camera crew has been assigned to get footage of the World Famous Gorilla Wrestler at work. The camera crew is in the truck with him and his dog, and they come across a small tree. The wrestler says to them, 'Just wait here, I'll be right back.'

He climbs the tree, wrestles with a gorilla for a while, then throws it to the ground. Quick as a flash, the man's dog jumps on the poor animal and has sex with it until it faints. The man throws it in the back of the van, and they drive on to a medium-sized tree with a medium-sized gorilla. And the same thing happens.

Then they're driving along, and there's a huge

tree with an absolutely massive gorilla in it. The man hands the cameraman a gun. 'What's this for?' the cameraman asks.

'Well, there's a small chance that I might lose the battle here. And if I do, shoot the dog!'

The animals were bored. Finally the lion had a great idea. 'Let's play the game the humans play. Football. I've seen it on TV.'

The lion's team received. They got their two firsts down and then had to punt. The mule punted and the rhino was back deep for the kick. He caught the ball, lowered his head and charged. First he crushed a road-runner, then two rabbits. He gored a wilderbeast, knocked over two cows, and broke through to the daylight, scoring six. Unfortunately they lacked a place kicker and the score remained 6-0.

Later in the first half the lion's team scored a touch-down and the mule kicked the extra point. The lion's team led at half-time.

The lion gave a pep-talk in the locker room. 'Look you guys, we can win this game. But we've got to keep the ball away from the rhino. He's a killer. Mule, when you kick off, be sure to keep it away from the rhino.'

The second half began. Just as the mule was about to kick off, the rhino's team changed formation and the ball went directly to the rhino. Once again, the rhino lowered his head and was off running. He stomped two gazelles, skewered a giraffe, bulldozed an elephant out of the way. It looked like he was home free when, suddenly, at the 20-yard line, he dropped down dead. There were no other animals in sight.

The lion went over to see what had happened. Right next to the dead rhino he saw a small centipede.

'Did you do this?' he asked the centipede.'

'Yeah, I did,' the centipede replied.

The lion yelled, 'Where the hell were you during the first half?'

'Get off my back. I was putting on my shoes!'

A tiger woke up one morning feeling magnificent. He felt so great he went outside and cornered a small monkey and roared at him, 'Who is the mightiest of all the jungle animals?' The terrified little monkey replied, 'You, of course. No one is mightier than you.'

A little while later it was a deer's turn. 'Who is the greatest and strongest of all the jungle animals?' roared the tiger. The deer just managed to stammer a reply. 'Oh great tiger, you are by far the mightiest animal in the jungle.'

On a roll, the tiger swaggered up to an elephant who was quietly munching on some weeds and roared at the top of his voice, 'Who is the mightiest of *all* the animals in the jungle?' The elephant grabbed the tiger with his trunk, picked him up, slammed him down, picked him up again and shook him until the tiger was just a blur of orange and black. Finally it threw the tiger into a nearby tree. The tiger fell out of the tree, staggered to his feet, looked at the elephant and said, 'Man, just because you don't know the answer, no need to get so pissed off!'

A blind man was waiting to cross the road when his guide dog peed on his leg. He reached into his pocket, took out a biscuit and gave it to the dog. A passerby who'd seen everything was very touched. 'That's very tolerant of you after what he just did.'

'Not really,' came the reply. 'I'm just finding out where his mouth is, so I can kick him in the nuts.'

A newly married couple inherited a parrot from an aged uncle. The parrot was very talkative and forever informing visitors as to what went on in the newly-weds' home. One evening after an embarrassing comment from the bird, the husband had had enough and said to the parrot, 'That's it. You're going to be covered up much earlier in future and if you take your cage cover off or embarrass us again, you're off to the zoo.'

A few days later the couple were preparing for a short trip and, as usual, the suitcase was too full to close. The husband said, 'I'll get on the top and jump up and down and see if you can get it.' After a bit the wife said, 'This is no good, I'll get on top and you see if you can get it.'

This still didn't work so the husband said, 'Tell you what, let's both get on top and bounce up and down – that'll get it.' With this, the parrot pulled off the cage cover and said, 'Zoo or no zoo, this I've gotta see!'

A man took his dog into a pub, bought a pint and settled down to watch football on the TV set above the bar. As luck would have it, it was a Fulham home game. After a one-sided match, Fulham lost, and the dog said, quite clearly, 'Oh, no – not again!'

The barman, startled, walked over to the owner and said, 'Did your dog just say "Oh, no – not again"?'

'Yes,' replied the owner blandly, 'he always says that when Fulham lose.'

'What does he say when Fulham win?'

'Don't know. I've only had him five years.'

A man goes into a pub with a pig under his arm. The barman spots him and says, 'That's the ugliest looking animal you've got there. Where on earth did you get it?

'Won it in a raffle,' says the pig.

A man was driving through the country, got thirsty and entered a pub. After a few minutes a large brown horse came clip-clopping in, sat down at a table, crossed its legs and ordered a coffee. Astonished, he asked the pub keeper if this wasn't just a little strange.

'Very,' he said. 'Normally it drinks a pint of beer.'

A pheasant was standing in a field chatting to a bull.

'I would love to be able to get to the top of yonder tree,' sighed the pheasant, 'but I haven't got the energy.'

'Well, why don't you nibble on some of my droppings?' replied the bull. 'They're packed with nutrients.'

The pheasant pecked at a lump of dung and found that it gave him enough strength to reach the first branch of the tree. The next day, after eating some more dung, he reached the second branch. And so on. Finally, after a fortnight, there he was proudly perched at the top of the tree. Whereupon he was spotted by a farmer who dashed into the farmhouse, emerged with a shotgun and blew the fuck out of the pheasant.

The moral of this story? Bullshit might get you to the top, but it won't keep you there.

Where do you find a tortoise with no legs?
Where you left it.

A horse walks into a bar and the bartender says,
'What a long face you have!'

A guy walks into a bar and puts his alligator on
the counter. The bartender says, 'You can't bring
that alligator in here.'
   'It's a pet alligator. Watch,' says the guy, tapping it
on its head. The 'gator opens its mouth wide. The
guy unzips his pants, pulls out his penis and puts it
in the alligator's mouth. He then taps the alligator
on the head and it closes its mouth gently on the
vulnerable member. Everyone in the bar is aghast.
He then taps the 'gator on the head again, it opens
its mouth and he puts his penis back in his pants.
   The guy says, 'I'll give anyone in the bar $50 to
do the same thing.' The patrons are very, very
quiet. Suddenly a drunken voice yells out,
'I ... I ... I'd like to do that. But I don't think I could
keep my mouth open that long!'

A baby harp seal walks into a bar. The bartender
says, 'What will you have, baby harp seal?' And the
baby harp seal says, 'Anything but Canadian Club on
the rocks.'

Two tall trees are growing in the woods. A small tree begins to grow between them and one big tree says to the other, 'Is that a son of a beech, or a son of a birch?'. The other says that he cannot tell.

A woodpecker lands on the small tree. One of the tall trees says, 'Woodpecker, you're a tree expert. Can you tell if that is a son of a beech or a son or a birch?' The woodpecker takes a taste of the small tree and replies, 'It is neither the son or a beech nor son of a birch. That, gentlemen, is the best piece of ash I've ever had my pecker in!'

A police dog responds to an ad for work with the FBI. 'Well,' says the personnel director, 'you'll have to meet some strict requirements. First, you must type at least 60 words per minute.' Sitting down at the typewriter, the dog types out 80 words per minute. 'Also,' says the director, 'you must pass a physical and complete the obstacle course.' This perfect canine specimen finishes the course in record time. 'There's one last requirement,' the director continues, 'you must be bilingual.' With confidence, the dog looks up at him and says, 'Meow!'

A farm family were gathering in the kitchen for breakfast. As the youngest son sat down, his mother told him he wasn't going to get anything to eat until he'd fed the animals. Angry, he thumped out the door and headed for the chicken coop. As he fed the chooks, he kicked each one in the head. Then it was off to the paddock to feed the cow. As she bent down to start on some fresh hay, he kicked her in the head. He poured slops into a trough for the pigs and, as they started eating, kicked them in the head. He then headed back to the kitchen and sat down. His mother was outraged. 'I saw what you did. Since you kicked the chickens you'll get no eggs for breakfast. And since you kicked the cow you'll get no milk. And no bacon or sausages because you kicked the pigs.'

His father came down the stairs and, nearly tripping on the cat, kicked it. The boy looked up at Mum and said, 'Are you gonna tell him or should I?'

Tired of driving, a salesman parked his car beside a paddock. Immediately a horse came to the fence and began to boast about his career. 'Yes, I'm a great horse. I've run in 25 races and won over $5 million. I keep my trophies in the barn.'

The salesman considered the value of owning a talking horse, found the farmer and started negotiations.

'Aah, you don't want that horse,' said the farmer.

'Yes, I do,' said the salesman, 'and I'll give you $100 000 for it.'

Without hesitation the farmer said, 'He's yours.'

Whilst writing out the cheque, the salesman

asked, 'By the way, why wouldn't I want your horse?'

'Because,' said the farmer, 'he's a liar. He hasn't won a race in his life.'

Two devout churchgoing women were chatting in front of the store when a dusty old cowboy rode up, tied his horse in front of the saloon, walked around behind it, lifted its tail and kissed it full on the rectum.

Disgusted, one of the women said, 'That's sickening. Why did you do that?'

To which the cowboy replied, 'I've got chapped lips.'

'Does that make them feel better?'

'No, but it stops me from licking them.

At a conference on the supernatural, one of the speakers asked, 'Who here has seen a ghost?' Most hands went up. 'And how many of you have had some form of interaction with a ghost?' About half the hands remained up. 'Okay, now how many of you have had physical contact with a ghost?' Three hands stayed up, and there was a slight murmur in the crowd.

'Well, that's very interesting. Let me ask if any of you have, how shall I put this, been intimate with a ghost.' One hand stayed up. The speaker was astonished. 'Sir, are you telling us that you've actually had sexual liaison with a ghost?'

The guy with his hand up suddenly looked embarrassed and said, 'Oh, I'm sorry. I thought you said goat.'

Two dogs are in a vet's waiting room. Each eyes the other with a combination of suspicion and sympathy.

'What are you here for?' the first dog asks.

'Well, I was feeling really bad the other day. And my master's six-year-old started bugging me. I tried to ignore the little shit, but was feeling so rotten that I bit his hand off.'

'I know exactly how you must have felt. So why are you here?'

'Well, they reckon I'm too vicious so I'm going to be ... you know ... I'm going to be desexed.'

'Oh dear, I'm sorry.'

'So, what are you in here for?'

'Oh, nothing really.'

'Go on, tell me. It'll take my mind off the operation.'

'Okay, well it's like this. The bitch next door was in heat and I was feeling really randy. Then my mistress came into the kitchen wearing a short skirt and no underwear and when she bent over to put some dog food in my bowl I just couldn't resist.'

'So you're here for the operation too?'

'No. I'm here to have my nails clipped.'

A society lady had a miniature schnauzer which was suffering from an ear infection. The vet told her that this was due to an ingrown hair and the best treatment would be to remove the hair with a depilatory cream. The woman went to a chemist and asked for assistance in selecting the best product. He explained that some were better for legs, while others were better for facial hair. He then asked, 'May I ask where you intend to use it?'

She replied, 'It's for my schnauzer.'

He said, 'Okay, use this brand. But don't ride a bike for two weeks.'

POLITICALLY INCORRECT

Air Force One crashes, instantly killing President Clinton, Vice President Gore and their wives. St Peter greets them personally at the Pearly Gates and informs them that they've been granted an audience with God. They are led by St Peter to a tremendous throne room and there, lo and behold, is the supreme being. 'And who might you be?' God asks the Vice President. 'I'm Albert Gore junior, Vice President of the United States of America.' 'Ah, yes, you've done much for the environment. Love your work. Come sit on my left.'

'And you there, who are you?' 'Your Holiness, I'm William Jefferson Clinton, President of the United States.' 'Right, you are a brave man who has confronted some difficult issues. Come sit on my right.'

'Now, who might you be?'

'My name is Hillary Rodham Clinton and *you* are sitting on *my* seat.'

Bill, Hillary and Al are flying from DC to the West Coast. Al says, 'Boy, I would like to drop a $100 bill out of the plane and make one person very happy.' Hillary replies, 'I would rather drop ten $10 bills out and make ten people very, very happy.'

Bill replies, 'I would drop 100 $1 bills and make 100 people really happy.'

The pilot, listening to all this, turns around and says, 'Why don't all three of you jump out and make 250 million people very happy?'

Why doesn't Hillary wear mini-skirts around the White House?
Because her balls would show.

What are the two worst things about Bill Clinton?
His face.

It's been discovered that Clinton was a test-tube baby. Apparently he wasn't worth a fuck back then either!

What did the band play at Clinton's inauguration?
Inhale to the chief.

Why is Bill Clinton apprehensive about going to the movies?

Because he's afraid the usherette will ask to see his stub.

Hillary came into the room with a big smile and a spring in her step. 'My, you're in a good mood,' said Bill, 'why are you so happy?'

'I just got back from my annual physical exam and the doctor said I had the breasts of a 25-year-old woman,' Hillary gushed.

'Did he say anything about your 46-year-old ass?' Bill asked. 'No,' said Hillary, 'your name wasn't mentioned.'

I'm glad I am an American, I'm glad I'm free. I wish I were a dog and Clinton was a tree.

Three high-school boys are walking down the street in Washington. Suddenly they see Bill Clinton go jogging by, and he's about to be hit by a car. They pull the President out of the way and save his life. Bill says, 'Thank you for saving me. I'll grant each of you a wish.'

The first boy says, 'I want to go Georgetown.' Bill pulls some strings and the boy gets admitted.

The second boy says, 'I want to get into West Point but it normally requires a congressional appointment.' So Bill calls up his Democratic friends in congress and gets the boy his appointment.

The third boy says, 'I want to be buried in Arlington National Cemetery.' Bill says, 'That's an odd request for a 17-year-old.' The boy says, 'Yeah, but when my father finds out I saved your life he's going to kill me.'

Hillary's being driven around Washington DC when she spots a little boy sitting in a park with a wagon. She thinks, A great press opportunity, and has her driver pull over. She gets out to talk to the boy and discovers that he has six little puppies in the wagon. She comments on how nice they are and the little boy says, 'Thank you, m'am, they're Democrats.' Of course Hillary is extremely pleased.

A few days later Bill decides to take one of his jogs down to McDonald's, which is close to the park, and Hillary mentions that if he should see a little boy with a wagon he should stop and talk to him. Bill sees the little boy with the wagon and puppies and says, 'What nice puppies those are.' The boy says, 'Thank you, sir, they're Republicans.' 'Wait a minute,' said Bill, 'Hillary told me they're Democrats.' The boy responds, 'Yes sir, but now their eyes are open.'

Bill Clinton is considering changing the Democratic Party emblem from a donkey to a condom, because it stands up to inflation, protects a bunch of pricks, halts production, and gives you a false sense of security while being screwed.

Bill Clinton's new revelations about his sex life: he's finally admitted to having sex with Gennifer Flowers a couple of times ... but he didn't come.

Why are people in Arkansas having peanut butter and jelly for Thanksgiving this year?
Because they sent their turkey to the White House.

Potential presidential candidates were meeting the Wizard of Oz. President Bush went first to see the Wizard and said, 'Everyone says I have no compassion or feeling. I wish to have a heart.' The Wizard said, 'So be it.'
The second was Dan Quayle. He said to the Wizard, 'People think I'm unintelligent and have no commonsense whatsoever. I wish to have a brain.' The Wizard said, 'So be it.'
The third was Ross Perrot. 'People say I have no confidence and lack conviction. I wish to have some courage.' The Wizard said, 'So be it.'
And then Bill Clinton approached. The Wizard

183

looked at him and said, 'Well, what do you want?'
To which Clinton replied, 'I'm here for Dorothy.'

Bumper sticker on an Arkansas car: If you can
read you this you're not from here.

How did Bill and Hillary Clinton meet?
They were dating the same girl in high school.

Why do they put Clinton's picture on the inside
of toilet bowls?
So the arseholes can see who they voted for.

If Bill and Hillary and Al and Tippa took a boat
ride and the boat capsized who would be saved?
The United States of America.

Why is Bill Clinton diverting federal funds from
improving schools to improving jails?
Because when his term is through, he won't be
going to school.

A man goes into a bar in Montana. He's watching TV over the bar and Bill Clinton comes on. He says out loud to no one in particular, 'If that guy isn't the biggest horse's arse I've seen, I don't know who is.'

A big cowboy comes down the bar and knocks him off his stool. He gets back up and starts watching TV again. This time Hillary comes on. He says, 'I thought Bill was bad, but Hillary is definitely the biggest horse's arse in the world.'

Another cowboy comes and knocks him off his stool. The guy's perplexed. He gets back on his stool and says to the bartender, 'Excuse me, I thought I was in a conservative state. Where am I? Clinton country?' 'No,' said the bartender, 'you're in horse country.'

Clinton is giving a speech. A member of the audience wakes up momentarily and asks, 'Has he finished yet?' A neighbour replies, 'He finished an hour ago, but he hasn't stopped.'

Chelsea asks Hillary, 'Mom, what did you have at the state dinner?'

'Some beef, some asparagus, and 7374 green peas.'

'Don't bullshit me, Mom. When did you count the peas?'

'While your father was giving his speech.'

Bumper sticker seen in Scotsdale, Arizona: Where the hell is Lee Harvey Oswald now that we really need him?

What's the difference between the Panama Canal and Hillary Clinton?
The Panama Canal is a busy ditch.

Clinton's walking his dog around the White House lawn. He walks it past the guards' post, and a marine says, 'Mr President, is that a new dog?' Clinton smiles and replies, 'Why yes, I got it for my wife.' The marine inspects the dog, looks up with a smile and says, 'Good trade.'

President Clinton and Vice President Gore were coming back from a health-care meeting in their limo when Gore asked, 'Hey Bill, what are you gonna do when you get back to the White House?'
The slickster replied, 'Well, I'm gonna tear off Hillary's panties.'
'Wow!' exclaimed Gore, 'I didn't know you and Hillary were so passionate.'
Clinton replied, 'We're not. It's just that the damn things are starting to cut into my waist.'

Hillary Clinton dies and goes to Heaven. St Peter approaches her and says, 'Hillary, I know you're Somebody down on Earth, but up here you're just another person and I'm swamped right now. So have a seat and I'll get back to you as soon as I can.'

Hillary sits down and begins looking around. She notices a huge wall that extends as far as the eye can see, and on that wall there are millions and millions of clocks. She can't help noticing that on occasion some of the clocks jump ahead 15 minutes. When St Peter returns she asks, 'What's the deal with the clock?' St Peter replies, 'There's a clock on the wall for every married man on Earth.'

Hillary asks, 'What does it mean when the clock jumps ahead 15 minutes?' St Peter replies, 'That means that the man that belongs to that clock has just committed adultery.'

'Hillary asks, 'Well, is my husband's clock on the wall?'

St Peter replies, 'Hell no. God has it in his office and is using it for an electric fan.'

A little old lady arrives at US Immigration. The official's question is, 'Do you advocate the overthrow of the government by violence or subversion?' She pauses for thought and says, 'Violence, I think.'

A bloke's been through a terrible divorce and as he leaves the courthouse says under his breath, 'It's about time I had some good luck.'

Whereupon, POOF! A genie appears. The genie says, 'You may have three wishes, but whatever you wish for your wife will get double.'

The man says he's agreeable and asks for $20 million. The genie points out that his wife will get $40 million. The man asks to be ten years younger. The genie points out that, now, his wife will be 20 years younger.

'And what is your third wish?' asks the genie.

'Beat me half to death.'

A man walking along a road in the bush comes across a shepherd with a huge flock of sheep. 'I'll bet you $100 against one of your sheep that I can tell you the exact number in this flock,' he says. The shepherd thinks it over and, because it's a big flock, takes the bet. The man says, '973.' The shepherd is astonished because that's exactly right. He says, 'Okay, I'm a man of my word, take an animal.' The man picks up a sheep and begins to walk away.

'Wait!' cries the shepherd. 'Give me a chance to get even. Double or nothing that I can guess your occupation.' The man agrees. 'You're an economist for a government think-tank,' says the shepherd. 'Amazing,' says the man, 'you're exactly right. But how did you work it out?' 'Well,' says the shepherd, 'put down my dog and I'll tell you.'

A mathematician, an accountant and an economist apply for the same job. The interviewer calls in the mathematician and asks him, 'What does 2 + 2 equal?' The mathematician replies, 'Four.' The interviewer asks, 'Four exactly?' 'Yes, four exactly.'

The interviewer then calls in the accountant and asks the same question. The accountant says, 'On average, four, give or take 10 per cent, but on average, four.'

Then the interviewer calls in the economist and poses the same question. 'What does 2 + 2 equal?' The economist gets up, locks the door, closes the shades, sits down next to the interviewer and says, 'What do you want it to equal?'

Three econometricians go hunting and come across a huge deer. The first econometrician fires, but misses, by a metre to the left. The second econometrician fires, but also misses, by a metre to the right. The third econometrician doesn't fire, but shouts in triumph, 'We got it! We got it!'

A civil engineer, a chemist and an economist are travelling in the countryside and, feeling weary, stop at a small inn. 'I've only two rooms, so one of you will have to sleep in the barn,' says the innkeeper.

The civil engineer volunteers to do so, and goes outside while the others go to bed. But in a short time he's knocking at the door. He says, 'There's a cow in that barn. I'm a Hindu and it would offend my beliefs to sleep next to a sacred animal.'

So the chemist says, 'Okay, I'll sleep in the barn.' Soon there's another knock – it's the chemist saying, 'There's a pig in that barn. I'm Jewish and cannot sleep next to an unclean animal.'

So the economist is sent to the barn. Soon there's even louder knocking. They open the door and see that it's the cow and the pig.

A party of economists were climbing the Alps and after several hours got hopelessly lost. One of them studied the map, turning it up and down, trying to identify distant landmarks, consulting his compass, squinting at the sun. Finally he said, 'Okay, see that big mountain over there?'

'Yes,' said the others.

'Well, according to the map, we're standing on top of it.'

Albert Einstein dies and meets three New Zealanders in the queue outside the Pearly Gates. To pass the time he asks their IQs. The first replies, '190.'

'Great,' says Einstein, 'we can discuss the contribution by Ernest Rutherford to atomic physics and my theory of general relativity.'

The second answers, '150.'

'Good,' says Einstein. 'I look forward to discussing the role of New Zealand's nuclear-free legislation and quest for world peace.'

The third New Zealander mumbles, '50.' Einstein pauses and then asks, 'So what is your forecast for the budget deficit next year?'

Why did God create economists?
In order to make weather forecasters look good.

Why did the economist cross the road?
It was the chicken's day off.

Two economists meet on the street. One enquires, 'How's your wife?' The other responds, 'Relative to what?'

Iconomists have forecast nine out of the last five recessions.

A totalitarian head of state asks for an economist with one arm to advise his government. Why? Because he was tired of economists who say,

'Well, on the one hand ... but on the other hand ...'

Three leading economists hired a Cessna to go hunting moose in northern Canada. The pilot reminded them that it was a small plane and they'd only be able to bring back one moose.

But the economists killed one each and, come Sunday, talked the pilot into letting them bring all three dead moose on board. Shortly after the takeoff, the plane stalled and crashed. In the wreckage, one of the economists woke up, looked around and said, 'Where the hell are we?'

'Oh, just about 100 metres east of the place we crashed last year.'

An economist:

Someone who didn't have enough personality to become an accountant.

Someone who knows a hundred ways to make love, but doesn't know any women.

An economist returns to his old university. He expresses interest in the current exam questions, and his old professor shows him some. To his astonishment, they're the same ones that he answered ten years ago. How come? The professor explains, 'The questions are always the same – only the answers change.'

Economics is extremely useful as a form of employment for economists.

A central banker walked into a pizzeria to order a Hawaiian. When the pizza was ready, the clerk asked him, 'Should I cut it into six pieces or eight pieces?' The central banker replied, 'I'm feeling really hungry. You'd better cut it into eight pieces.'

The first law of economists: For every economist, there exists an equal and opposite economist.
The second law of economists: They're both wrong.

An economist is an expert who will know tomorrow why the things he predicted yesterday didn't happen today.

A study of economics usually reveals that the best time to buy anything is last year.

193

It was the final May Day in the Soviet Union with Gorbachev reviewing the tanks and the troops and the planes and the missiles. Finally ten men marched by dressed in black. 'Are they spies?' asked Gorby. 'They are economists,' replied the KGB director. 'Imagine the havoc they will wreak when we set them loose on the Americans.'

If an economist and a tax inspector were both drowning and you could only save one of them, would you go to lunch or read the paper?

Why do economists carry their diplomas on their dashboards?
So they can park in the handicapped parking.

An economist died in poverty and many local futures traders donated to a fund for his funeral. The CEO of a bank was asked to donate a dollar. 'Only a buck?' he said. 'Only a buck to bury an economist? Here's a cheque. Go bury 1000 of them.'

A physicist, a chemist and an economist are stranded on an island with nothing to eat.

Miraculously, a can of soup washes ashore. The physicist says, 'Let's smash open the can with a rock.' The chemist says, 'Let's build a fire and heat the can first.' The economist says, 'Let's assume that we have a can opener ...'

An Australian, an Englishman and a Japanese were discussing their respective countries over a drink. The Englishman mentioned that British medicine had progressed so far that doctors had recently taken a single liver, cut it into six pieces and then transplanted it into six separate men. This had resulted in six new workers in the job market.

The Japanese guy said that in his country doctors had cut a lung into 12 pieces, transplanted these into 12 people in need of healthy lungs, thereby putting 12 new people in the job market.

Not to be outdone, the Australian said, 'That's nothing. In my country, we took one arsehole, made it Prime Minister, and now there are five million people in the market for a job.'

A priest, a psychologist and an economist are playing golf. They get behind a very slow twosome who, despite having a caddy, take all day to line up their shots. To make matters worse, they're four-putting every green. By the eighth hole the three men are complaining loudly about the slow players ahead. The priest says, 'Holy Mary, I pray that they should take some lessons before they play again.' The psychologist says, 'There are some people who just like to play golf slowly.' The economist says, 'I really didn't expect to spend this much time playing a round of golf.'

By the ninth hole, they've had it. The psychologist goes to the caddy and demands that they be allowed to play through. The caddy explains that his two golfers are blind, that both are retired firemen who lost their eyesight saving people in a fire.

The priest is mortified. 'Here I am a man of the cloth and I've been swearing at the slow play of two blind men.' The psychologist is also embarrassed. 'I'm a man trained to help others with problems and I've been complaining about the slow play of two blind men.' The economist ponders the situation. Finally he goes to the caddy and says, 'Listen, next time they should play at night.'

Margaret Thatcher died and arrived at the Pearly Gates where she was confronted by St Peter with his clipboard.

'Name?' asked St Peter.

'Baroness Thatcher,' she replied.

Peter checked through all the names on the clipboard but couldn't find the baroness's. 'I'm sorry, you can't come in. Your place is downstairs in Hell.'

The imperious baroness turned and walked down the stairs. A short time later the phone rang. 'Hello, Pete, it's the Devil speaking. You'll have to take that bloody woman. She's only been here ten minutes and she's closed half the furnaces to reduce capacity.'

President Clinton has, as we all know, a deep commitment to marriage. Ever anxious to be politically correct, he recently rewrote the vows for a staffer's nuptials. He circled 'till death us do part' and wrote 'too morbid – do you want to alienate every sick person in America?'

When he got to 'I take you to be my lawful wedded wife', he deleted 'wife' and inserted 'partner', warning 'do not use sexist expressions'. And next to 'for better, for worse, for richer, for poorer', he wrote 'polarising – how about the middle ground?'

A man goes into hospital for a vasectomy. Prior to the operation, he's led into an exam room by a nurse who immediately drops to his knees and goes down on him.

He's astounded and, afterwards, asks, 'Why did you do that?'

'Well, we found it's the most efficient way to empty the seminal ducts,' she replies.

She then has him laid on a trolley, and wheels him towards the operating theatre. On the way he is astounded to see a ward full of men, all vigorously masturbating.

'What's this?'

'Oh, they're on Clinton's new health plan,' she explains.

Three men were telling stories around the campfire. Their conversation turned to medical miracles.

First man: 'There's a guy who lives just up the street from me. He used to work in construction. One day he got his hand run over by a bulldozer. Crushed it flat. Yet today, thanks to the doctors, he's a concert pianist.'

Second man: 'That's nothing. I knew a guy in college, the laziest bum on Earth. Very fat, out of shape. He was trying to bum a ride one day and got hit by a truck. Broke just about every damn bone in his body. But they managed to put him back together and now he's been chosen to run in the marathon in the Atlanta Olympics.'

Third man: 'Well, I knew this poor retarded kid. Couldn't do a whole lot. But someone at the munitions factory took pity on him and gave him a job as a stock boy. He was working in the warehouse one day and got locked in. It was pitch black and he couldn't find the door. And not being very bright, he lit a match. The whole joint went sky high. All they could find of him was his arsehole and his eyebrow. From those little bits they were able to put him back together and today that kid is the Governor of Massachusetts.'

A guy was lost in the mall by the Washington Monument. He stopped a cop and asked, 'What side is the State Department on?' The cop answered, 'Ours, I hope.'

A stockbroker in New York gets tired of his colleague's stories of going duck hunting each year. They boast of their prowess in the hunt and how many ducks they bag. Not to be outdone, he decides he's going hunting and buys the most expensive shotgun available. He spends a fortune on hunting clothes and gear, gets his licence and sets off.

After an exasperating day of tromping through the marshes and briars without seeing a single duck, he heads back to his car. On the way he sees a duck fly overhead. He raises his gun, blazes away at it and actually hits it. The duck falls into a nearby farmyard.

As the hunter starts to climb over the fence to retrieve his kill, he's confronted by a farmer who says, 'Where in the hell do you think you're going, city boy?'

'I'm going to get my duck.'

'My property, my duck,' says the farmer.

'Oh come on, I've been out here all day and that's the only duck I've seen. I shot it. It's my duck.'

The farmer again says, 'My property, my duck.'

They argue for a few minutes and finally the farmer says, 'I'll tell you what. We'll settle this country-style.'

'What's that?' the stockbroker asks warily.

'Well, I'll kick you in the balls as hard as I can and then you kick me in the balls as hard as you can, and we keep this up and the last man standing keeps the duck.'

Not wanting to return empty-handed, the stockbroker finally agrees. The farmer, wearing heavy workboots, kicks the guy in the balls with all his might. The stockbroker's eyes roll back in his head as he coughs and wheezes and struggles to stay on his feet. Composing himself somewhat, he says to the farmer, 'Okay, now it's my turn.'

The farmer replies, 'You can have the duck.'

GROOVE NET

What do Ethiopians and Yoko Ono have in common?

They're both living off dead beetles.

Have you heard about Michael Jackson's new book?

It's called *The Ins and Outs of Child Rearing*.

What's the difference between Michael Jackson and a grocery bag?

One is white, made out of plastic, and dangerous for kids to play with. And the other you carry your groceries in.

How can you tell if Michael Jackson has company? There's a ferris wheel parked outside his house.

The world's best and most famous conductor made a small mistake while conducting the New York Symphony Orchestra. The audience didn't notice, the orchestra didn't notice either, but he knew he'd made the mistake and decided that he should retire. Once the performance had finished, he turned and faced the audience and said, 'Ladies and gentlemen, this is my last performance as a world-class conductor. I'm now announcing my retirement.'

After a few minutes' silence from the shocked audience and orchestra, he was greeted with boos and hisses. He walked from the stage, only to be met by his manager, standing in between two gorilla-sized bodyguards. 'Oh no, you don't,' his manager said, 'you're not retiring.'

Forced back to work by his manager, he endured week after week of conducting he no longer wanted to do. While lying in bed one night with his wife of many years, he turned to her and said, 'Dear, would you be able to get me a small handgun?'

'Yes, dear,' she said, and he rolled over and went to sleep.

Sure enough, at his next performance, the conductor had a small handgun concealed in his jacket. Once the concert had finished, he turned to the audience and said, 'I'm announcing my retirement for the second time. This is my last performance.'

The tuba player from the orchestra stood up and shouted, 'You can't be serious!' and the conductor whipped out his handgun and shot the tuba player dead. It wasn't long before the police arrived and the conductor was taken away.

Days later, the conductor was taken to court. 'How do you plead to the charge of first-degree murder?' the judge enquired. 'Guilty, your Honour,' the conductor replied. 'Do you realise the sentence for first-degree murder in this state is death by electrocution?' the judge asked. The conductor thought for a moment, but came to the conclusion that death would surely be better than continuing on like he was. 'Yes, your Honour,' the conductor said.

While being strapped into the electric chair, one of the guards came to the conductor and said, 'You may have one last request before we terminate your life. What would you like?' After pondering a few seconds, the conductor replied, 'A silver platter with a dozen bananas.' His request was granted, and the conductor scoffed the bananas.

The room was emptied, and the switch was flicked. The conductor's hair stood on end, but he survived! As one guard was about to flick the switch again, he was stopped. 'He survived the chair and the law says we have to let him go.'

The conductor left the building, only to be greeted by his manager and the two gorilla-sized bodyguards. 'Back to work,' his manager said.

More weeks of forced conducting went by. Lying

in bed again one night with his wife, he asked, 'Dear, could you get me a grenade?'

'Yes, dear,' she replied.

At his next performance, the conductor waited until the end of the concert, the grenade tucked neatly in his undies. 'For the third time, I'm announcing my retirement!' he yelled. He took out the grenade, pulled the pin, and threw it into the audience. The grenade exploded, killing 23 members of the crowd. The police arrived, and he was taken away again.

'You again?' asked the judge. 'I thought I'd sentenced you to death not long ago.' The conductor shrugged. 'Okay, how do you plead to 23 counts of first-degree murder?' the judge asked. 'Guilty to all counts,' replied the conductor.

While the settings were changed to triple the voltage of the current going to the chair, the conductor was granted another last request.

'A silver platter with two dozen bananas,' was his answer. He scoffed the bananas, the room was evacuated and the switch was flicked. It appeared that they'd manage to kill him this time, but the conductor regained consciousness when they were about to remove his body. His manager and the two gorilla-sized bodyguards were waiting for him as he left the building. 'Back to work!'

The weeks dragged on, and the conductor couldn't take it any more. 'Dear, could you get me a missile launcher?' he asked his wife as they lay in bed.

'Yes, dear,' she replied.

He didn't even wait for the concert to start. 'Fuck

yas all!' he screamed, and launched a missile into the New York Symphony Orchestra, killing all 190 band members. The army was called in this time, and he was dragged away.

'Jesus Christ, you again? You're supposed to be DEAD!' the judge roared. The conductor just shrugged. 'May I ask how you plead for 190 counts of first-degree murder?'

'Guilty as sin!' the conductor screamed. 'The bastards deserved it!' He was hauled away.

A public announcement was issued to all local residents warning that there would be a short out in the power. Meanwhile, the city's electrical engineers were busy rerouting a massive dose of voltage into the electric chair. Once again, the conductor was granted a last request. 'Three dozen bananas on a silver platter,' he said. He scoffed the bananas, the building was completely vacated, and the electric chair was activated by remote control, some two kilometres away. The building exploded, reducing it to rubble. They fished through the ruins to find the conductor's ruined body.

His funeral was held some days later and as the casket was being lowered into the grave there was a knock on the coffin lid. Women fainted as the conductor crawled out of the coffin – alive!

He was taken to a large press conference. One reporter stood up and asked, 'You've survived three visits to the electric chair. How did you do it?'

'I've tried telling people before,' he said. 'I'm just a bad conductor.'

A violist is sitting in the front row crying hysterically. The conductor asks the violist what's wrong. The violist answers, 'The second oboe loosened one of my tuning pegs.' The conductor says, 'Well, that does seem a bit childish. But it's nothing to get so upset about. Why are you crying?' To which the violist replies, 'He won't tell me which one.'

How many musicians does it take to screw in a light bulb?
I don't know, big daddy, but hum a few bars and I'll fake it.

What did the drummer get in his IQ test?
Drool.

What's the difference between a violin and a viola?
There's no difference. The violin just looks smaller because the violinist's head is so big.

Why are viola jokes so short?
So violinists can understand them.

How do you tell the difference between a violinist and a dog?
 The dog knows when to stop scratching.

How many second violinists does it take to change a light bulb?
 None. They can't get up that high.

Why is a violinist like a scud missile?
 Both are offensive and inaccurate.

Why don't viola players suffer from piles?
 Because arseholes are in the first violin section.

How do you make a cello sound beautiful?
 Sell it and buy a violin.

Two bass players were engaged for a run of *Carmen*. After a couple of weeks they agreed to each take an afternoon off so that they could watch the matinée performance from the front of house. Joe duly took his break. Back in the pit that evening, Mo asked how it was. 'Great,' said Joe. 'You know that bit where the music goes BOOM boom boom boom? Well there are some guys up top singing a terrific song about a bullfighter at the same time.'

Why are harps like elderly parents?
Both are unforgiving and hard to get in and out of cars.

How do you get piccolos to play in unison?
Shoot one.

Why is a bassoon better than an oboe?
The bassoon burns longer.

What is a burning oboe good for?
Setting a bassoon on fire.

Why did the chicken cross the road?
To get away from the bassoon recital.

Why is an 11-foot concert grand better than a studio upright?

Because is makes a bigger kaboom when dropped over a cliff.

What is the definition of 'nerd'?

Someone who owns their own alto clarinet.

What do you call a bass clarinetist with half a brain?

Gifted.

What's the difference between a saxophone and a lawnmower?

Lawnmowers sound better in small ensembles. The neighbours are upset if you borrow a lawnmower and don't return it. The grip.

What's the difference between a trumpet player and the rear end of a horse?

I don't know either..

In an emergency, a jazz trumpeter was hired to play solos with a symphony orchestra. Everything was great through the first movement when she had some really hair-raising solos, but in the second movement she started improvising madly when she wasn't supposed to play at all. After the concert the conductor came round looking for an explanation. She said, 'I looked in the score and it said 'tacit' – so I took it.'

What's the difference between a bass trombone and a chainsaw?
Vibrato, plus it's easier to improvise on a chainsaw.

How do you know when a trombone player is at your door?
The doorbell drags.

What is a gentleman?
Someone who knows how to play the trombone, but doesn't.

What do you call a trombonist with a beeper?
An optimist.

What's the difference between a dead trombone player lying in the road and a dead squirrel lying in the road?

The squirrel was on his way to a gig.

What kind of calendar does a trombonist use for his gigs?

Year-At-A-Glance.

What's the difference between a French horn section and a '57 Chevy?

You can tune a '57 Chevy.

A woman had gone a long, long time without so much as the hope of a relationship. When she finally picked up a good-looking guy and went out with him, her friends were curious as to how it went.

'What's he like?' a friend asked.

'Oh, he's fine I guess. He's a musician, you know.'

'Did he have class?'

'Well, most of the time, yes. But I don't think I'll be going out with him again.'

'Oh, why not?'

'Well, he plays the French horn, so I guess it's just habit, but every time we kiss, he sticks his fist in my rear!'

Why are orchestra intermissions limited to 20 minutes?
So you don't have to retrain the drummers.

What do you call someone who hangs out with musicians?
A drummer.

How do you know when a drummer is knocking at your door?
The knock always slows down.

Why do bands have bass players?
To translate for the drummer.

What's the difference between a drummer and a terrorist?
Terrorists have sympathisers.

What do drummers use for birth control?
Their personalities.

If you threw a violist and a soprano off a cliff, who would hit the ground first?

The violist. The soprano would have to stop halfway down to ask directions. Still, who cares.

What's the difference between a soprano and a terrorist?

You can negotiate with a terrorist.

What's the difference between a soprano and a pirahna?

The lipstick.

What's the difference between a soprano and a pit bull?

The jewellery.

How many sopranos does it take to change a light bulb?

Just one. She holds the bulb and the world revolves around her.

What's the difference between a Wagnerian soprano and the average All-Pro offensive lineman?
Stage makeup.

What is the difference between a soubrette and a cobra?
One is deadly poisonous, and the other is a reptile.

How do you tell if a Wagnerian soprano is dead?
The horses seem relieved.

What's the first thing a soprano does in the morning?
Gets up and goes home.

What's the difference between a soprano and a Porsche.
Most musicians have never been in a Porsche.

A jazz musician dies and goes to Heaven, where an angel takes him by the hand and says, 'Hey man, welcome! You've been elected to the Jazz Allstars

of Heaven – right up there with Satchmo, Miles,
Django, all the greats. And we've got a gig tonight!
Only one problem – God's girlfriend gets to sing.'

What do you see if you look up a soprano's
skirt?
  A tenor.

How do you put a sparkle in a soprano's eye?
  Shine a flashlight in her ear.

Where is a tenor's resonance?
  Where his brain should be.

What's the definition of a male quartet?
  Three men and a tenor.

What's the difference between a World War and
a high school choral performance?
  The performance causes more suffering.

Why do high school choruses travel so often?
Keeps assassins guessing.

There's nothing I like better than the sound of a banjo, unless of course it's the sound of a chicken caught in a vacuum cleaner.

What's it mean when a guitar player is drooling out of both sides of his mouth?
The stage is level.

How do you get a guitar player to play softer?
Give him some sheet music.

Why do bagpipe players walk while they play?
To get away from the noise.

How many country and western singers does it take to change a light bulb?
Three. One to change the light bulb and two to sing about how great the old one was.

What happens if you play blues music backwards?
  Your wife returns to you, your dog comes back to life, and you get out of prison.

What does it say on a blues singer's tombstone?
  I didn't wake up this morning.

How many sound men does it take to change a light bulb?
  One, two, three. One, two, three ...

Two musicians are driving down the road when they glance into the rear vision and, to their horror, see the Grim Reaper sitting in the back seat. He informs them that they've had an accident and have both died. But before he takes them off into Eternity, he'll grant each musician one last request – something to remind them of their past life on Earth.
  The first says that he was a country and western musician and would like to hear eight choruses of 'Achy-Breaky Heart' as a last hurrah. The second musician says, 'I was a jazz musician ... kill me now.'

What's the difference between a bull and a symphony orchestra?

The bull has the horns in front and the arsehole in the back.

A conductor and a violist are standing in the middle of the road. Which one do you run over first, and why?

The conductor. Business before pleasure.

Why are conductors' hearts so coveted for transplants?

They've had so little use.

What's the difference between a conductor and a sack of fertiliser?

The sack.

What's the difference between a symphony conductor and Dr Scholl's Foot Pads?

Dr Scholl's Foot Pads buck up the feet.

What's the difference between a pig and a symphony orchestra conductor?
    There are some things a pig just won't do.

What's the ideal weight for a conductor?
    About two and a half pounds, including the urn.

A musician calls a symphony orchestra's office to talk to the conductor. 'I'm sorry, he's dead,' comes the reply. The musician calls back 30 times, always getting the same reply from the receptionist. At last she asks him why he keeps calling. 'I just like to hear you say it.'

A musician arrives at the Pearly Gates. 'What did you do when you were alive?' asks St Peter.
    'I was the principal trombone player of the City of Birmingham Orchestra.'
    'Excellent, we have a vacancy in our celestial symphony orchestra for a trombonist. Why don't you turn up at the next rehearsal?'
    So when the time for the next rehearsal comes, our friend presents himself with his heavenly trombone. As he takes his seat, God moves, in a mysterious way, to the podium and taps his baton to bring the players to attention. Our friend turns

to the angelic second trombonist and whispers, 'So what's God like as a conductor?'

'Oh, he's okay most of the time, but occasionally he thinks he's von Karajan.'

It was the night of a grand concert and all the celebrities and notables had turned up to hear it. But around 8 o'clock there was still no sign of the conductor. The theatre manager was desperate, fearful of refunding everyone's money. He went backstage and asked the musicians if any of them could conduct. None of them could. He went around and asked the staff if any of them could conduct. No luck. He started asking people in the lobby, in the hope that maybe one of them could conduct the performance. No luck.

He went outside and started asking everybody passing by if they could conduct. No luck whatsoever. By now the concert was 20 minutes late in starting and the crowd were getting restless and would soon be demanding their money back.

The desperate manager looked around and spied a cat sitting on a fire hydrant, a dog peeing on a tree and a horse standing in the street. 'Oh, what the heck,' he exclaimed, 'what do we have to lose?'

So the manager went up to the cat and asked him, 'Mr Cat, do you know how to conduct?' The cat meowed, 'I don't know. I'll try.' But although it tried really hard it couldn't stand upright on its hind legs.

The manager sighed and thanked the cat and

then asked the dog, 'Mr Dog, do you think you can conduct?' The dog woofed, 'Let me see.' But although it managed to stand on its hind legs and wave its front paws around, it couldn't keep upright long enough to last through an entire movement. 'Nice try,' the manager told the dog, and turned in utter desperation to the horse.

'Mr Horse, how about you? Can you conduct?' The horse looked at him for a second, and without a word turned around, presented its hind end and started swishing its tail in perfect 4-4 time.

'Thank Christ!' yelled the manager. 'The concert can go on.' However, the horse then dropped a load of plop onto the street. The assistant manager was horrified and told the manager, 'We can't have this horse conduct. What would the orchestra think?'

The manager looked first at the horse's rear end and then at the plop lying in the street and replied, 'Trust me – from this angle, the orchestra won't even know they have a new conductor.'

Once upon a time there was a blind rabbit and a blind snake. One day the blind rabbit was happily hopping down the path towards his home when he bumped into someone. Apologising profusely, he said, 'I'm blind and didn't see you there.'

'Perfectly all right,' said the snake. 'I'm blind too, and couldn't see to step out of your way.'

They conversed in a friendly fashion and finally the snake said, 'This is the best conversation I've had with anyone for years. Would you mind if I felt you to see what you're like?'

'No,' said the rabbit, 'feel away.'

So the snake wrapped himself round the rabbit and snuggled his coils and said, 'Ummmm, you're soft and warm and fuzzy and cuddly and those ears! You must be a rabbit.'

'That's right,' said the rabbit. 'May I feel you?'

'Go right ahead.'

And the snake stretched himself out full-length on the path. The rabbit stroked the snake's body and then drew back in disgust.

'Shit,' he said, 'you're cold, and slimy, you must be a conductor!'

'**M**ummy,' said the little girl, 'can I get pregnant by anal intercourse?'

'Of course you can,' her mother replied, 'how do you think conductors are made?'

There were two people walking down the street. One was a musician, the other didn't have any money either.

What's the first thing a musician says at work? Would you like fries with that?

St Peter is checking people at the Pearly Gates. The first is a Texan. 'Tell me, what have you done in your life?' asks St Peter.

'Well, I struck oil,' says the Texan, 'so I became rich, but I didn't sit on my laurels. I divided all my money among my entire family in my will, so our descendants are set for about three generations.'

St Peter says, 'Very good, come in.'

The second guy in line says, 'I struck it big in the stock market, but I didn't just provide for my own like that Texan guy. I donated $5 million to Save the Children.'

'Wonderful,' says St Peter. 'Who's next?'

A third guy has been listening, and says timidly with a downcast look, 'Well, I only made $5000 in my entire lifetime.'

'Heavens,' said St Peter, 'what instrument did you play?'

St Peter's checking people into Heaven. He asks a man, 'What did you do on Earth?'

The man replies, 'I was a doctor.'

St Peter says, 'Fine, go right through the Pearly Gates.'

'Next. What did you do on Earth?'

'I was a schoolteacher.'

'Go right through those Pearly Gates. And what did *you* do on Earth?'

'I was a musician.'

'Go round the side, up the freight elevator, through the kitchen.'

What's the difference between a seamstress and a violist?
The seamstress tucks up the frills.

What's the difference between a seamstress and a soprano?
The seamstress tucks and frills.

Definition of a string quartet: A good violinist, a bad violinist, an ex-violinist and someone who hates violinists, all getting together to complain about composers.

How is lightning like a violist's fingers?
Neither one strikes in the same place twice.

How do you keep a violin from getting stolen?
Put it in a viola case.

What's the difference between a viola and a coffin?
The coffin has the dead person on the inside.

What do you do with a dead violist?
  Move him back a desk.

What's the difference between a viola and a trampoline?
  You take your shoes off to jump on a trampoline.

What's the difference between a viola and an onion?
  No one cries when you cut a viola.

What's the definition of 'perfect pitch'?
  Throwing a viola into a dumpster without hitting the rim.

Why do violists stand for long periods outside people's houses?
  They can't find the key and they don't know when to come in.

How can you tell when a violist is playing out of tune?
  The bow is moving.

Why is playing the viola like peeing in your pants? They both give a nice warm feeling without making any sound.

Why is a viola solo like premature ejaculation? Because even when you know it's coming, there's nothing you can do about it.

Why don't violists play hide and seek? Because no one will look for them.

What do a viola and a law suit have in common? Everyone is happy when the case is closed.

A violist and a cellist were standing on a sinking ship. 'Help,' cried the cellist, 'I can't swim.' 'Don't worry, said the violist, 'just fake it.'

A violist came home and found his house burned to the ground. When he asked what happened the police told him, 'Well, apparently the conductor came to your house and – ' The violist's eyes lit up and he interrupted excitedly, 'The conductor? Came to *my* house?'

A viola player decides he's had enough of being a viola player, the butt of all jokes. So he decides to change his instrument. He goes into a shop and says, 'I want to buy a violin.' The man behind the counter looks at him for a moment and then says, 'You must be a viola player.'

The viola player is astonished. 'Well, yes I am, but how did you know?'

'Well, this is a fish and chip shop.'

A man went on a safari in darkest Africa. The native guides took him deep into the jungle where they could hear the screeching of birds and the howling of wild animals. After a few days of travel he was being driven crazy by the constant drumming noise in the background. He asked the leader of the guides what the drumming was. He got no answer. Just a stony silence. They travelled deep into the jungle and the drumming got louder. But nobody would explain it.

Finally, one morning, after days of ever-louder drumming, there was a sudden silence. Whereupon the native guides screamed and hid in the undergrowth. 'What's wrong? Why have the drums stopped?' the man asked.

The native guides chorused, 'Very bad.'

'Why?'

'When drum stops, very bad. Next comes viola solo!'

SEEING THE LIGHT

How many Windows programmers does it take to change a light bulb?

Four hundred and seventy-two. One to write WinGetLightBulbHandle, one to write WinQueryStatusLightBulb, one to write WinGetLightSwitchHandle ...

How many managers does it take to change a light bulb?

'We've formed a task force to study the problem and why light bulbs burn out, and figure out what, exactly, we as supervisors can do to make the bulbs work smarter, not harder.'

How many Tech Support folk does it take to change a light bulb?

We have an exact copy of the light bulb here, and it seems to be working fine. Can you tell me what kind of system you have? Okay, now exactly how dark is it? Okay, there could be four or five things wrong ... have you tried the light switch?

How many Microsoft technicians does it take to change a light bulb?
Three. Two to hold the ladder and one to screw the bulb into a faucet.

How many Microsoft vice presidents does it take to change a light bulb?
Eight: one to work the bulb and seven to make sure Microsoft gets $2 for every light bulb ever changed anywhere in the world.

How many testers does it take to change a light bulb?
We just noticed the room was dark; we don't actually fix the problem.

How many developers does it take to change a light bulb?

The light bulb works fine on the system in my office.

How many C++ programmers does it take to change a light bulb?

You're still thinking procedurally. A properly designed light bulb object would inherit a change method from a generic light bulb class, so all you'd have to do is send a light bulb change message.

How many shipping department personnel does it take to change a light bulb?

We can change the bulb in seven–ten working days; if you call before 2 p.m. and pay an extra $15, we can get the bulb changed overnight. Don't forget to put your name in the upper right-hand corner of the light bulb box.

How many Microsoft engineers does it take to change a light bulb?

None, Bill Gates will just redefine Darkness (TM) as the new industry standard.

How many monkeys does it take to change a light bulb?

Two. One to do it, and one to scratch his bum.

How many Californians does it take to screw in a light bulb?
Five. One to screw in the light bulb, and four to share the experience.

How many New Yorkers does it take to change a light bulb?
None of your fucking business. Get owta my way!

How many Englishmen does it take to change a light bulb?
What do you mean change it? It's a perfectly good light bulb! We've had it for 100 years and it's worked just fine.

How many Ukrainians does it take to screw in a light bulb?
They don't need to. They glow in the dark.

How many African-Americans does it take to screw in a light bulb?

Two. One to hold the bulb, and one to drive the pink Cadillac in sight circles.

How many Iranians does it take to change a light bulb?

One hundred. One to screw it in and 99 to hold the house hostage.

How many Israelis does it take to screw in a light bulb?

Sixty-four to storm the room and take control of it, one to forcibly eject the old bulb and another to screw it in.

How many Australians does it take to screw in a light bulb?

Sixteen. One to change the bulb and 15 to stand around saying, 'Goodonya mate.'

How many dead politicians does it take to change a light bulb?

As many as possible.

How many Bill Clintons does it take to change a light bulb?

None. He'll only promise change.

How many Dan Quayles does it take to screw in a light bulb?

One, but it has to be a pretty dim bulb.

How many libertarians does it take to screw in a light bulb?

None. If you want to sit in the dark, that's your business.

How many Russian leaders does it take to change a light bulb?

Nobody knows. Russian leaders don't last as long as light bulbs.

How many Marxists does it take to change a light bulb?

None. The seeds of revolution and change are within the light bulb itself.

How many Maoists does it take to change a light bulb?

One to screw in the bulb and 1000 to chant, 'Fight Darkness!'

How many Apple employees does it take to change a light bulb?

Seven. One to screw it in and six to design the T-shirts.

How many Apple programmers does it take to change a light bulb?

Only one. But why bother? The light socket will be obsolete in six months anyway.

How many editors does it take to change a light bulb?

Two. One to screw in the bulb and one to issue a rejection slip to the old bulb.

How many cafeteria staff does it take to change a light bulb?

Sorry. We closed 18 seconds ago, and I've just cashed up.

How many librarians does it take to change a light bulb?
Don't know, but I could look it up for you.

How many supermarket cashiers does it take to change a light bulb?
Are you kidding? They won't even change a $5 bill.

How many Mafia members does it take to change a light bulb?
Three. One to change the light bulb and one to kill the witness.

How many Teamsters does it take to change a light bulb?
Eighteen. You got a problem with that?

How many bureaucrats does it take to change a light bulb?
Two. One to screw it in and one to screw it up.

How many astronomers does it take to take change a light bulb?
None. Astronomers prefer the dark.

How many university professors does it take to change a light bulb?
Just one. But once they get tenure, they don't change any more.

How many football players does it take to change a light bulb?
The entire team. And they all get a semester's credit for it.

How many psychologists does it take to change a light bulb?
Just one. But the light bulb has to really *want* to change.

How many chiropractors does it take to change a light bulb?
Just one, but it takes 30 visits.

How many jugglers does it take to change a light bulb?

One, but it takes at least three light bulbs.

How many magicians does it take to change a light bulb?

Depends on what you want to change it into.

How many circus performers does it take to change a light bulb?

Four. One to change the bulb and three to sing, 'Ta da!'

How many actors does it take to change a light bulb?

Nine. One to climb the ladder and replace the bulb, eight to stand around grumbling, 'That should be *me* up there!'

How many actresses does it take to change a light bulb?

One. But you should have seen the line outside the producer's hotel room.

How many movie directors does it take to change a light bulb?

Just one, and when he's done, everyone thinks that his last light bulb was much better.

How many screenwriters does it take to change a light bulb?

Why do we have to change it?

How many mystery writers does it take to change a light bulb?

Two. One to screw it in almost all the way and another to give it a surprise twist at the end.

How many poets does it take to change a light bulb?

Three. One to curse the darkness, one to light a candle and one to change the bulb.

How many fishermen does it take to change a light bulb?

Five. And you should have seen the light bulb! It must have been *this* big!

How many Einsteins does it take to change a light bulb?

That depends on the speed of the change and the mass of the bulb. Or vice versa, of course. It just might be easier to leave the bulb in and change the room. It's all relative.

How many heterosexual males does it take to screw in a light bulb in San Francisco?

Both of them.

How many gay men does it take to screw in a light bulb?

Three. One to screw in an Art Deco bulb and two to shriek, 'Fabulous!'

How many lesbians does it take to change a light bulb?

Two. One to do it and one to make a video documentary about it.

How many evolutionists does it take to change a light bulb?

Only one, but it takes eight million years.

How many pessimists does it take to change a light bulb?

None. Why bother? It's just going to burn out anyway.

How many Carl Sagans does it take to change a light bulb?

Billions and billions.

How many Jewish mothers does it take to change a light bulb?

'That's all right, I'll sit in the dark.'

How many *real* men does it take to change a light bulb?

None. Real men aren't afraid of the dark.

How many Christians does it take to change a light bulb?

Three, but they're really only one.

How many Christian Scientists does it take to change a light bulb?

None, but it takes at least three to sit and pray for the old one to come back on.

How many pro-lifers does it take to change a light bulb?

Six. Two to screw in the bulb and four to testify that it was lit from the moment they began screwing.

How many Pygmies does it take to screw in a light bulb?

At least three.

How many auto mechanics does it take to screw in a light bulb?

Six. One to force it with a hammer, and five to go out for more bulbs.

How many bankers does it take to screw in a light bulb?

Four. One to hold the bulb and three to try and remember the combination.

How many investment brokers does it take to screw in a light bulb?

'My God, it burnt out! Sell all my G.E. stock now!'

How many Zen Buddhists does it take to screw in a light bulb?

Two. One to screw in the bulb, and one to not screw in the bulb.

How many cops does it take to screw in a light bulb?

None. It turned itself in.

How many database people does it take to screw in a light bulb?

Three. One to write the light bulb removal program, one to write the light bulb insertion program, and one to act as a light bulb administrator to make sure nobody else tries to change the light bulb at the same time.

How many disarmament folk does it take to screw in a light bulb?

They won't because:

1. If we change our bulb, they will just change theirs to a brighter one, so where will it all end?
2. We already have enough bulbs to illuminate the entire world three times over.
3. We shouldn't spend money for light bulbs as long as anyone is hungry anywhere.
4. We don't know what effect all of this artificial light will have on the future of mankind.
5. Nature provides us with all the light we need, we just haven't learned to husband it yet.
6. Artificial light isn't aesthetically correct.
7. The candle is more traditional, and it uses no electricity.
8. It is the responsibility of the federal government to provide light to all Americans, without regard to race, age, creed, colour, sex, religion, socio-economic status, national origin or need.

How many doctors does it take to screw in a light bulb?

That depends on whether it has health insurance.

How many existentialists does it take to screw in a light bulb?

Two. One to screw it in and one to observe how the light bulb itself symbolises a single incandescent beacon of subjective reality in a netherworld of endless absurdity reaching out towards a maudlin cosmos of nothingness.

How many fatalists does it take to screw in a light bulb?

What does it matter? We're all gonna die anyway.

How many feminists does it take to screw in a light bulb?
1. That's not funny!
2. Two. One to change the bulb and one to write about how it felt.
3. Three. One to screw it in and two to talk about the sexual implications.
4. Four. One to change it, and three to write about how the bulb is exploiting the socket.
5. Three. One to change the bulb, and two to secretly wish they were the socket.
6. Two. One to screw in the light bulb and one to kick the balls off any man trying to help the first one.

How many fundamentalists does it take to screw in a light bulb?

The Bible doesn't mention light bulbs.

How many junkies does it take to screw in a light bulb?

'Oh wow, is it like dark, man?'

How many lesbians does it take to screw in a light bulb?

Three. One to screw it in and two to talk about how much better it is than with a man.

How many modern artists does it take to screw in a light bulb?

Four. One to throw bulbs against the wall, one to pile hundreds of them in a heap and spray-paint it orange, one to glue light bulbs to a cocker spaniel, and one to put a bulb in the socket and fill the room with light while all the critics and buyers are watching the fellow smashing the bulbs against the wall, the fellow with the spray gun, and the cocker spaniel.

How many netheads does it take to tell yet another light bulb joke?

One thousand, six hundred and twenty-two. One to tell the original joke, and the rest to give some minor variation of it.

How many psychoanalysts does it take to screw in a light bulb?

How many do you think it takes?

How many Reaganists does it take to screw in a light bulb?

Two. One to screw it in, and one to send the bill to the next generation.

How many Roman Catholics does it take to screw in a light bulb?

Two. One to screw it in, and another to repent.

How many Russians does it take to screw in a light bulb?

That's a military secret.

How many lawyers does it take to change a light bulb?

Such number as may be deemed necessary to perform the stated task in a timely and efficient manner within the strictures of the following agreement:

Whereas the party of the first part, also known as 'the lawyers' and the party of the second part, also known as 'the light bulb' do hereby and forthwith agree to a transaction wherein the party of the second part (light bulb) shall be removed from the current position as a result of failure to perform previously agreed upon duties, i.e. the lighting, elucidation, and otherwise illumination of

251

the area ranging from the front (north) door, through the entry way, terminating at an area just inside the primary living area, demarcated by the beginning of the carpet, any spillover illumination being at the option of the party of the second part (light bulb) and not required by the aforementioned agreement between the parties. The aforementioned removal transaction shall include, but not be limited to, the following steps:

1. The party of the first part (lawyer) shall, with or without elevation at his option, by means of a chair, step stool, ladder or any other means of elevation, grasp the party of the second part (light bulb) and rotate the party of the second part (light bulb) in a counter-clockwise direction, said direction being non-negotiable. Said grasping and rotation of the paty of the second part (light bulb) shall be undertaken by the party of the first part (lawyer) to maintain the structural integrity of the paty of the second part (light bulb), notwithstanding the aforementioned failure of the party of the second part (light bulb) to perform the customary and agreed upon duties. The foregoing notwithstanding, however, both parties stipulate that structural failure of the party of the second part (light bulb) may be incidental to the aforementioned failure to perform and in such case the party of the first part (lawyer) shall be held blameless for such structural failure insofar as this agreement is concerned so long as the non-negotiable directional codicil (counter-clockwise) is observed by the party of the first part (lawyer) throughout.

2. Upon reaching a point where the party of the

second part (light bulb) becomes separated from the party of the third part ('receptacle'), the party of the first part (lawyer) shall have the option of disposing of the party of the second part (light bulb) in a manner consistent with all applicable state, local and federal statutes.

3. Once separation and disposal have been achieved, the party of the first part (lawyer) shall have the option of beginning installation of the party of the fourth part ('new light bulb'). This installation shall occur in a manner consistent with the reverse of the procedures described in step one of this self same document, being careful to note that the rotation should occur in a clockwise direction, said direction also being non-negotiable and only until the party of the fourth part ('new light bulb') becomes snug in the party of the third part (receptacle) and in fact becomes the party of the second part (light bulb).

Note: The above described steps may be performed, at the option of the party of the first part (lawyer), by said party of the first part (lawyer), by his or her heirs and assigns, or by any and all persons authorised by him or her to do so, the objective being to produce a level of illumination in the immediate vicinity of the aforementioned front (north) door consistent with maximisation of ingress and revenue for the party of the fifth part, also known as 'The Firm'.

How many Chicago school economists does it take to change a light bulb?

None:

1. If the light bulb needed changing, the market would already have done it.
2. The darkness will cause the light bulb to change by itself.
3. If the government would just leave it alone, it would screw itself in.
4. There is no need to change the light bulb. All the conditions for illumination are in place.
5. They're all waiting for the unseen hand of the market to correct the lighting disequilibrium.
6. Because, look! It's getting brighter! It's definitely getting brighter!

Or:

Just one, but it really gets screwed.

Or:

A thousand: ten theoretical economists with different theories on how to change the light bulb, and 990 empirical economists labouring to determine which theory's the correct one, while everyone is still in the dark.

How many MBAs does it take to change a light bulb?

'Only one if you hire me. I can actually change the light bulb myself. As you can see from my resumé, I've had extensive experience changing light bulbs in my previous positions. My only weakness is that I'm compulsive about changing light bulbs in my spare time.'

How many doctoral students does it take to change a light bulb?

'Should have an answer for you in about five years.'

LAWYERS AND OTHER CRIMINALS

s the highway patrolman approached the accident site, he found that the entire driver's side of the BMW had been ripped away, taking with it the driver's arm. The injured yuppie, a lawyer obviously in shock, kept moaning, 'My car, my car,' as the officer tried to comfort him. 'Sir,' the patrolman said gently, 'I think we should be more concerned about your arm than your car.'

The driver looked down to where his arm should have been, then screamed, 'My Rolex! My Rolex!'

little old lady walked into a branch of Chase Manhattan Bank holding a large paperbag. She told the teller that she had $3 million in the bag and wanted to open an account. But first, she insisted on meeting the president of the bank. After looking into the bag and seeing a huge amount of money that might well have amounted to $3 million, the teller called the president's office.

The lady was ushered into the president's presence. She explained that she liked to know the people that she did business with. The president asked her how she'd come into such a large amount of cash. 'Was it an inheritance?'

'No,' she replied, 'I bet.'

'You bet?' repeated the president. 'On horses?'

'No,' she replied, 'on people.'

Seeing his confusion, she decided to demonstrate. 'I'll bet you $25 000 that by 10 a.m. tomorrow your balls will be square.' The bank president immediately accepted the bet and for the rest of the day was very, very careful. He decided to stay home that evening and take no chances.

Next morning he checked himself in the shower to make sure that everything was okay. Everything was. He went to work and waited for the little old lady to come in at 10 and give him his $25 000.

At 10 a.m. sharp she was escorted into his office with a younger man whom she introduced as her lawyer. 'Well,' she asked, 'what about our bet?'

'I don't know how to tell you this,' he replied, 'but I'm the same as I always have been, only $25 000 richer.'

The lady requested that she be able to see for herself and the president, thinking this was reasonable, dropped his trousers. She then instructed him to bend over and grabbed hold of him. Yes, everything was normal. As the president adjusted his clothing, he noticed her lawyer banging his head against the wall. 'What's wrong with him?' the president asked.

'Oh him,' she replied, 'I bet him $100 000 that by 10 this morning I'd have the president of Chase Manhattan Bank by the balls.'

Mickey Mouse was trying to convince the judge to give him a divorce from Minnie. 'I'm sorry, Mickey,' said the judge, 'but your claiming Minnie is crazy is not a valid reason for me to grant a divorce.'

'I didn't say she was crazy,' said Mickey, 'I said she was fucking Goofy.'

A burglar breaks into an apartment on Fifth Avenue, opposite the Met. He's sure that nobody's home but, just in case, keeps the lights off. While he searches for the wall safe he hears a voice saying, 'I can see you! Jesus can see you too!' He freezes in his tracks. Doesn't move a muscle.

A couple of minutes pass. The voice repeats, 'I can see you! Jesus can see you too!' The burglar takes out his flashlight, switches it on, looks around the room. He sees a birdcage with a parrot in it. 'Did you say that?'

The parrot says again, 'I can see you! Jesus can see you too!'

'Ah, so what. You're just a fucking parrot,' says the burglar.

'I may be just a parrot,' replies the bird, 'but Jesus is a fucking doberman!'

The three bears returned from a stroll in the woods to find the door of their little house wide open. Cautiously they went inside. After a while Daddy Bear said, 'Somebody's been eating *my* porridge.'

Mummy Bear yelled, 'Somebody's been eating *my* porridge!'

Little Baby Bear rushed in. 'Bugger the porridge. Someone's nicked the video.'

A big city lawyer was called in on a case between a farmer and a large railroad company. The farmer had noticed his prize cow missing from the field through which the railroad passed and filed suit against the railroad company for its value. The case was to be tried before a JP in a backroom of the general store, and the attorney immediately cornered the farmer and tried to have him settle out of court. Finally the farmer agreed to take 50 per cent of what he was claiming.

After the farmer signed the release and took the cheque, the young lawyer couldn't help but gloat a little. He told the farmer, 'I hate to tell you this but I put one over on you in there. I couldn't have won the case. The engineer was asleep and the fireman was in the caboose when the train went through your farm that morning. I didn't have a single witness to put on the stand.'

The farmer replied, 'Well, I tell you. I was a little worried about winning that case myself. Because that damn cow came home this morning.'

A golfer sets up for a tee shot with a row of trees and an out-of-bounds on the right side. He slices wildly and the ball heads off in the direction of the trees. About 15 minutes later, a highway patrolman approaches him. 'Is this your ball?'

'Yes, I think it is.'

'Well,' says the officer, 'it went over the trees and through the window of a house. It hit a cat and the cat ran out the front door. A school bus was driving by at the time and the driver, trying to miss the cat, hit a tree. The bus exploded into flames and there were no survivors.'

'Oh my god, that's terrible,' said the golfer. 'Is there anything I can do?'

The policeman replied, 'Well, you might try keeping your left arm a little straighter and start your down swing with your hips.'

PROSECUTOR: Did you kill the victim?

DEFENDANT: No I didn't.

PROSECUTOR: Do you know what the penalties are for perjury?

DEFENDANT: Yes I do. And they're a hell of a lot better than the penalty for murder.

Lawyers are people who can write a 10 000-word document and call it a brief.

What's the difference between a lawyer and a prostitute?
A prostitute will usually quit screwing you when you're dead.

What's black and brown and looks good on a lawyer?
A doberman.

What do you call 1000 lawyers chained together at the bottom of the ocean?
A good start.

Why do they always bury lawyers 12 feet deep?
Because deep down, lawyers are okay.

A tourist wandered into an antique shop in San
Francisco's China Town. It was poorly lit and the
shelves were groaning with fascinating and intriguing
objects. Picking through them he discovered a
marvellously detailed life-size bronze sculpture of a
rat. It was so lifelike, so vividly detailed, that he
couldn't resist it. He asked the shop owner for the
price. '$12 for the rat, sir,' said the shop owner,
'and $1000 more for the fascinating story behind it.'
'You can keep the story, old man,' the tourist
replied, 'but I'll take the rat.'

He left the store with the bronze rat under his
arm and as he crossed the street, two live rats
emerged from a sewer drain and fell into step
behind him.

The tourist looked over his shoulder and began
to walk faster. But with every step there seemed to
be yet another rat following him. By the time he'd
walked a few blocks, there were hundreds of them
at his heels. People began to point and shout. And
he began to panic.

He walked faster and faster and soon began to
run as multitudes of rats swarmed from sewers,
vacant lots, basements and abandoned cars. Finally,
he panicked and ran full tilt towards the waterfront
at the bottom of the hill.

The rats kept up squealing hideously. There must
have been millions of them so that by the time he
reached the water's edge there was a trail blocks
long behind him – and a deafening squeaking and
squealing filled the air.

Gathering his last skerrick of strength, he climbed
up on the lightpost, and hurled the bronze rat into

the bay, as far as he could heave it. Whereupon the seething tide of rats surged over the breakwater into the sea, and drowned.

When he gathered himself together, he made his way back to the antique shop. 'Ah, so you've come back for the rest of the story,' said the shop owner, with a wise smile.

'No,' replied the tourist. 'But I was wondering if you happened to carry bronze lawyers?'

How can you tell when a lawyer is lying?
His lips are moving.

Why won't sharks attack lawyers?
Professional courtesy.

What do you have when a lawyer is buried up to his neck in sand?
Not enough sand.

What's the difference between a lawyer and a bucket full of shit.
The bucket.

What is the definition of a shame?
When a busload of lawyers goes off a cliff.
What's the definition of a crying shame?
There is an empty seat.

What do you get when you cross the Godfather
with a lawyer?
An offer you can't understand.

Why is it that many lawyers have broken noses?
From chasing parked ambulances.

Where do you find a good lawyer?
In the cemetery.

What's the difference between a lawyer and a
gigolo?
A gigolo only screws one person at a time.

What's the difference between a lawyer and a
vampire?
A vampire only sucks blood at night.

Why do lawyers wear neckties?

To keep the foreskin from crawling up their chins.

How many law professors does it take to change a light bulb?

You need 250 just to lobby for the research grant.

If you see a lawyer on a bicycle, why wouldn't you swerve to hit him?

It might be your bicycle.

A little boy asks his mother, 'Mum, do prostitutes have babies?'

'Of course, sweetie, where do you think all the lawyers come from?'

A customer visits a brain store. 'How much for engineer brain?'

'$3 an ounce.'

'How much for doctor brain?'

'$4 an ounce.'

'How much for lawyer brain?'

'$100 an ounce.'

'Why is lawyer brain so much more?'
'Do you know how many lawyers you need to kill to get an ounce of brain?'

A grade school teacher was asking students what their parents did for a living. 'Tim, you're first,' she said. 'What does your mother do all day?'

Tim stood up proudly and said, 'She's a doctor.'

'That's wonderful. How about you, Annie?'

Annie shyly stood up, shuffled her feet and said, 'My father is a mailman.'

'Thank you, Annie,' said the teacher. 'What about your father, Billy?'

Billy proudly stood up and announced, 'My daddy plays piano in a whorehouse.'

The teacher was aghast and promptly changed the subject to geography.

Later that day she went to Billy's house and rang the bell. Billy's father answered the door. The teacher explained what his son had said and demanded an explanation. Billy's father said, 'I'm actually an attorney. But how can I explain a thing like that to a seven-year-old?'

A lawyer died and arrived at the Pearly Gates. To his dismay, there were thousands of people ahead of him in the line to see St Peter. To his surprise, St Peter left his desk at the gate and came down the long line to where the lawyer was, and greeted him warmly. Then St Peter and one of his assistants took the lawyer by the hands and guided him up the front of the line and into a comfortable chair by his desk. The lawyer said, 'I don't mind all this attention, but what makes me so special?'

St Peter replied, 'Well, we've added up all the hours for which you billed your clients, and by my calculation you must be around 193 years old.'

A lawyer and a physician had a dispute over precedence. They referred it to Diogenes, who gave it in favour of the lawyer as follows: 'Let the thief go first and the executioner follow.'

'How can I ever thank you?' gushed a woman to Clarence Darrow, after he had solved her legal troubles.

'My dear woman,' Darrow replied, 'ever since the Phoenicians invented money there has been only one answer to that question.'

The Pope and a lawyer find themselves together before the Pearly Gates. After a small quantum of time which is spent discussing their respective professions, St Peter shows up to usher them to their new Heavenly station. After passing out wings, harps, halos and such, St Peter decides to show them to their new lodgings. After only a brief flight from the gates, Peter brings them down on the front lawn of a palatial estate with all sorts of lavish trappings. This, Peter announces, is where the lawyer will be spending eternity. 'Wow!' says the Pope, 'if he's getting a place like this, I can hardly wait to see mine!' They take flight once again and, as Peter leads on, the landscape below begins to appear more and more mundane until they finally land on a street lined with brownstone houses. Peter indicates the third on the left as the Pope's new domicile and turns to leave, wishing the pontiff his best. The Pope, in a mild state of astonishment, cries out, 'Hey, Peter! What's the deal here? You put that lawyer feller in a beautiful estate home and I end up in this dive?'

Peter looks at the pontiff amusedly and replies, 'Look here, old fellow. This street is practically encrusted with spiritual leaders from many eras and religions. We're putting you here so you guys can get your dogma together. That other guy gets an estate because he's the first damned lawyer to make it up here!'

Carlson was charged with stealing a Mercedes Benz and, after a long trial, the jury acquitted him. Later that day Carlson came back to the judge. 'Your Honour,' he said, 'I wanna get out a warrant for that dirty lawyer of mine!'

'Why?' asked the judge. 'He won your acquittal. What do you want to have him arrested for?'

'Well, your Honour,' replied Carlson, 'I didn't

have the money to pay his fee, so he went and took the car I stole.'

'You seem to have more than the average share of intelligence for a man of your background,' sneered the lawyer at a witness on the stand. 'If I wasn't under oath, I'd return the compliment,' replied the witness.

A judge in a small city was hearing a drink-driving case and the defendant, who had both a record and a reputation for driving under the influence, demanded a jury trial. It was nearly 4 p.m. and getting a jury would take time, so the judge called a recess and went out in the hall looking to impanel anyone available for jury duty. He found a dozen lawyers in the main lobby, and told them that they were a jury. The lawyers thought this would be a novel experience and so followed the judge back to the courtroom. The trial was over in about ten minutes and it was very clear that the defendant was guilty. The jury went into the jury room, the judge started getting ready to go home, and everyone waited.

After nearly three hours, the judge was totally out of patience and sent the bailiff into the jury room to see what was holding up the verdict. When the bailiff returned, the judge said, 'Well, have they got a verdict yet?'

The bailiff shook his head and said, 'Verdict? Hell, they're still doing nominating speeches for the foreman's position!'

Diogenes went to look for an honest lawyer. 'How's it going?' someone asked. 'Not too bad,' said Diogenes. 'I still have my lantern.'

A woman and her little girl were visiting the grave of the little girl's grandmother. On their way back to the car, the little girl asked, 'Mummy, do they ever bury two people in the same grave?'

'Of course not, dear,' replied the mother. 'Why would you think that?'

'The tombstone back there said "Here lies a lawyer and an honest man".'

The defendant who pleads his own case has a fool for a client, but at least there will be no problem with fee-splitting.

Two guys, George and Harry, set out in a hot air balloon to cross the Atlantic Ocean. After 37 hours in the air, George says, 'Harry, we better lose some altitude so we can see where we are.'

Harry lets out some of the hot air in the balloon, and the balloon descends to below the cloud cover. George says, 'I still can't tell where we are. Let's ask that guy on the ground.'

So Harry yells down to the man, 'Hey, could you tell us where we are?' And the man on the ground yells back, 'You're in a balloon, 100 feet up in the air.' George turns to Harry and says, 'That man must be a lawyer.' Harry says, 'How can you tell?'

'Because the advice he gave us is 100 per cent accurate, and totally useless.'

For three years, a young attorney had been taking his brief vacations at a country inn. The last time, he'd finally managed an affair with the innkeeper's daughter. Looking forward once again to an exciting few days, he dragged his suitcase up the stairs of the inn, then stopped short. There sat his lover with an infant on her lap!

'Helen, why didn't you write when you learned you were pregnant?' he cried. 'I would have rushed up here, we could have got married, and the baby would have my name!'

'Well,' she said, 'when my folks found out about my condition, we sat up all night talkin' and talkin' and decided it would be better to have a bastard in the family than a lawyer.'

God decided to take the Devil to court and settle their differences once and for all. When Satan heard this, he laughed and said, 'And where you think you're going to find a lawyer?'

Santa Claus, the Tooth Fairy, an honest lawyer and an old drunk are walking down the street together when they simultaneously spot a $100 bill. Who gets it? The old drunk, of course. The other three are mythological creatures.

A lawyer named Strange was shopping for a tombstone. After he had made his selection, the stonecutter asked him what inscription he would like on it.

'Here lies an honest man and a lawyer,' responded the lawyer.

'Sorry, but I can't do that,' replied the stonecutter. 'In this state, it's against the law to bury two people in the same grave. However, I could put "Here lies an honest lawyer".'

'But that won't let people know who it is,' protested the lawyer.

'Certainly will,' retorted the stonecutter, 'people will read it and exclaim, "That's Strange!"'

At a convention of biological students, one student remarks to another, 'Did you know that in our lab we have switched from mice to lawyers for our experiments?'

'Really?' the other replied. 'Why did you switch?'

'Well, for three reasons: first, we found that lawyers are far more plentiful; second, the lab assistants don't get so attached to them; and thirdly, there are some things even a rat won't do. However, it's far more difficult to apply our findings to human beings.'

What do you call a lawyer with an IQ of 50?
Your Honour.

What do you call a lawyer who's gone bad?
Senator.

In front of you stand four men: Adolf Hitler, Idi Amin, Saddam Hussein and a lawyer. You're holding a gun which contains only three bullets. Who do you shoot?
Use all three bullets on the lawyer.

What is the difference between a lawyer and a vulture?
  The lawyer gets Frequent Flyer miles.

How many lawyers does it take to roof a house?
  Depends on how thin you slice them.

How do you get a lawyer out of a tree?
  Cut the rope.

What is it that a goose can do, a duck can't and a lawyer should?
  Stick his bill up his arse.

What's the difference between a catfish and a lawyer?
  One's a bottom-crawling scum sucker, and the other's just a fish.

Why did the lawyer cross the road?
  To get to the car accident on the other side.

Did you hear about the terrorist who hijacked a 747 full of lawyers?

He threatened to release one every hour if his demands weren't met.

What does a lawyer and a sperm have in common?

Both have about a one in three million chance of becoming a human being.

Why does California have so many lawyers and New Jersey so many toxic waste dumps?

New Jersey got to pick first.

Why did the post office recall the new 'lawyer' stamps?

Because people couldn't tell which side to spit on.

Did you hear about the lawyer from Texas who was so big when he died that they couldn't find a coffin big enough to hold the body?

They gave him an enema and buried him in a shoe box.

How many lawyers does it take to change a light bulb?

Sixty-five: 42 to sue the power company for failing to prevent the surge that took the bulb out in the first place, 14 to sue the electrician who wired the house, and nine to sue the bulb manufacturer.

Why has the Baptist Church quit baptising lawyers?

Because they can't get the ring out of the baptismal tub.

A defence attorney in a Northern California murder case says he believes Max the parrot may hold the answer to who smothered Jane Gill to death in her bedroom two years ago. But an attempt to get the African grey parrot's testimony into evidence last week was blocked by the judge. Max was found dehydrated and hungry in his cage two days after Gill's murder. After the parrot was coaxed back to health at a pet shop, the shop's owner said the bird began to cry out, 'Richard! No, no, no!' The man charged in the case is Gill's business partner, and his name is not Richard. He says he is innocent. Gary Dixon, a private investigator working on the case, surmised that the bird is now in a witness protection program. 'Max's identity has been changed and he is now a macaw.'

ATTORNEY: At the scene of the accident, did you tell the constable you had never felt better in your life?

FARMER: That's right.

ATTORNEY: Well then, how is it that you are now claiming you were seriously injured when my client's auto hit your wagon?

FARMER: When the constable arrived, he went over to my horse, who had a broken leg, and shot him. Then he went over to Rover, my dog, who was all banged up, and shot him. When he asked me how I felt, I just thought that under the circumstances it was a wise choice of words to say I've never felt better in my life.

The lawyer is standing at the gates to Heaven and St Peter is listing his sins:

1. Defending a large corporation on a pollution suit when he knew they were guilty.
2. Defending an obviously guilty murderer because the fee was high.
3. Overcharging fees to many clients.
4. Prosecuting an innocent woman because a scapegoat was needed in a controversial case.

And the list goes on for quite a while. The lawyer objects and begins to argues his case. He admits all these things but argues, 'Wait, I've done some charity in my life also.'

St Peter looks in his book and says, 'Yes, I see. You once gave a dime to a panhandler and you once gave an extra nickel to the shoeshine boy. Correct?'

The lawyer gets a smug look on his face and replies, 'Yes.'

St Peter turns to the angel next to him and says, 'Give this guy 15 cents and tell him to go to Hell.'

It's been discovered that lawyers are the laval stage of politicians.

A small town that cannot support one lawyer can always support two.

The trouble with the legal profession is that 98 per cent of its members give the rest a bad name.

Four surgeons were taking a coffee break and discussing their work. The first one said, 'I think accountants are the easiest to operate on. You open them up and everything inside is numbered.'

The second said, 'I think librarians are easiest to operate on. You open them up and everything inside is in alphabetical order.'

The third one said, 'I like to operate on

electricians. You open them up and everything inside is colour coded.'

The fourth one said, 'I like to operate on lawyers. They are heartless, spineless, gutless, and their heads and their arses are interchangeable.'

The scene is Heaven, with three men standing at the Pearly Gates. St Peter says to the first man, 'Let's see, you're Mr Jones, the engineer. We've been expecting you. Please follow me.' St Peter leads him down a hall to a door marked 101. 'This is where you'll be staying, Mr Jones,' says St Peter. Inside is a dank, dark, cold, musty room. Water is dripping from the walls where torture equipment is dangling. And chained to the centre of the floor is a growling, savage dog. Mr Jones nervously steps in as a loud voice cries from above, 'Mr Jones, you have sinned!' St Peter slams the door and returns to the remaining two men.

'And you are Mr Smith, the doctor,' says St Peter. 'You are in room 102. Please follow me.' A door opens into a room which is dark and dank with water dripping down the walls and horrible torture equipment hanging everywhere. And, once again, a growling, snarling dog is chained to the centre of the floor. As Mr Smith enters weeping, a voice from above cries, 'Mr Smith, you have sinned!' St Peter slams the door and returns to the last man.

'And you must be Mr Brown, the lawyer. We've been waiting for you. You are in room 103. Please follow me.' When they get to room 103, St Peter opens the door to reveal another dark, musty, gloomy room with torture equipment hanging from the slimy walls. But in the centre of the room stands Bo Derek. As the lawyer steps into the room, the voice cries out, 'Bo Derek! You have sinned!'

The lawyer died having not lived a wholly admirable life. He found himself at the gates of Hell. 'Welcome,' announced the Devil, greeting him warmly. 'Glad you could join us. As this is your last taste of free will, you're allowed to choose which of three possible places in which to spend Eternity.' There were three doors behind the Devil. He opened the first. Flames shot into the room and the lawyer could see thousands of people amidst the fire. 'No,' said the lawyer, 'not this one.'

The Devil opened the second door. The lawyer could see an infinity of people working at an immense rock pile. They were all being whipped as they hammered the large boulders into smaller ones. 'No, again,' said the lawyer.

Finally the Devil opened the third door which showed vast numbers in a lake with vomit up to their chins. All of them were chanting, 'Don't make waves! Don't make waves!'

'That's awful,' commented the horrified lawyer.

'You think that's bad,' asked the Devil. 'You should see it when the angels spend the weekend here with their motorboats!'

A dying man gathered his lawyer, doctor and clergyman to his bedside and handed each of them an envelope containing $25 000 in cash. He made each promise that after his death they would place the three envelopes in his coffin. He told them that he wanted to have enough money to enjoy the afterlife.

Next week the man died. At the wake the lawyer, doctor and clergyman each placed an envelope in the coffin and bid their friend farewell.

Three months later the three met by chance. The clergyman, feeling guilty, confessed that there was only $10 000 in the envelope he'd placed in the coffin. Rather than waste all the money, he'd sent $15 000 to a mission in South America. He asked for their forgiveness.

Moved by the gentle clergyman's sincerity, the doctor confessed that he, too, had kept some of the money for a worthy medical charity. His envelope, he admitted, had only had $8000 in it.

The lawyer was seething with self-righteous outrage. He expressed his deep disappointment in the felonious behaviour of two of his oldest and most trusted friends. 'I am the only one who kept his promise to our dying friend. My envelope contained my personal cheque for the entire $25 000.'

In the middle of the night, in the middle of nowhere, two cars collide and a fair amount of damage is done, although neither driver is hurt. It's impossible to assess blame for the accident. One driver is a doctor and the other a lawyer. The lawyer calls the police on his cellular phone. They'll be here in ten minutes.

It's cold and damp and both men are shaken. The lawyer offers the doctor a drink of brandy from a hip flask. The doctor gratefully accepts and hands it back to the lawyer, who puts it away. 'Aren't you going to have a drink?' the doctor says. 'After the police get here,' replies the lawyer.

A truck driver used to amuse himself by running over any lawyer he saw walking on the side of the road. Every time he saw a lawyer walking, he'd swerve to hit him. And there'd be a loud thump. Then he'd swerve back on the road. He found this immensely enjoyable.

One day the truck driver was driving along when he saw a priest hitchhiking. He pulled the truck over and asked the priest, 'Where are you going, Father?'

'I'm going to the church in the next town.'

'No problem, Father, I'll give you a lift. Climb in.'

The happy priest climbed in to the passenger's seat and the truck continued on its way. Suddenly the driver saw a lawyer walking down the road and swerved to hit him. But remembering there was a priest in the truck, he swerved back at the last minute. However, even though he was certain he'd missed the lawyer, he still heard a loud thud.

Not understanding where the noise came from, he glanced in his mirrors and when he didn't see anything, turned to the priest and said, 'I'm sorry, Father. I almost hit that lawyer.'

'That's okay,' replied the priest, 'I got him with the door.'

An airliner was having engine trouble and the pilot told the cabin crew to have the passengers prepare for an emergency landing. A few seconds later he asked the flight attendant if everyone was buckled in and ready. 'All set back here, captain,' came the reply, 'except for one lawyer who's passing out business cards.'

A very good man dies and as a reward for an honourable, charitable life, goes to Heaven. When he arrives, St Peter meets him with a warm welcome. 'Since you were such a good person in life,' says the saint, 'you may enter.'

'Thank you. But before I come in, could you tell me what to expect? What kind of people are here?'

'All kinds,' replied St Peter.

'Well, are there any convicted criminals in Heaven?'

'Yes, some.'

'Are there any communists in Heaven?'

'Yes, there are.'

'Are there any Nazis in Heaven?'

'Just a few.'

'Well, are there any lawyers in Heaven?'

And St Peter said, 'What? And ruin it for everyone else?'

A monster was on trial, facing a possible life sentence. So his lawyer bribed a juror to hold out for a lesser charge. After hours of deliberation the jury returned a verdict carrying a maximum of ten years in prison. Afterwards, the lawyer approached the corrupted juror. 'You had me so worried. When the jury was out so long I was afraid you couldn't pull it off.'

'I was worried, too,' answered the juror. 'The others all wanted to acquit him.'

A man went into a Chamber of Commerce in a small town. Obviously distressed, he asked the man at the counter, 'Is there a criminal attorney in town?'

The man replied, 'Yes, but we can't prove it yet.'

A farmer walks into an attorney's office wanting to file for divorce.

'May I help you?'

'Yes, I want to get one of those day-vorces.'

'Do you have any grounds?'

'Yeah, I've got about 140 acres.'

'No, you don't understand, do you have a case?'

'No, I've got a John Deere.'

'No, you don't understand, I mean do you have a grudge?'

'Yeah, I've got a grudge. That's where I park my John Deere.'

'No, sir, I mean do you have a suit?'

'Yes sir, I've got a suit. I wear it to church every Sunday.'

'Well sir, does your wife beat you up or anything?'

'No sir, we both get up at 4.30 a.m. Together.'

'Well, is she a nagger or anything?'

'No, she's a little white gal, but her last kid was a nagger. That's why I want this day-vorce.'

I broke a mirror in my house. I'm supposed to get seven years of bad luck. But my lawyer thinks that he can get me five.

Undistinguished and often shabby in appearance, Ulysses S. Grant did not recommend himself to strangers by looks. He once entered an inn in Galena, Illinois, on a stormy winter's night. A number of lawyers in town for a court session were clustered around the fire. One looked up as Grant appeared and said, 'Here's a stranger, gentlemen, and by the looks of him he's travelled through Hell itself to get here.'

'That's right,' said Grant cheerfully.

'And how did you find things down there?'

'Just like here,' replied Grant, 'lawyers all closest to the fire.'

A mature woman was discussing her forthcoming and fourth wedding with a priest. 'Father, how am I going to tell my husband that I'm still a virgin?'

'Child, you've been a married woman for many years. Surely that cannot be.'

'Well, Father, my first was a psychologist and all he wanted to do was talk about it. The next one was in construction and he always said he'd get to it tomorrow. The last one was a gynaecologist and all he did was look. But this time, Father, I'm marrying a lawyer, and I'm sure I'm going to get screwed.'

A devout couple were about to get married when a tragic car accident ended their lives. When they got to Heaven they asked St Peter if he could arrange for them to be married, since it was what they'd hoped for in life. He thought about it and agreed but said they'd have to wait.

About 100 years later St Peter sent for them and they were married in a simple ceremony.

Thirty years later, they discovered that, perhaps, it would be better not to spend all eternity together. They returned to St Peter and said, 'We thought we'd be happy forever but now believe we have irreconcilable differences. Is there any way we can get divorced?'

'Are you kidding?' said St Peter. 'It took me 100 years to get a priest up here to marry you. I'll never get a lawyer.'

Three persons arrive at Heaven and St Peter greets them before the Pearly Gates. 'Welcome to Heaven. We have just one last thing to do before you enter. Are you ready for your last test?'

The first person says, 'I've prepared for this moment for 80 years.'

'Okay,' says St Peter, 'spell God.'

'G-O-D.'

'Very good. Enter your eternal reward.'

The second person says, 'That was easier than I thought. I'll take my test now.'

'Okay,' says St Peter, 'spell love.'

'L-O-V-E.'

'Excellent. Enter your eternal reward.'

The third person, a lawyer, says, 'Boy, this is gonna be a snap. Give me my test.'

'Okay,' says St Peter, 'spell "prorhipido-glossomorpha".'

There was a terrible accident at a railroad crossing. A train smashed into a car, pushed it almost a kilometre down the track. Fortunately no one was killed but the driver took the train company to court. At the trial the engineer insisted that he'd given the driver ample warning by waving his lantern back and forth for nearly a minute. He stood up and convincingly demonstrated how he'd done it. The court believed his story and the suit was dismissed.

'Congratulations,' the lawyer said to the engineer afterwards. 'You did superbly under cross-examination.'

'Thanks,' he said, 'but he sure had me worried.'

'How's that?' the lawyer asked.

'I was afraid he was going to ask if the damn lantern was lit.'

A lawyer had a jury trial in a difficult business case. The client was out of town when the jury came back with its decision. The lawyer immediately sent a telegram to his client reading: JUSTICE TRIUMPHED.

The client wired back: APPEAL AT ONCE!

A lawyer was asked if he'd like to become a Jehovah's Witness. He declined, as he hadn't seen the accident, but said that he would still be interested in taking the case.

Two young women who hadn't seen each other for a long time met shopping. One said to the other, 'Chloe, it's been so long. I heard you got married.'

'Yes,' the second woman said, 'I married a lawyer, and an honest man too.'

'Hmm,' said the first woman, 'isn't that bigamy?'

A lawyer was doing a cross-examination of a defendant. The lawyer said, 'Now, isn't it true that on the fifth of November last year you rode naked through the streets on top of a dust cart, letting off fireworks and singing 'I Did It My Way' very loudly?'

The defendant asked, 'What was that date again?'

A lawyer was approached by the Devil. The Prince of Darkness said he could fix it so that the lawyer would win all of his court cases, make twice as much money, work half as hard, be appointed to the Supreme Court by the age of 49 and live to be 90. All he had to do was promise the Devil his soul, the soul of his wife, of his children, and the souls of all his ancestors. The lawyer thought for a minute before asking, 'So, what's the catch?'

There were two brothers. One went to business school and became a banker, the other went to law school and became a lawyer. They drifted apart, completely losing touch with each other. The banker did very well, becoming vice president of a large bank with many branches. One day the banker realised the lawyer's 50th birthday was coming up. He felt he should try to locate his missing brother. He sent letters off to various bar associations and finally his efforts were rewarded. He received a letter that his brother was vice president and general counsel for a small circus in Kansas. No phone number – the circus didn't have a telephone.

So the banker flew to Kansas City and took a bus to Topeka. There he asked a cabdriver for help. The cabdriver drove the banker to the outskirts of town and then to a smaller town and then to a little village. At the far end of the village was a sad, dilapidated little circus covered with dust. All the trucks and trailers needed a paint job. The circus wasn't second-rate. Not even third-rate. And there he found his brother's trailer, with his name on the door, and, in wobbly lettering, 'Vice President and General Counsel'.

The banker knocked on the door. The lawyer opened it. The brothers tearfully embraced and each told the other what they'd been doing over the last 25 years. After 30 minutes of this the lawyer consulted his watch and said, 'Time to give the elephant an enema.'

'What?' asked the banker as the lawyer dressed himself in a rain slicker. 'Time to give the elephant his enema,' repeated the lawyer.

'What are you talking about?' asked the banker.

'Well,' said the lawyer, 'the circus has fallen on hard times. We didn't have the money for liability insurance. Last year, after the circus had its parade through a small town, an old man slipped on some shit the elephant had left on the street. He broke his leg. We were sued. We lost. And the payment to the old man just about wiped us out. We couldn't afford another claim like that. It would ruin us. And there's a parade this afternoon.'

With that, the lawyer walked outside, grabbed a fire hose, inserted the nozzle in the elephant's bum and turned on the hydrant. Almost immediately, after a deep abdominal rumble, the elephant sprayed the lawyer from head to toe with shit.

The banker watched these proceedings in utter disbelief. At first he couldn't speak. But then he said to his brother, 'Please, please, PLEASE. You don't have to do this. Come with me. I have a good position with the bank. I can get you a clean job as a teller. Maybe even as a loan officer.'

The lawyer, wiping the shit off his face, shouted: 'What! And give up the practice of law?'

A lawyer and an engineer were fishing off the Barrier Reef. The lawyer said, 'I'm here because my house burnt down and everything I owned was destroyed by the fire.'

'That's a coincidence,' said the engineer. 'I'm here because my house and all my belongings were destroyed by a flood, and my insurance company also paid for everything.'

The lawyer looked puzzled. 'How do you start a flood?'

A Russian, a Cuban, an American and a lawyer are in a train. The Russian takes a bottle of the best vodka out of his pack, pours some into a glass, drinks it and says, 'In Russia, we have the best vodka in the world. Nowhere in the world can you find vodka as good as the one we produce in Ukraine. And we have so much of it, that we can just throw it away.' With that, he opens the window and throws the rest of the bottle through it. All the others are quite impressed.

The Cuban takes a pack of Havanas from his pocket, lights one and says, 'In Cuba we have the best cigars in the world: Havanas. Nowhere in the world are there so many and so good cigars and we have so much of them that we can just throw them away.' Saying that, he throws the pack of Havanas through the window. Once again, everybody is impressed.

The American takes a deep breath, stands up, opens the window and throws the lawyer through it.

What was O.J.'s favourite play when he was in the Buffalo Bills?

Cut left, then slash right!

Knock, knock.
Who's there?
O.J.

O.J. who?
That's fine, you're on the jury.

O.J. was seen running through the airport, jumping over seats and babies and strollers, to catch his plane to Chicago. A rental agent was frantically running after him yelling, 'Mr Simpson, Mr Simpson, you forgot your bloody glove.'

Did you hear about O.J.'s new movie? It's called *Sex, Knives and Athletic Tape*.

Why did O.J. do it?
He was practising for a part in the new movie, *Jock the Ripper*.

Why do they call him O.J?
Because he beats the pulp out of his women.

There's a new drink about in the bars now, called the Bloody Nicole. It's the same thing as a Bloody Mary, but instead of adding tomato juice, you add O.J.

O.J. wants the jury to come to his golf club and see how bad his slice is.

The defence claims that O.J. was acting on the advice of his marriage counsellor. After the last attempt at reconciliation failed, the counsellor told O.J. to take another stab at it.

O.J. Simpson gets sent to jail and is laying in his cell, depressed. His cellmate says to him, 'Hey, it's not all that bad. We've a lot of activities around here. Do you like sports?'
'Hell, yes,' says O.J.
'Do you like football?'
'Hell, yes,' says O.J.
'You'll like Mondays then. Do you like baseball?'
'Hell, yes,' says O.J.
'Great, you'll love Wednesdays then. Are you gay?'
'Hell, no,' says O.J.
'Pity. You're going to hate Fridays.'

O.J.'s introduced to his new cellmate, a huge, nasty looking guy doing consecutive life sentences. He says to O.J., 'Look here, we're gonna get somethin' straight off da bat. Are you gonna be the husband oh da wife?'

O.J. says, 'What?'

The guy gets real mad and says, 'Are you gonna be da husband oh da wife?'

O.J. thinks fast and says, 'I'll be the husband.'

The guy then says, 'Okay. Now get down on yo' knees and suck your wife's dick!'

What do O.J. Simpson and Michael Jackson have in common?

They are both missing a glove.

What did Michael Jackson say to O.J. Simpson?

'Don't worry, I'll take care of the kids.'

Did you hear that John Wayne Bobbitt called O.J. last night? He wanted O.J. to know that he knows what it feels like to be separated from a loved one.

What do you get when you put Lorina Bobbitt, Tammy Faye and O.J. Simpson in the same room?

A butcher, a Bakker and a licence plate maker.

Why did O.J. sit in the Bronco for so long?
Because Rodney King told him not to get out of the car.

What would you have if O.J. was put in the cell with David Koresh and Jeffrey Dahmer?
You'd have a complete breakfast: cereal, toast and O.J.

The greatest marketing idea of the century: His and Her knives endorsed by O.J. Simpson and Lorina Bobbitt.

What's the only thing worse than being married to Lorina Bobbitt?
Being divorced from O.J. Simpson.

What does O.J. stand for?
Obdurate Jerk
Obligatory Jokes
Obsessively Jealous
Odourous Journalism
Out Joyriding
Outlook: Jail

What are the three worst words to hear from
O.J. Simpson?
  I love you.

Did you hear about the new O.J. breakfast special?
  It's eggs, steak and prune juice. First, you
beat it, then you stab it with a knife, then you get
the runs.

It's one thing to kill your ex-wife, but another thing
to take a victory lap around the city afterwards.

After looking all over LA, they finally found
12 people who had never seen O.J. Simpson,
never heard of O.J. Simpson and had no idea who
O.J. Simpson is or was. They're all professors at
USC.

O.J. went into the hospital for a biopsy. When the
doctor pulled out his scalpel, O.J. said, 'You call that
a knife?'

magine someone walking round with his hands together behind his back, wiggling his fingers. Someone asks, 'What's this?'

'O.J. Simpson signing autographs.'

'O.J. my man, haven't seen you in a while. How's Nicole?'

'I think she's dead.'

'What do you mean, you think she's dead?'

'I dunno. The sex is still the same, but the dishes are piling up in the sink.'

Did you hear that O.J. is merchandising to help pay for his defence?

But there's a problem with the O.J. watches. There seems to be an hour missing, from 10 p.m. to 11 p.m.

What do Nicole Brown Simpson and the Australian yacht in the America's Cup have in common?

They both went down in under two and a half minutes.

O.J. Simpson's lawyers report to their client, 'We have good news and bad news. The bad news is that your blood has been DNA tested as being the blood at the murder scene. The good news is that your cholesterol's fine.'

Police are now saying that O.J.'s no longer a suspect because they found a Superbowl ring at the murder scene.

Why did O.J. go to Chicago?
To find a clean towel.

A certain wealthy lawyer had a summer house in the country, to which he retreated for several weeks of the year. Each summer, he would invite a different friend to spend a week or two at the house, which was in a backwoods section of Maine.

On one particular occasion, he invited a Czechoslovakian friend to stay. The friend, eager to get a freebee off a lawyer, agreed. Early one morning, they decided to pick berries for their breakfast. As they gathered berries, along came two huge bears, a male and a female. The lawyer, seeing the two bears, immediately dashed for cover. His friend, however, wasn't so lucky, and the male bear reached him and swallowed him whole.

The lawyer ran back to his Mercedes, tore into town as fast as he could, and got the local sheriff.

The sheriff grabbed his shotgun and rushed back to the berry patch with the lawyer. Sure enough, the two bears were still there. 'He's in that one!' cried the lawyer, pointing to the male, while visions of lawsuits from his friend's family danced in his head. He just had to save his friend.

The sheriff looked at the bears and, without batting an eyelid levelled his gun, took careful aim and shot the female. 'What did you do that for?' exclaimed the lawyer. 'I said he was in the other!'

'Exactly,' replied the sheriff, 'and would you believe a lawyer who told you the Czech was in the male?'

Reports today indicate that O.J. Simpson has told his Defence Attorney, Johnny Cochrane, 'I'll kill that fucking dog with my bare hands if they bring it to court!'

What's the difference between Christopher Reeve and O.J.?

At least O.J. will walk.

Did you hear that Jeffrey Dahmer escaped from jail?

He was last seen heading towards Oklahoma City in an A-1 steak sauce truck.

What did Ron Goldman say to Nicole Simpson as they were going to Heaven?

Here are your fucking sunglasses.

A doctor, a lawyer and an architect were arguing about who had the smartest dog. They decided to settle the issue by getting all the dogs together and seeing whose could perform the most impressive feat. 'Okay, Rover,' ordered the architect, and Rover trotted over to the table and in four minutes constructed a complete scaled model of a cathedral out of toothpicks. The architect slipped Rover a cookie, and everyone agreed that it was a pretty impressive performance.

'Hit it, Spot,' commanded the doctor. Spot lost no time in performing an emergency Caesarian on a cow. Three minutes later the proud mother of a healthy little heifer was all sewn up and doing fine. Not bad, conceded the onlookers, and Spot got a cookie from the doctor.

'Your turn, Fella,' said the lawyer. Over went Fella, humped the other two dogs, took their cookies, and went out to lunch.

PADDIES AND POLAKS

A man walks into a bar and orders a glass of Polish vodka. A man sitting next to him remarks, 'That's a coincidence. I, too, am enjoying a Polish vodka. Since I arrived from the old country, this is the only bar in which I have found it.' To which the first replies, 'Old country! I'm from the old country. Let me buy you another!'

As the drinks are being poured, one of the men asks, 'What part of the old country are you from?'

'Krakow,' replies the other.

'This is weird,' said the first. 'I, too, am from Krakow! Let's get another shot.'

After the new round arrives, the first asks, 'So, pal, what did you do back in Krakow?'

'Not much, really. I came here right out of high school. I graduated from the Lech Walesa Technical Academy in '81.'

'This is eerie,' replies the other. 'I'm Walesa Tech. '81. Let's get another shot.'

But the bartender says, 'Slow down fellas, I gotta

make a call.' The bartender calls his wife and tells her that he'll be late getting home. When she inquires as to the cause, he replies, 'Oh, the friggin' Liszjewski twins are here again!'

A pigmy went to his first cricket match and was describing it to his witch-doctor on his return. 'It was a beautiful sunny Sunday,' he said. 'A big crowd of people had gathered around this big field of grass. In the middle there was a thin strip of mowed grass. And there were three sticks at either end. And a man in a long overcoat came out with two men in sweaters. And he tossed something silvery into the air. They went out and in came 11 men in sweaters and white pants. One of them was padded and had great big gloves. Then out came two men with pads on their legs and small gloves holding big sticks. They took positions at either end of the strip and another man came running towards them and threw a red ball at the person holding the stick. And at that very minute it started to pour. Those white men sure know how to make rain.'

A Pole, a Brit and an American rob a bank. Afterwards, each hides in a different tree. The cops go to the American's tree and say, 'Who's up there?' The American guy says, 'Tweet, tweet.' The cops say, 'Oh, just a bird.' They go to the British guy's tree and say, 'Who's up there?' The British guy says, 'Meow, meow.' 'Oh, that's just a cat,' the cops say. So they go to the Polish guy's tree and say, 'Who's up there?' The Polish guy says, 'Mooooooo!'

An Oregonian, a Californian and a Texan were out camping. They were lazing around the campfire when the Texan pulled out a bottle of Tequila and, after taking a couple of swallows, threw the bottle up in the air, pulled out his six-shooter and neatly shot the bottle. The Californian noted that there'd still been some Tequila left in the bottle, but the Texan replied, 'That's okay, we have plenty of Tequila where I come from.'

The Californian promptly brought out his bottle of White Zinfandel, took two swallows, threw it up in the air and shot it with a 9mm semi-automatic Glock pistol with a 15-shot clip, stating, 'We have plenty of this where I come from.'

The Oregonian took all this in and finally opened a bottle of Henry's Blue Boar Irish Ale. He downed the entire bottle, threw it up in the air, shot the Californian with a 12-gauge shotgun and deftly caught the bottle. The Texan's jaw dropped nearly to his silver buckle and his eyes widened. The Oregonian seemed puzzled at the reaction. 'It's okay, we've plenty of Californians where I come from and I can get a nickel for the bottle.'

An Englishman, an American and a Scot were in a café drinking tea. A fly came up and landed in the Englishman's tea. The man scooped the fly out, called the waiter and said, 'I say, there's a fly in my tea.'

As the waiter came back with a fresh cup of tea for the Englishman, a fly landed in the American's tea. 'Damn!' the American shouted, standing up. 'There's a fly in my @*#&$! tea!' Again the waiter headed off for a fresh cup.

Just as the waiter was coming back with the American's tea, a fly landed in the Scot's tea. 'I notice there's a fly in your tea,' the waiter said hurriedly. 'Do you want me to get you another cup?'

'No,' said the Scot, who scooped the fly out of his cup and, holding it by its wings, shook it and said, 'Spit it out, ye wee bugger!'

An American, a Russian and an Israeli are waiting to order in a restaurant. The waiter says, 'Excuse me, but I've got bad news. There's a shortage of meat.' The Russian asks, 'What's meat?' The American asks, 'What's a shortage?' The Israeli asks, 'What's excuse me?'

A Frenchman and an Italian were sitting next to an American on an overseas flight. They began discussing their home lives. 'Last night I made love to my wife four times,' the Frenchman bragged. 'This morning she made me delicious crêpes and told me how much she adored me.'

'Last night I made love to my wife six times,' said the Italian. 'This morning she made me a wonderful omelette and told me she could never, never love another man.'

The Frenchman turned to the silent American. 'And how many times did you make love to your wife last night?'

'Once,' he replied.

'Only once!' said the Italian. 'And what did she say to you this morning?'

'Don't stop.'

An American tourist went into a restaurant in a Spanish provincial city for dinner, and asked to be served the specialty of the house. When the dish arrived, he asked what kind of meat it contained.

'Sir, these are the *cojones*,' the waiter replied.

'The what?' exclaimed the tourist.

'They are testicles of the bull killed in the ring today,' explained the waiter.

The tourist gulped but tasted it anyway and found it to be delicious. Returning the following evening, he asked for the same dish. After he finished the meal, the tourist commented to the waiter, 'Today's *cojones* are much smaller than the ones I had yesterday.'

'True, sir,' said the waiter. 'You see, the bull, he does not always lose.'

A zoo acquires one of an endangered species of gorilla. Right from the outset she's very bad tempered, very difficult to handle. The zoo's vet announces she's in heat. But what to do? There's no male of her species available. Whereupon the zoo administrators remember that one of their zookeepers, an Irishman called O'Reilly who is responsible for cleaning animals' cages, is notorious for his ability to satisfy females. Perhaps they could persuade him to satisfy the gorilla.

So they approach O'Reilly with a proposition. Would he be willing to screw the gorilla for $500? O'Reilly asks for the night to think things over and on the following day says that he'll accept the offer on three conditions. 'Firstly, I don't want to have to kiss her. Secondly, I want any offspring to be raised Roman Catholic.'

The zoo administration quickly accedes to these conditions. But what could be third? 'Well,' says O'Reilly, 'you've got to give me some time to come up with the $500.'

Two retired English officers were sitting in their armchairs in a London club reading their respective papers. 'By jove,' said one, looking over the top of *The Times*, 'do you remember old Carruthers during the War? I thought he'd died, but it turns out they've found him after 40 years living up a tree with a gorilla.'

'I say. Male or female gorilla?'

'Female of course. Nothing queer about old Carruthers.'

A young man of the upper class took a walk in Soho on a very windy day. As he passed a young woman, the wind caught her skirt and lifted it above her head. The man said, 'Oh, it's airy, isn't it?' The young woman replied, 'Yeah, what the 'ell did you expect? Feathers?'

Mulligan and Sean were taking a little stroll. 'At my funeral,' said Mulligan, 'I want you to pour a bottle of Irish Whisky over me grave.'

'I'll be glad to,' said Sean. 'But would you mind if it passes through me kidneys first?'

Paddy and Mick landed themselves a job at a sawmill. Just before morning tea, Paddy yelled, 'Mick! I lost me finger!'

'Have you now?' says Mick. 'And how did you do it?'

'I just touched this big spinning thing here like thi– Damn! There goes another one!'

O'Connell was staggering home with a pint of booze in his back pocket when he slipped and fell heavily. Struggling to his feet, he felt something wet running down his leg. 'Please, God,' he implored, 'let it be blood.'

313

'Ah, Sean,' said Michael McStain, 'how'd ye be comin' by that glorious black eye, me lad?'

Sean O'Malley shook his head and replied, "Tis the damndest thing. I was over at Molly's house, dancin' with the lovely lass, when her father walked in.'

'An' old Master Callahan is thinking that dancin' is an evil thing, cured by a black eye, is that it?'

'Na, na, Michael. The old man's deaf, an' couldn't hear th' music.'

'Hello, Pan American Airlines?' said Big Mick Lonegan. 'Could ye be tellin' me how long it takes to fly from Boston to Dublin?'

The voice on the telephone said, 'I'll see sir, just a minute.'

'Ahh, 'tis fast, to be sure. Thank ye,' Mick said as he hung up.

Paddy O'Shea got friendly with some of the local Boston Irish, and they took him to an upscale Irish pub.

'Amazin', just amazin', that's what America is,' he said, looking with delight into his glass. 'Never have I been seein' an ice cube with a hole in it!'

'Oi sure have,' said his host, Michael Sullivan. 'Bin married to one fer 15 years.'

An Irishman buys a packet of peanuts. He hands one to his wife. After a while, she asks for another. 'What for? They all taste the same.'

Two Irishmen were working on a building site digging a ditch. The foreman was at them all the time to keep busy. No breaks, just work, work, work. Finally one of the Irishmen noticed that the foreman left around 3.00 every afternoon. So they started leaving at 3.15.

The next day when the foreman left at 3.00, the workmen left at 3.15. One of them, Pat, arrived home, walked into the house, opened the bedroom door, and discovered the foreman in bed with his wife. He immediately ran back to the building site and dug like mad until 5.00.

The next day Pat told his mate, 'Listen, we can't knock off work any more at 3.15. I almost got caught.'

Paddy is on holidays with his girlfriend in Las Vegas. After paying a fortune for tickets they go to a night club where Paddy has been assured they'll be able to mingle with the stars. Sure enough the place is full of them and the conversation is very exciting.

'Hi ya, Madonna!'
'How do, Clint?'
Far from being impressed, Paddy's girlfriend is

annoyed that Paddy doesn't know any of the stars, and that nobody's interested in talking to them. On a visit to the toilet Paddy finds himself standing beside Frank Sinatra. Paddy explains the problem, tells him he's been a fan ever since 'On The Town' and has all his records. Would Mr Sinatra please help him out? All he has to do is walk past Paddy's table and say, 'How ya Paddy?' For once, Frank is in a good mood and agrees.

Twenty minutes later Frank walks up to the table where Paddy and his girlfriend are sitting talking. 'Hey Paddy,' shouts Frank. Paddy looks up and says, 'Fuck off, Frank, can't you see I'm talking to my girlfriend?'

Two women are walking down the Falls Road in Belfast. One says to the other, 'Don't them soldiers look stupid wearing camouflage in the middle of the city?' To which the other replies, 'What soldiers?'

Two IRA volunteers are waiting in ambush for an English patrol. It's due to pass at midday but hasn't arrived by 1.00. Then it's 2.00, and finally 3.00. Seamus is getting worried. 'God, Sean, they're awful late. I hope nothing's happened to them!'

Paddy heard that a fortune could be made by working as a lumberjack in Canada. So off he goes. After some weeks, he arrives at a lumberjack camp and asks the foreman for a job.

'Okay sonny, but you'll have to do a test first. If you can chop down 100 trees tomorrow, you're hired.'

So next day, Paddy gets his chainsaw and happily saws away all day. When the trees are counted Paddy only has 98. 'Oh, well,' says the foreman, 'you'll get another chance tomorrow.'

Next day, same story, 99 trees. 'I don't believe this,' says the foreman, 'a big strong fella like yourself should be able to cut down 100 trees in a day. You get one more chance, and I'll join you to show you the trick of it.'

Next day, Paddy and the foreman go into the forest. Upon arrival at a nice spot the foreman puts the chainsaw on the ground and starts the engine. Says Paddy, 'Holy Jesus! Where's the noise coming from?'

Paddy visits the hospital. 'I want to be castrated!' he demands cheerfully.

'Are you sure about this?' the doctor asks. 'Have you discussed it with your wife?'

'Yes, yes! I've thought about this for a long time. Let's get it over with!'

So the operation is performed. On his way home from hospital Paddy meets Mick.

'Well, hello Paddy! I haven't seen you for a

couple of days,' Mick says as they shake hands.

'No, I've been in hospital.'

'Well, that's funny. I'm on my way there right now!'

'Really? What's up?'

'I'm going to be vaccinated.'

'Oh shit! That's what it's called!'

How do you get a one-armed Irishman out of a tree?

You wave to him.

A bloke pulls up to a petrol station in Ireland and asks for five litres of petrol. The attendant replies they don't sell petrol.

'Don't sell petrol? What sort of garage is this? Well, check the oil for me.'

The attendant says they don't sell oil.

'What? Top up the radiator for me then.'

The attendant says they don't have any water, that in fact the garage is just a front for the IRA.

'Okay, then blow my tyres up.'

A young man was living on one side of London but his job was on the other. After a few years he bought himself one of the most expensive cars on the market. It was dazzlingly duco'd, had a very loud horn, went extremely fast, and all the girls watched as he drove by.

But living in London had its problems. He rarely had the chance to drive the car at top speed. So he decided to ferry the car to Ireland where, he thought, he could get away with a bit of high-speed driving.

Just out of Dublin he pressed down on the accelerator and sent the car rocketing to 140, 150, 160 kph. Then suddenly, as if they'd appeared from nowhere, he saw a man and a donkey crossing the road. They were so unused to traffic that they hadn't bothered to look. He swerved the car to the right missing them both but couldn't stop. He crashed through a fence and hit an old oak in a nearby field. The old man said to the donkey, 'Sure, an' we just got outta that field in toime, didn't we!'

How do you tell the Italians at a cock fight?
    They're the ones betting on the duck.
And how can you tell if the Mafia's involved?
    The duck wins.

A gondolier was floating down a canal singing 'O Solo Mio'. God looked down and wondered what would happen if he took half the gondolier's brain away. He did and the gondolier sang O so, o so. So God wondered what would happen if he took away the rest of the gondolier's brain, and he started singing 'When Irish Eyes Are Smiling.'

Guido goes to the godfather. Could he find a job for his nephew, due to arrive from Sicily? 'No problems,' says the godfather.

'Sir, I should tell you that the boy is deaf and dumb.'

'That's okay,' said the capa. 'We'll give him a job as a bagman and he won't need to talk.'

The boy had been working for several months picking up numbers-game receipts when the Don called Guido into his office. 'That little scumbag nephew of yours has been skimming from the collections,' he roared. 'I figure he's stolen about $600 000 by now and I want it back.'

Guido found his nephew and in sign language warned the boy of the godfather's rage. 'He's very upset with you and wants to see us both right away.' The boy followed his uncle to the Don's office and Guido signed to the lad, 'The godfather wants to know where the money is you stole from him.'

The boy shrugged his shoulders as if he knew nothing about it. Whereupon the don pulled a .357 magnum from the drawer, pointed it at the boy's head and bellowed, 'Tell that little puke he's got ten seconds to tell you where the money is or I'll blow his head off.'

The boy's eyes widened and he quickly signed to his uncle, 'I stashed the money under the basement stairs at your house.'

'Well,' the don demanded, 'what did the little shit say?'

Guido replied, 'He says he doesn't think you have the guts to pull the trigger.'

One day I'ma gonna Malta to bigga hotel. Ina morning I go down to eat breakfast. I tella waitress I wanna two pissis toast. She brings me only one piss. I tella her I want two piss. She say go to the toilet. I say, you no understand, I wanna piss onna my plate. She say you better no piss onna plate, you sonna ma bitch. I don't even know the lady and she call ma sonna me bitch!

Later I go to eat at a bigga restaurant. The waitress brings me a spoon and a knife, but no fock. I tella her I wanna fock. She tell me everyone wanna fock. I tell her you no understand, I wanna fock on the table. She say you better not fock on the table, you sonna ma bitch.

So, I go back to my room inna hotel and there is no shits onna my bed. I call the manager and tella him I wanna shit. He tell me to go to toilet. I say you no understand. I wanna shit on my bed. He say you better not shit onna bed, you sonna ma bitch.

I go to the checkout and the man at the desk say, peace on you. I say piss on you too, you sonna ma bitch, I gonna back to Italy!

Sam makes a confession to his wife. 'Sadie, the doctor says I've got disherpes.' Sadie looks it up in her home medical dictionary. 'Sam, not to worry,' she says. 'It says here that disherpes is a disease of the Gentiles.'

Schwartz and Goldstein decide to set up business but are told they'll do better if they have less foreign-sounding names. Schwartz thinks about this for a long, long time and decides to go for Smith. Goldstein also goes for the name of Smith and they call their business Smith & Smith.

First day, first phone call: 'May I speak to Mr Smith,' to which the receptionist replies, 'Which Mr Smith do you want? Schwartz or Goldstein?'

A young Jew and an old Jew are travelling on a train. The young Jew asks, 'Excuse me, sir, what time is it?' The old Jew doesn't answer.

'Excuse me, sir, what time is it?' The old Jew keeps silent.

'Sir, forgive me for interrupting you all the time, but I really want to know what time it is. Why won't you answer me?'

The old Jew says, 'Son, the next stop is the last on this route. I don't know you, so you must be a stranger. If I answer you now, according to Jewish tradition I have to invite you to my home. You're handsome and I have a beautiful daughter. You will both fall in love and you'll want to get married. And tell me, why would I want a son-in-law who can't even afford a watch?'

Moshe goes to a tailor to try on his new bespoke suit. But the arms are too long. 'No problems,' says the tailor, 'just bend them at the elbow and hold them out in front of you. See, now it's fine.'

'But the collar's up around my ears.'

'Nothing, nothing. Just hunch your back up a little. No, a little more. Per'

'But I'm stepping on my cuffs!'

'Bend your knees a little to take up the slack. Look in the mirror – the suit fits perfectly.'

Twisted like a pretzel, Moshe lurches out of the store and Rebecca and Florence see him go by.

'Look,' says Rebecca, 'that poor man.'

'Yes,' says Florence, 'but what a beautiful suit.'

It's Yom Kippur, the holiest day of the Jewish calendar. As it draws to a close in a small synagogue, the Rabbi is praying fervently. 'God, oh God, I am nothing before you.' The cantor joins in, 'God, oh God, I am nothing before you.' Whereupon the beadle, inspired by their piety and fervour, cries out, 'Oh God, I am nothing before you.'

The cantor raises his eyebrows, looks at the Rabbi and says, 'Look who thinks he's nothing!'

A Polak returns from work and finds his wife in bed with a friend. He raves, he rants, he pulls a pistol out of his pocket and holds it up to his own head. Whereupon his wife starts laughing uncontrollably. 'Don't laugh, bitch,' he yells. 'You're next!'

How did the Polak burn his face?
Bobbing for French fries.

Men will go to extraordinary lengths to prove their manhood. Witness Frenchman Pierre Pumpille of Lyon, who recently shunted a stationary car two metres by head-butting it. 'Women thought I was a god,' he explained from his hospital bed. But he was a sissy compared to Polish farmer, Krystof Azninsky, who staked a strong claim to being Europe's most macho man by cutting off his own head.

Azninsky, 30, had been drinking with some friends when it was suggested they strip naked and play some 'men's games'. They began by hitting each other over the head with frozen swedes, but then one man seized a chainsaw and cut off the end of his foot. Not to be outdone, Azninsky grabbed the saw and, crying, 'Watch this then,' swung at his own head and decapitated himself. 'It's funny,' said one companion, 'because when he was young he put on his sister's underwear. But he died like a man.'

A young Polak wants to try out for his high school's football team. He seeks out the coach, who asks him if he can block.

The Polak runs into a telephone pole and shatters it.

The coach asks the Polak a few more questions before throwing him a football. The coach asks, 'Can you pass that?'

The Polak replies, 'You bet, sir. If I can swallow it, I can pass it.'

The Polak apprentice, assisting in building a house, takes a nail from the box and looks at it. He tosses it over his shoulder and picks up another one which he nails into the board in front of him. He picks up the next nail, looks at it and throws it over his shoulder. His boss says, 'What the hell are you doing? Those were all brand new nails. Why are you throwing half of them away?'

'Boss, I know they're new. But some of them are pointing in the wrong direction.'

To which the boss says, 'You Polish idiot. Those are for the other side of the house!'

Polish loan sharks lend out all their money and skip town.

A Polish firing squad stands in a circle.

The new Polish navy has glass bottom boats, to see the old Polish navy.

Have you seen a Polish mine detector? He puts his fingers in his ears and starts stamping on the ground with his foot.

Why did the Polak cross the road?
He couldn't get his dick out of the chicken.

Two Polish guys rent a boat and go fishing on a lake. They're amazed by the number of fish they catch, so one says to the other, 'We'll have to come back here tomorrow.'
'But how will we remember where the spot is?'
The first guy takes a can of spray paint, paints an X on the bottom of the boat, and says, 'We'll just look for this X tomorrow.'
The other guy says, 'You idiot. How do you know we'll get the same boat?'

747 recently crashed in a cemetery in Poland. So far Polish officials have retrieved 2000 bodies.

An English guy is driving with a Polish guy as a passenger. He pulls over because he's worried that his turn signal isn't working, and asks the Polish guy to step out of the car and check the lights while he tests them. The English guy turns on the turn signal and says, 'Is it working?' To which the Polish guy responds, 'Yes, it's working. No, it's not working. Yes, it's working. No, it's not working.'

Three men are travelling in the Amazon: a German, an American and a Polak. Unfortunately, they are captured by some Indians. The head of the tribe says to the German, 'What do you want on your back for your whipping?' The German responds, 'I will take oil.' They put oil on his back and a large Indian whips him ten times. When he's finished the German has huge welts on his back and can hardly move.

The Indians haul him away and say to the Polak, 'What do you want on your back?'

'I'll take nothing!' says the Polak, and stands there straight, taking his ten lashings without a flinch.

'What will you take on your back?' the Indians ask the American, who says, 'I'll take the Polak.'

A Polak wanted to join an amateur basketball team. The coach decided to give him a chance. 'I'll give you three questions. If you come back in a week and answer them all correctly you're on the team.'

'Great,' said the Polak.

'Here are your questions. First, how many days are there in a week that begin with the letter T? Second, how many seconds are there in a year? And third, how many Ds are there in the Rudolph the Rednosed Reindeer?'

Next week the Polak came back.

'So how many days in the week start with T?' The Polak said, 'Two.'

'Very good,' said the coach, 'and what are they?'

'Today and tomorrow.'

'Hmmm, okay,' said the coach. 'How many seconds in a year?'

'Twelve.'

'Twelve! How the hell did you come up with 12?'

'Well,' said the Polak, 'there's the 2nd of January, the 2nd of February, the 2nd of – '

'Okay, okay,' said the coach. 'Now how many Ds in Rudolph the Rednosed Reindeer?'

'That's easy. Three hundred and sixty-five.'

'What!' cried the coach. 'How did you get that figure?' To which the Polak sang, 'De-de de-de de-de-de.'

A Polak goes to a carpenter. 'Can you build me a box that's two inches high, two inches wide and 50 feet long?'

'Well,' said the carpenter, 'it could be done, I suppose, but what would you want a box like that for?'

'Well,' said the Polak, 'a neighbour moved away and forgot some things. So he's asked me to send him his garden hose.'

A Polak is learning how to skydive. The instructor tells the Polak to jump out of the plane and pull his ripcord. The instructor explains that he himself will jump out right behind him so that they can go down together.

The time comes. The instructor reminds the Polak that he will be right behind him. The Polak jumps from the plane and, after a few seconds, pulls the ripcord. Then the instructor jumps too. He pulls his ripcord but the parachute doesn't open. The instructor, frantically trying to get his parachute open, plummets past the Polak. The Polak, seeing this, undoes the straps to his parachute. 'So you wanna race, eh?'

An Englishman, a Frenchman and a Polak were captured by the Germans and thrown into prison. Fortunately the guard is kindly and says, 'I'm going to lock you away for five years but I'll let you have anything you want now. Before I lock you away.'

The Englishman said, 'I'll have five years' supply of

beer.' His wish is granted and they lock him away with his beer.

The Frenchman says, 'I'll have five years' supply of brandy.' His wish is granted and they lock him away with his brandy.

The Polak says, 'I'll have five years' supply of cigarettes.' His wish is granted and they lock him away with his cigarettes.

Five years later the war is over, and the Americans arrive. They release the prisoners. The Englishman staggers out totally drunk. Then the Frenchman rolls out, rather inebriated. Then they release the Polak, who comes out and says, 'Has anyone got a light?'

A Polish guy is walking along the beach at Cannes. There are many beautiful women lying in the sun and he wants to meet one. But try as he might, the women don't seem interested. Finally he walks up to a French guy who is surrounded by adoring women. 'Excuse me,' he says to the Frenchman, 'I've been trying to meet one of these women for about an hour now and I can't seem to get anywhere. You're French, you know these women. What do they want?'

'Maybe I help you a leetle beet,' says the Frenchman. 'What you do ees, you go to zee store, you buy a leetle bikini sweeming suit, you walk up and down zee beach, you meet a girl very qweekley zees way.'

'Thanks,' says the Polish guy and goes off to the

store. He buys a skimpy red bathing suit, puts it on, goes back to the beach. He parades up and down but still has no luck. So he goes back to the Frenchman. 'I'm sorry to bother you again, but I went to the store, got a swimsuit and I still haven't been able to meet a girl.'

'Okay,' says the Frenchman, 'I tell you what you do. You go zee store, you buy potato. You put potato in sweeming suit and walk up and down zee beach. You will meet girl very, very qweekley zees way.'

'Thanks,' says the guy. He goes to the store. Buys a potato. Puts it in the swimsuit. But after marching up and down for an hour, the women are still avoiding his gaze. So he goes back to the Frenchman. 'Look, I got the suit, I put the potato in it. I walked up and down the beach. Still nothing. What more can I do?'

'Well,' says the Frenchman, 'maybe I can help you a leetle beet. Why don't you try moving zee potato to the front of the sweeming suit?'

A man goes to a brothel. The madam is out of women, but since the guy is Polish, she thinks she can get away with an inflatable doll. He'll never know the difference. But because she's never tried this before, she waits outside the door. After five minutes the Polak comes out. 'How was it?' asks the madam.

'I don't know,' says the Polak. 'I bit her on the bum and she farted and flew out the window.'

331

How do you know if a Polak has been using a computer?

There's white-out on the screen.

A Polish guy is walking down the street carrying a brown paper bag. He runs into one of his friends who asks, 'Hey, what do you have in the bag?'

The man tells his friend that he has some fish in the bag.

His friend says, 'Well, I'll make you a bet. If I can guess how many fish you have in the bag, you'll have to give me one.'

The Polish man says, 'I'll tell you what. If you can tell me how many fish I have in this bag, I'll give you both of them.'

Who wears a dirty white robe and rides a pig?

Lawrence of Poland.

Did you hear about the tragedy in Poland?

In Poland's largest shopping mall there was a terrible outrage. People were stuck on the escalators for four hours.

A Polak, an African-American and a white guy were driving through a desert when they ran out of gas. They decided to start walking to the nearest town, 50 miles back, to get some help.

A rancher was sitting on his front porch that evening when he saw the white guy top the horizon and walk towards him. The rancher noticed that the white guy was carrying a glass of water. The rancher said, 'Hi, there. What are you doing carrying a glass of water through the desert?'

The white guy explained his predicament and said that as he had a long way to go, he might get thirsty, so that's why he was carrying the water.

A little while later the rancher noticed the African-American walking toward him with a loaf of bread in his hand. 'What are you doing?' asked the rancher.

The man explained the situation and said that as he had a long way to go, he might get hungry, and that's why he had the bread.

Finally, the Polak appeared, dragging a car door through the sand. More curious than ever, the rancher asked, 'Hey, why are you dragging that car door?'

'Well,' said the Polak, 'I have a long way to go, so if it gets too hot, I'll roll down the window.'

P olish Airlines Flight 113 was descending for a landing at an airport unknown to the pilot, who suddenly exclaimed to the co-pilot, 'Holy cow! Look how short the runway is! I've never seen one that short!'

The co-pilot yelled, 'Wow! You're right! That's incredible! Are you sure we can make it?'

'Well, we better, we're almost out of fuel.'

The pilot got on the intercom and notified the passengers to put their heads between their knees and prepare for an emergency landing. Then he set the flaps down and slowed the plane to just over stall-speed. The jumbo jet came screaming in, on the ragged edge of control. The pilot's hands were sweating, the co-pilot was praying. They touched down and came screeching to a halt just before the edge of the runway, the tyres smoking. 'Whew! That was close!' yelled the pilot. 'That runway was short!'

'Yeah!' said the co-pilot, 'and wide too!'

A Polak was suffering from constipation, so his doctor prescribed suppositories. A week later the Pole complained to the doctor that they didn't produce the desired results. 'Have you been taking them regularly?' the doctor asked. 'What do you think I've been doing,' the Pole said, 'shoving them up my arse?'

How do you know you're flying over Poland? There's toilet paper hanging on the clotheslines.

Did you know that Poland has just bought 10 000 septic tanks?

As soon as they learn how to drive them, they're going to invade Russia.

Did you hear about the Polak who thought his wife was going to kill him?

On her dressing table he found a bottle of Polish Remover.

Three men applied for a job as a detective. One was Polish, one was Jewish and one was Italian. Rather than ask the standard questions during the interview, the chief decided to ask each applicant just one question and base his decision upon that answer.

When the Jewish man arrived for his interview, the chief asked, 'Who killed Jesus Christ?' The Jewish man answered without hesitation, 'The Romans killed him.' The chief thanked him and he left.

When the Italian man arrived for his interview, the chief asked the same question. The Italian replied, 'Jesus was killed by the Jews.' Again, the chief thanked the man, who then left.

When the Polish man arrived for his interview, he was asked the same question. He thought for a long time before saying, 'Could I have some time to think about it?' The chief said, 'Okay but get back to me tomorrow.'

When the Polish man arrived home, his wife asked, 'How did the interview go?' He replied, 'Great, I got the job, and I'm already investigating a murder!'

A Polak was jumped by two muggers. He fought desperately but was finally subdued. The muggers went through his pockets. 'You mean you fought like that for 57 cents?' asked one of the muggers incredulously.

'Is that all you wanted,' moaned the Pole, 'I thought you were after the $400 in my shoe.'

Kowalski and Lisjewski are hard at work cleaning out the sewer on a sweltering day in July, beneath the streets of the Bronx. Kowalski says, 'I really hate this crummy, smelly job, shovellin' shit!'

Lisjewski says, 'Yeah, me too. I hate it!'

Kowalski says, 'How come you and me is down here underground shovelling shit and breaking our backs, when Rafaelli is up there sittin' in the truck with the air-conditioner on, smokin' cigarettes and readin' the newspaper? That's what I'd like to know!'

Lisjewski says, 'You know what I'm gonna do? I'm going up there and I'm gonna say to that Rafaelli just like I said it to you, and then we'll see what he's got to say.'

Lisjewski says, 'Yeah, go up there and tell 'im what you said.'

So Kowalski brushes the muck off his pants, climbs up the ladder to the street and goes over to the truck. Rafaelli says, 'Whaddaya want, Kowalski? And hurry up, it's hot out here.'

Kowalski says, 'Well, I just wanna know one thing, Rafaelli. How cum me 'n Lisjewski is down there underground shovellin' shit, and yer up here in the air-conditionin', smokin' cigarettes all day? How come?'

Rafaelli smiles and says, 'Is that all you wanted to know? That's real easy, Kowalski.' He holds his hand out in front of the heavy iron truck bed and says, 'Okay, Kowalski, hit my hand real hard.'

Kowalski unloads a huge haymaker of a punch and, of course, Rafaelli pulls his hand away quickly. Kowalski smashes his fist against the truck.

'Okay, Kowalski,' says Rafaelli, 'that's the reason why I get to stay up here in the truck, and you and Lisjewski gotta shovel shit in the sewer. Do you get it now?'

Kowalski nods and returns to the ladder, rubbing his hand. When he gets back down into the tunnel, Lisjewski is waiting for him. 'What'd he say, Kowalski? How come izzit that Rafaelli gets to sit up there in the truck, and we gotta come down here and shovel shit?'

Kowalski says, 'I don't know if you're gonna be able to undertand this, but I'll try to explain it just like Rafaelli told me. Now, hit my hand real hard.' and Kowalski holds his hand up in front of his face ...

An Italian, an American and a Polak are captured by the French and are taken to the guillotine. The executioner places the Italian on the block and asks if he has any last words. The Italian replies, 'I pray to the Virgin Mary that I may live.' The blade drops, and stops a mere inch from the Italian's neck. Amazed, the French let him go.

Next, the American is put in position and asked if he has any final words. He replies, 'In the name of Jesus Christ, please have mercy.' They drop the blade, and again it stops, just an inch from the American's neck. In disbelief, they let him go free.

Then the Polak is placed on the block, and they ask if he has any last words. He says, 'Yeah, you've got a knot in your rope.'

A Polak is hired to paint the lines on the road. On the first day he paints ten miles, and his employers are amazed. But, the second day he painted just five, and on the third day, he painted only a mile of the road.

Disappointed, his boss asks what the problem was. The Polak replies, 'Well, sir, every day I have to walk farther and farther to get back to the paint bucket.'

There are three construction workers eating lunch on top of a building. An Italian, a Polak, and an Asian. The Italian has a meatball hero, the Asian has noodles, and the Polak has knockwurst. The Italian and the Asian are tired of having the same lunches every day. The Italian says that if he gets a meatball hero the next day he will throw it off the building. The Asian says that if he gets noodles tomorrow he will also throw it off the building. The Polak says that if he gets knockwurst tomorow he will throw it off the building.

Sure enough, the Italian and the Asian open their lunchboxes the next day and find they have a meatball hero and noodles respectively, and both throw their lunches off the building. Without opening his lunchbox, the Polak throws his sandwich off the building, too. The other guys ask him how he knew it was knockwurst again without even looking. He responds, 'Because I pack my own lunch.'

Why did the Polak sell his waterskis?
Because he couldn't find a lake with a hill in it.

Two Polaks are flying across Europe in a three-engined 727. The pilot announces, 'Folks, we just had one engine go out. But don't worry, this plane can fly just fine on two engines, but we're going to be about an hour late getting into Warsaw.'

An hour later the pilot gets on the intercom again. 'Sorry, but a second engine just went out. But please don't worry. This plane is designed to fly safely on one engine. But we will be about two hours late getting into Warsaw.'

After that announcement one Polak looks at the other and says, 'Well, I sure hope the third engine doesn't go out. Otherwise we'll be up here all night.'

Did you hear about the Polish airliner that crashed?

It ran out of coal.

What is 200 yards long and eats cabbage?

A Polish meat queue.

Two Polish peasants are loitering by the side of the road one day when a tourist pulls up in his car. He winds down the window and asks, 'Do you speak English?' The peasants both shrug their shoulders. The tourist then tries, '*Parlez vous Francais?*' Again the peasants plainly don't understand. The tourist then shows off his skill by trying German, Russian, Italian and Spanish, but to no avail. Finally he drives off in disgust. One peasant comments in Polish, 'It must be wonderful to be able to speak so many languages.' The other retorts, 'Pah! Look how far it got him!'

What did the Polish people light their houses with before they used candles?

Electricity.

An American, a Frenchman and a Polak are lined up in front of a firing squad, awaiting execution. The American is first. He points behind the firing squad and shouts, 'Flood!' When the soldiers turn to look, he escapes.

The Frenchman quickly devises his plan and shouts, 'Tornado!' He escapes as well.

The Polak, thinking he has caught on, yells, 'Fire!'

A tribe of Native Americans named all women according to the animal hide with which they made their blanket. So one woman was known as Squaw of the Buffalo Hide, while another was Squaw of the Deer Hide. And there was a particularly strong woman who was known as Squaw of the Hippopotamus Hide. She was as large and powerful as the animal from which her blanket was made.

Year after year, the woman would enter the tribal wrestling tournament and easily defeat all challenges from the Squaw of the Buffalo Hide, the Squaw of the Deer Hide, the Squaw of the Horse Hide and the Squaw of the Bear Hide. One year, two of the squaws petitioned the chief to allow them to enter their sons as a wrestling tandem in order to defeat the Squaw of the Hippopotamus Hide.

341

When the match began, it became clear that the squaw had finally met an opponent that was her equal. The two sons wrestled and struggled vigorously. The match lasted for hours without a clear victor but finally the chief intervened and declared that, in the interests of the health and safety of the wrestlers, he would declare a winner.

He retired to his tepee, contemplated the great struggle and found it extremely difficult to decide a winner. After much deliberation, he came out and announced his decision.

'The Squaw of the Hippopotamus Hide is equal to the sons of the squaws of the other two hides.'

A missionary was sent to spread the good word in Bongo Bongo, but found little success. He approached the king to see what would be necessary to engender co-operation. The king had seen pictures of European kings and queens sitting on thrones, and told the missionary that he would have the entire tribe converted if only he could have a golden throne. The missionary wrote to the Home Mission Board to tell them of this marvellous opportunity, and they sent him a throne. No, it wasn't solid gold, but the king liked it very much, and the whole tribe converted. The missionary was regarded as a hero by fellow evangelists.

In his later years, however, the king got arthritic and decided that sitting on his hard, golden throne was exacerbating his aches and pains, so he stashed the throne up in the attic of his grass shack.

Trouble is, one day the throne came crashing through the ceiling and squashed the old king.

Which only goes to show that people who live in grass houses shouldn't stow thrones.

Who killed more Indians than Custer?
Union Carbide.

What's the difference between yoghurt and Australia?
Yoghurt has a real live culture.

How many South African policemen does it take to break an egg?
None. It fell down the stairs.

It's the first day back at school after the summer holidays and all the little children are fidgeting about with excitement.

TEACHER: Okay, kids, we'll begin the year by discussing what we did over the holidays. Joey, what did you do?

JOEY: Well, Miss, I had a wonderful time. Every morning I would go down to the beach and play in the sand.

TEACHER: Very good Joey, if you can spell 'sand' I'll give you a Mars Bar.

JOEY: Mmmmh ... s-a-n-d.

TEACHER: Very good Joey, here's a Mars Bar. Sally, what did you do over the holidays?

SALLY: Well, Miss, I would go down to the beach and play in the sand too. Sometimes Joey and I would go for a paddle in the sea.

TEACHER: Lovely. If you can spell 'sea' you can have a Mars Bar.

SALLY: S-e-a.

TEACHER: Good Sally, have a Mars Bar. Now what about you Leroy? What did you get up to?

LEROY: Well, Miss, I also went down to the beach, but none of the other kids would play with me 'cause my skin's a different colour.

TEACHER: Oh, poor, poor Leroy. How dreadful. That's racial hatred for you. If you can spell 'prejudice' you can have a Mars Bar.

President Reagan visited India and was touring the countryside with Rajiv Gandhi. Reagan couldn't help but notice people shitting in the open. Wanting to help, he produced his cheque book and offered a donation to build a few toilets. This embarrassed Ghandi enormously, but he felt it was undiplomatic to refuse.

A few months later, Ghandi visited the US and he hoped to see someone shitting out in the open, so that he could put Reagan in a similarly embarrassing position. Finally, fortunately, he found one man squatting in public view. Delighted, Ghandi offered Reagan a donation for building a toilet.

'Oh, he has his own toilet,' Reagan said, 'but he insists on shitting like this. He's the Indian Ambassador.'

An Eskimo has a broken snowmobile, so he brings it in to be serviced. After checking it out, the service mechanic says, 'It looks like you blew a seal.'

The Eskimo looks at him and says, 'No, that is just frost on my moustache.'

CYBERKIDS

One of Johnny's favourite pastimes was hiding in the wardrobe while his mother entertained her lover. One day Johnny's dad came home early, so his mum shoved her lover into the wardrobe and Johnny struck up a conversation.

JOHNNY: Sure is dark in here.

MAN: Yeah kid, it sure is.

JOHNNY: Wanna buy a football?

MAN: I don't think so, kid.

JOHNNY: You really should buy this football.

MAN: What the hell for?

JOHNNY: It might make me forget I saw you here.

MAN: Okay, kid, how much?

JOHNNY: A hundred bucks.

MAN: What! Okay, but keep your mouth shut.

The guy paid and left as soon as the coast was clear. Next week Johnny was in the wardrobe again, Mum's lover was pounding away again, when Dad came home early again. So the man winds up in the

349

closet again, and Johnny starts talking to him.

JOHNNY: Sure is dark in here.

MAN: Yeah kid, it sure is.

JOHNNY: Wanna buy a football helmet?

MAN: Let me guess. A hundred bucks and you'll forget you saw me. Right?

JOHNNY: Right.

The guy pays up and takes off as soon as he can.

Later that week Johnny's dad tells Johnny to get his football and helmet so that they can play some ball. 'I can't Dad, I sold them for two hundred bucks,' says Johnny. Dad says, 'Johnny, you're a lying little cuss and you're going to pay for that one.' And sends him off to confession.

Johnny sits in the confessional, the door shuts, and the window opens to the priest. 'Sure is dark in here,' Johnny says.

The priest replies, 'Listen kid, I'm out of money and I don't even like football.'

A father was walking with his young son in the park when they came upon two dogs having sex. The boy asked his dad what the dogs were doing. He said they were making a puppy.

A couple of days later the boy walked in on his parents who were having sex on the couch. He asked his father what they were doing. He said that they were making a baby.

The boy replied, 'Can you turn Mummy over? I'd much rather have a puppy.'

It was obvious to Mum and Dad that the only way to pull off a Sunday afternoon quickie without their ten-year-old son hanging around was to send him out on the balcony. So they ordered him to report on all the neighbourhood activities.

The boy began his commentary. 'There's a car being towed from the parking lot,' he said.

'An ambulance just drove by.'

'It looks like the Andersons have company,' he called out.

'Max is riding a new bike and the Coopers are having sex.'

Mum and Dad shot up in bed. 'How do you know that?' the startled father asked.

'Their kid is standing out on the balcony too.'

A priest was walking down the street when a small boy approached from the other direction carrying a bottle of acid. The priest was afraid that the child might injure himself, so he offered to trade a bottle of holy water for the dangerous fluid. 'What will holy water do?' asked the boy.

'Well,' replied the priest, 'I rubbed this on a woman's belly and she passed a baby.'

To which the boy replied, 'That's nothing. I rubbed this on a cat's arse and it passed a motorcycle.'

'**D**ad, what is politics?'

'Politics? Well, consider our home. I am the wage earner, so let's call me Capitalism. Your mother is the administrator of the money, so we'll call her Government. We take care of you and your needs, so we'll call you the People. We'll call the maid the Working Class, and your baby brother the Future. Do you understand so far?'

'I'm not really sure, Dad, I'll have to think about it.'

Late that night, the boy's sleep was disturbed by the crying of his baby brother. He got up and found that the baby had soiled its nappy. He went to his parents' room and found his mother fast asleep, and then discovered that his father was bonking the maid so vigorously that they didn't hear his knocks on the door. He returned to his bed and went to sleep.

Next morning he reported to his father, 'Dad, I now think I understand what politics is.'

'Good, my boy. Explain it to me in your own words.'

'Well, while Capitalism is screwing the Working Class and the Government is sound asleep, the People are being completely ignored and the Future is full of shit.'

There was a kid who hung around the local grocery store where the bigger boys always teased him. They said he was two bricks shy of a load, two pickles shy of a barrel, dumber than a box of rocks, that his belt didn't go through all the loops, that the lights were on but no one was home, that his elevator didn't go all the way to the top, or that his elevator did go all the way to the top but no one got off.

To prove the kid's stupidity, the bigger boys frequently offered him a choice between a nickel and a dime. He'll always take the nickel, they said, because it's bigger.

The grocer took the kid aside and said, 'Those boys are making fun of you. They think you don't know a dime is worth more than a nickel. Are you grabbing the nickel because it's bigger? Or what?'

The kid looked at the grocer and whispered, 'No. But if I took the dime they'd quit doing it.'

'Jimmy, did your mother help you with your homework last night?' the teacher asked.

'No, she did it all.'

Little Johnny was sitting in class one day. All of a sudden he needed to go to the bathroom. He yelled out, 'Miss Jones, I need to take a piss.'

'Now, Johnny, that is not the proper word to use in this situation. The correct word you want to use is "urinate". Please use the word "urinate" in a sentence correctly, and I will allow you to go.'

Little Johnny thinks for a bit. 'You're an eight — but if you had bigger tits you'd be a ten.'

■ like kids, but I don't think I could eat a whole one.

Five-year-old Johnny is running around the house making life miserable for his mother. She says, 'Johnny, why don't you go across the street and watch them build the house. Maybe you can learn some new things.'

Johnny disappears for about four hours and when he returns his mother asks, 'Did you learn anything interesting today?'

'I learned how to hang a door,' Johnny replies.

'That's great! How do you do that?'

'Well, first you get the son of bitch. Then you slap the piece of shit up there but it's too fucking small. So you shave a cunt hair off here and a cunt hair off there and put the goddamn thing up.'

Johnny's mother is floored by his language. 'You go to your room and wait until your father gets home!'

Later, Johnny's dad goes into his room and says, 'I understand you got in a little trouble today.'

'All I did was tell Mom how to hang a door.'

'Why don't you tell me?' Dad asks.'

Well, first you get the son of bitch. Then you slap the piece of shit up there but it's too fucking small. So you shave a cunt hair off here and a cunt hair off there and put the goddamn thing up.'

Dad screams, 'That's it, young man. You go get a switch from the backyard.'

Johnny looks at his dad and says, 'Fuck you, that's the electrician's job.'

There were two young brothers talking in their backyard waiting for their mother to make them lunch. One was four, the other three.

FOUR: I'm getting pretty old now, I think I can start cussing.

THREE: Oh yeah?

FOUR: Yeah, I think I'm going to start saying damn whenever I feel like it.

THREE: You know what?

FOUR: What?

THREE: I think I'm getting pretty old, I'm going to start cussing too.

FOUR: Oh yeah? What are you going to say?

THREE: I'm going to say arse.

Their mother calls them in for lunch and asks the four-year-old, 'What do you want for lunch?'

'Oh damn, I think I'll have some spaghetti-o's.'

The mother was aghast. She took the four-year-old by the ear to the bathroom, washed his mouth out with soap, spanked him and put him in his room and slammed the door.

She returned to the kitchen and asked the three-year-old, 'What do you want for lunch?'

'I don't know, Mom but you can bet your arse it won't be spaghetti-o's.'

A bright, well-behaved little boy lived with his parents and grandparents in suburbia. One evening, the boy's father passed outside his bedroom window and was pleased to hear him kneeling beside his bed saying his prayers. He finished off with:

God bless Mummy
God bless Daddy
God bless Grandma
Ta ta Grandpa.

The father thought this form of prayer a little strange, but was so pleased that his son was praying of his own accord that he thought nothing more of it. Until, that is, Grandpa passed away with a stroke during the night.

A few weeks later, he again overheard his son's prayers:

God bless Mummy
God bless Daddy
Ta ta Grandma.

Sure enough, the next morning they found the little boy's grandmother had had a heart attack in the middle of the night and passed away.

Several weeks later the father overheard his son say:

God bless Mummy
Ta ta Daddy.

The father was stricken with grief. What had he done to deserve such a short life! He was still in the prime of life.

So great was his turmoil, that he didn't get a wink of sleep all night. He got up in the morning expecting disaster to strike at any time. He drove extra carefully to work that morning, and stayed in his office all day.

On his return home, he poured out his worries to his wife. He'd had an awful day, grief-stricken, worried, and he just wanted to get it over with. But his wife had no time for him. 'You think *you've* had a bad day. I've been waiting for you to get back to help me out. I've had a terrible day today. I got up this morning and opened the front door to find the milkman lying dead on the porch ...'

IS THERE A DOCTOR IN THE MOUSE?

The other day Ray Charles went to the doctor for a check-up. After the examination, the doctor told Ray, 'I have some good news and some bad news.' Ray said, 'Give me the bad news first.'

The doctor said, 'I'm afraid we got some bad results from one of your tests, and we are going to have to operate and cut off your left testicle.'

Ray sort of winced, pondered a bit and said, 'Well, what's the good news?'

To which the doctor replied, 'You still got the right one baby, uhh huhh.'

Did you hear about the gynaecologist who quit his job and went into interior decoration?

He could wallpaper the whole house through the keyhole.

Two gynaecologists meet at a conference. As usual, they tell each other what cases they have had during the past year:

'Well, I had a patient with breasts just like melons.'

'Incredible! So big?'

'Yes.'

'But I had a patient with a clitoris just like a lemon.'

'Wow. So big?'

'No, so sour.'

Twins are born.

Mother happy.

Father happy.

Mother: 'Just look at the lovely babies ...'

Father takes one by the head, and the little neck breaks.

Doctor rushes in. 'How could you DO that?'

Father: 'It was easy. Look!'

Dave's office insisted that he go to the doctor's for a complete physical. Worried that the doctor might notice that his hearing was getting worse, Dave asked his wife to come along. After a long wait they finally got to see the doctor, who checked Dave's pulse, heart rate and blood pressure. 'Dave, I'll need to do some additional tests. I'll need a urine sample, a stool sample and a sperm sample.'

Dave turned immediately to his wife and

whispered, 'What? What did he say?'

'Don't worry about it,' she said, 'just leave your underpants.'

A world-famous urologist believed he could diagnose any disease simply by looking at a urine sample. To test his prowess, a friend with tennis elbow peed into a jar and then got additional donations from his wife, daughter and his dog. The next morning, he jerked off in it as well.

He gave the bottle to the famous urologist and was told he'd be called in a few days with the results.

Finally the urologist called and said, 'It was a tough case but I think I've solved it.'

'What's wrong with me?' the man asked.

'Well, your wife has the clap, your daughter is pregnant, your dog has worms and if you quit playing with yourself, you wouldn't have tennis elbow.'

A guy goes to his doctor for a check-up. After a lot of tests the doctor says, 'I've got some bad news and some good news. After going over all your tests, I've discovered that you've a latent homosexual personality.'

'Oh, my God, that's awful,' says the guy. 'So what's the good news?'

The doctor says, 'Well, I think you're kinda cute.'

A nurse in the maternity ward asked the young med student why he was so enthusiastic about obstetrics. 'When I was in medical rotation,' he said, 'I thought I was suffering from heart attacks, asthma and itch. In surgery I was sure I had ulcers. In the psychiatric ward I thought I was losing my mind. Now, in obstetrics, I can relax!'

A fellow goes to the doctor and says, 'Doctor, I have this problem that I'm always farting all of the time. Although they don't smell, they do make loud noises, and it's affecting my social life.' The doctor gives him some pills and asks him to return next week.

He returns and says, 'Those pills did no good. In fact they made things worse. I still fart as much, but now they smell terrible.'

To which the doctor replied, 'Good! Now that we have your nose working again, let's work on your farting.'

There was a businessman, and he was feeling really crook, so he went to see the doctor about it. The doctor said to him, 'Well, it must be your diet. What sort of greens do you eat?' And the man replied, 'Well, actually, I only eat peas. I hate all other green foods.'

The doctor was quite shocked at this and said, 'Well, man, that's your problem. All those peas will be clogging up your system, you'll have to give them up!'

The businessman said, 'But how long for, I mean I really like peas!'

And the doctor replied, 'Forever, I'm afraid.'

The man was quite shocked by this, but he gave it a go and sure enough, his condition improved and he pledged that he would never eat a pea again.

One night years later, he was at a work convention and getting quite sloshed. One of his workmates said, 'Well, ashually, I'd love a cigarette, cozi avint ad a smoke in four years. I gave it up.'

The barman said, 'Really? I haven't had a game of golf in three years because it cost me my first marriage. So I gave it up!'

And the businessman said, 'Thash nuvving. I haven't ad a pea in six years.'

The barman jumped up screaming. 'Okay, everyone who can't swim, grab a table.'

An elderly couple went into a doctor. They told the doctor, 'We're having some trouble with our sex life. Could you watch and offer some suggestions?'

The doctor replied, 'I'm not a sex therapist. You should find someone else.'

The couple said, 'No, no, we trust you.'

After watching them have sex, the doctor said, 'You don't seem to be having any troubles. I wish

365

my sex life was as good. I can't give you any suggestions.'

This was repeated the next week and the following week. The exasperated doctor finally said, 'You aren't having any trouble. Is this your idea of kinky sex?'

The man replied, 'No, actually the problem is if we have sex at my house, my wife will catch us. If we have sex at her house, her husband will catch us. The motel charges us $50, and we can't afford that. You only charge $35, and Medicare pays half of that.'

Bill and Bruce were cutting wood when Bruce cut his arm off. Bill wrapped it in a plastic bag and took it to a surgeon who said, 'I'm an expert at reattaching limbs. Come back in a few hours.'

So he came back in a few hours and the surgeon said, 'I finished faster than I expected. Bruce is down at the local pub.'

Bill went to the pub and saw Bruce throwing darts. A few weeks later, Bill and Bruce were cutting wood again and this time Bruce amputated his leg. Bill put it in a plastic bag and took it back to the surgeon who said, 'Legs are a bit more difficult. Come back in six hours.'

Six hours later Bill returned and the surgeon said, 'No worries, Bruce is down playing soccer.' And lo and behold, so he was, kicking goals.

A few weeks later, Bruce had an even worse accident and cut off his head. Bill put the head in a plastic bag and took the rest of his friend to the surgeon who said, 'Well, I don't know. Heads can be really tough. But come back in 12 hours.'

Twelve hours later the surgeon said, 'I'm sorry, your friend died.' Bill said, 'That's okay, I understand. As you said, heads are tough.'

To which the surgeon replied, 'Oh no. The surgery went fine. But Bruce suffocated in the plastic bag.'

A fellow had been suffering from terrible headaches. Finally he went to the doctor, who gave him a thorough examination. 'Well, I'm not sure exactly what's causing the problem, but we've found a cure. You'll have to be castrated.'

The man, needless to say, was horrified. 'No, doctor, I prefer to suffer the headaches.'

But as time passed, they got worse and worse and finally he was driven back to the surgery. 'Okay, I'll have the operation.'

Afterwards the man was very depressed and his doctor told him, 'I recommend you begin a new life – start fresh from this point.'

Taking the advice, the man went to a men's shop for new clothes. The salesman said, 'Let's start with the suit. Looks like you'd take about a 38-regular.'

'That's right,' said the man. 'How did you know?'

'Well, when you've been in the business as long as I have, you get pretty good at sizing a man up. Now for the shirt, looks like a 15-long.'

'Exactly,' said the man.

'And for underpants, I'd say a size 36.'

'Well, there's your first mistake,' said the man. 'I've worn 34s for years.'

'No, you're a size 36 if ever I've seen one,' said the salesman.

'I ought to know,' the man replied. 'I take 34.'

'Well, if you insist,' said the salesman. 'But they're going to pinch your balls and give you headaches.'

A woman went to her physician for a follow-up visit after he'd prescribed testosterone for her. She was a little worried about some of the side effects. 'Doctor, the hormone you've been giving me has been a help but I'm afraid you're giving me too much. I've started growing hair in places I've never grown hair before.'

The physician said, 'A little hair growth is a perfectly normal side effect of testosterone. Just where has it appeared?'

'On my balls.'

A woman was going to marry one of those chauvinists who wanted a virgin, so she went to a physician and asked him to reconstruct her hymen. He told her it would cost around $500 but there was another way that would cost only $50. She agreed to try the cheap way, paid her money and the doctor went to work on her for some time.

After the honeymoon, she returned to the doctor and told him everything was perfect. It had hurt a lot and there'd been a little bleeding. She asked him how he'd done it. 'I tied your pubic hair.'

A woman goes to a doctor's office for a check-up. As she takes off her blouse he notices a red H on her chest. 'How did you get that mark?' asks the doctor.'

'Oh, my boyfriend went to Harvard. He's so proud of it that he never takes off his Harvard sweatshirt, even when we make love.'

A couple of days later another girl arrives for a check-up. As she takes off her blouse the doctor notices a blue Y on her chest. 'How did you get that mark?'

'Oh, my boyfriend went to Yale. He's so proud of it, he never takes off his Yale sweatshirt. Not even when we make love.'

A couple of days later a third girl comes in for a check-up. As she takes off her blouse he notices a green M on her chest. 'Do you have a boyfriend at Michigan?' asks the doctor.

'No, but I have a girlfriend at Wisconsin. Why do you ask?'

A woman goes to the doctor and says, 'I've got a bit of a problem. But I'll have to take off my clothes to show you.' She goes behind the screen and disrobes.

'Well, what is it?' asks the doctor.

'It's a little bit embarrassing,' she replies. 'See, two green circles have appeared on the inside of my thighs.'

The doctor examines her, consults his text books but is just about to give up. Then, suddenly, he says, 'Have you been having an affair with a gypsy?'

The woman blushes and confesses, 'Well, actually I have.'

'That's the problem,' says the doctor. 'Tell him his earrings aren't gold.'

A mute was walking through the city one day when he came upon a friend who'd been similarly afflicted. In sign language he enquired how his friend was doing. His friend spoke to him. 'Oh, can that hand-waving shit. I can talk now,' he said.

Astonished, the mute asked for details. It seems his friend had gone to a doctor who, seeing no physical damage, had put him on a treatment program.

Gesturing wildly, the mute asked his friend to ring the specialist and make an appointment for the very next day.

After an examination, the specialist confirmed that there was no permanent damage. The mute was essentially in the same condition as his friend, and there was absolutely no reason why he couldn't be helped as well.

'Let's have the first treatment right now,' signed the excited mute.

'Very well,' replied the specialist. 'Go into the next room, drop your pants and lean over the examination table. I'll be right in.'

The mute did as instructed and the doctor sneaked in with a broomstick, a mallet and a jar of Vaseline. A brief procedure resulted in the mute jumping from the table, screaming, 'AAAAAaaaaaaa!'

'Very good,' smiled the specialist. 'Next Tuesday we move on to B.'

A guy walks into a shrink's offices and says, 'Doctor, doctor, please help me. I'm convinced I'm a dog.' The shrink replies, 'Well, why don't you just get on the couch and we'll talk about it.'

The guy says, 'Can't. I'm not allowed on the couch.'

Two psychiatrists met in the corridor of the hospital. One says, 'Good morning.'

'What exactly did he mean by that?' the other wonders.

A man started a new job in a pickle factory, but after a week he had to visit the psychiatrist. 'I've got to leave the pickle factory,' he said, 'every time I start work I have an inexplicable desire to put my prick in the pickle slicer.'

The psychiatrist told him to relax and go back to work. But after a week the man came back, saying his urge had got worse. Once again, the psychiatrist calmed him down and sent him back to work.

The next week the man came back looking really dejected and said, 'I finally did it. I put my prick in the pickle slicer.'

'What happened?' asked the psychiatrist.

'The boss came in and caught me and I got the sack.'

'What about the pickle slicer?' asked the psychiatrist.

'Oh,' said the man, 'she got the sack as well.'

A patient thinks he's George Washington. He finishes up one session by telling the psychiatrist, 'Tomorrow we'll cross the Delaware and surprise them when they least expect it.' As soon as he's gone, the shrink picks up the phone and says, 'King George, this is Benedict Arnold. I have the plans.'

A woman with a problem goes to a psychologist, but she's very hesitant about describing it. Eventually he manages to glean that she thinks she might be sexually perverted.

'What kind of perversion are we talking about?'

'Well. I like to be ... no, no. I'm sorry, doctor, but I'm too ashamed to talk about it.'

'Come, come, my dear. I'm a psychologist. I've been dealing with these problems for decades. So just tell me what's the matter.'

The woman tries to explain, but gets so embarrassed that she blushes furiously and looks on the verge of collapse. At this point the psychologist has a bright idea. 'Look, I'm a bit of a pervert myself. So if you show me what your perversion is, I'll show you what mine is.'

The woman considers the offer for a few moments and agrees. 'Well, my perversion is ... my perversion ... I like to be kissed on the bottom!'

'Shit, is that all!' says the psychologist. 'Look, go behind the screen, take off all your clothes and I'll come round and show you what my perversion is!'

The woman obeys and after undressing behind the screen, gets down on all fours in the hope of having her bottom kissed. After 15 minutes, nothing has happened so she peers around the screen to see the psychologist sitting behind his desk, with his feet on the table, reading a newspaper and whistling.

'Excuse me,' says the woman, 'I thought you said you were a pervert.'

'Oh, I am,' says the psychologist. 'I've just shat in your handbag.'

An anthropologist came home after spending a year on a South Sea island. His friends asked him if he had anything unusual to report. He replied that one tribe had invented palm leaf suppositories to cure constipation. 'How good are they?' he was asked.

'Well,' he said, 'with fronds like that, who needs enemas?'

What do you call three people in wheelchairs on top of each other?

A vegetable rack.

CRUISING THE
SUPERHIGHWAY

As a little girl is coming out of school, a man pulls up in his car, winds down the window and says to her, 'I'll give you a sweet if you'll get in the car with me.'

The little girl says, 'No, I'm not getting in the car.'

The next day the man pulls up again, winds down the window and says, 'I'll give you two sweets if you'll get in the car with me.'

The little girl says, 'No, I'm not getting in the car.'

The third day the man pulls up and offers her a whole bag of sweets if she'll get into the car.

'No, Dad,' replies the girl, 'there's no way I'm getting into the Lada!'

Having troubles with her VW Beetle, a woman pulled over to the side of the road and opened the hood. To her astonishment, there was nothing there. Another woman with a VW Beetle stopped to see if she could help. The first woman said, 'Well, it seems I don't have an engine.'

The second woman replied, 'That's okay. I've got a spare one in the boot.'

A driver tucked this note under the windshield wiper of his automobile. 'I've circled the block for 20 minutes. I'm late for an appointment, and if I don't park here I'll lose my job. Forgive us our trespasses.'

When he came back he found a parking ticket and this note: 'I've circled the block for 20 years, and if I don't give you a ticket, I'll lose my job. Lead us not into temptation.'

A man in a Porsche 911 stops at a stoplight and a guy on a scooter pulls up next to him. The guy on the scooter leans over and takes an admiring look at the inside of the Porsche and tells the driver that he has a really hot car. Well, the light turns green so the driver of the Porsche decides to show off and he peels out and leaves the guy on the scooter in the dust. Then, all of a sudden, he sees the scooter zip past him. So, being a little cocky, the Porsche driver floors it again and blows past the guy on the scooter. A few seconds later, he again sees the scooter zip past him. By now he's a little irate as well as a little miffed that the scooter keeps passing him. So he floors it until he is going over

160 kmh. He thinks to himself there's no way the scooter could catch him now. But then he looks in the rearview mirror and sees the scooter starting to catch up. He then decides to find out what that scooter really is, and slams on his brakes. The scooter crashes into the Porsche. After the dust has settled, the Porsche driver sees the scooter driver lying on the road and goes over to him and asks how he could go as fast as the Porsche on a little wimpy scooter. The dying man replies, 'I can't really, but my suspenders were caught in your side mirror ...'

A Lada stops suddenly on a highway. A Jaguar crashes into it. And behind that, a Rolls Royce crashes into the Jag. The Rolls Royce driver steps out of his car, and complains, 'You fool, my radiator grille is broken. It will cost me one day of income!'

Complains the Jaguar driver, 'The front of my car is squeezed, it will cost me one month of salary!'

Says the Lada driver, 'My car is completely smashed. I will have to work one year to buy myself a new one!'

Answers the Rolls Royce driver, 'Fancy anyone buying such an expensive car!'

W hat's the difference between a Lada and AIDS? You can still palm AIDS off to someone else.

How can you double the worth of a Lada?
By filling its gasoline tank.

Why is a Lada so handy during the Finnish winter?
You don't need seatbelts – you freeze tightly to the seat.

Why do they give away free TVs with Ladas?
So you've got something to do while waiting for the mechanic to come and fix it.

What do you call a Lada with a turbo?
A Skoda.

What do you call someone who buys a secondhand Lada?
A scrap dealer.

What does a Lada buyer do to look sophisticated?
Wears dark glasses.

But how do you tell the Lada buyer from all the other people with dark glasses?

He's the one with the white stick.

What's the difference between two Jehovah's Witnesses and a Lada?

You can shut the door on two Jehovah's Witnesses.

Man walks into a service station and asks the mechanic, 'Do you have a windscreen wiper for a Lada?'

The mechanic scratches his head, thinks for a bit and replies, 'Well, it seems to be a reasonable swap – yes, I do.'

In the middle of Spain, a Lada is driving along and meets a donkey. The donkey, never having seen a Lada before, asks, 'What are you?'

The Lada says, 'I'm a car, what are you?'

The donkey says, 'I'm a horse.'

What do you call a Lada at the top of a hill?

A miracle.

Three guys die and are awaiting admission into Heaven. St Peter says to them, 'I've only one question before you enter. Were you faithful to your wives?'

The first guy answers, 'Yes, I never even looked at another woman.' St Peter says, 'See that Rolls Royce over there? That's your car to drive while you're in Heaven.'

The second guy says, 'Once I strayed, but I confessed to my wife and she forgave me and we worked it out.' St Peter says, 'See that new Buick over there? That's your car to use in Heaven.'

The third guy says, 'I have to admit, St Peter, I chased every bit of tail I could and was with a lot of women.' St Peter says, 'That's okay. You were basically a good guy. So that old VW Bug over there is yours to use while you're in Heaven.'

The three guys climb into the cars and drive through the Pearly Gates.

A few weeks later, the second and third guys are driving along in the Buick when they see the first guy's Rolls Royce parked outside a bar. They stop and go into the bar and find him with empty bottles all around him, face buried in his hands. 'Buddy, what could possibly be so bad?' they say. 'You're in Heaven, you drive a Rolls Royce, and everything is great.'

He says, 'I saw my wife here yesterday.'

The other two say, 'But that's great! What's the problem?'

'She was driving a Lada.'

The atomic scientist was so exhausted from the lecture circuit that he let his chauffeur give one of his lectures while he dressed as the chauffeur. During the question and answer period there came a very difficult question. Holding his composure, the chauffeur-turned-atomic-scientist responded, 'That question is so ridiculously simple to answer, I'm going to have my chauffeur answer it for you.'

A very dignified man enters a Swiss Bank and enquires about taking out a loan for 2000 Swiss francs.

'What security can you offer?' the banker enquires.

'Well, my Rolls Royce Silver Ghost is parked out front. I'll be away for a few weeks. Here are the keys.'

Four weeks later the dignified man returns to the bank and pays off the loan. 2024 francs, including interest.

'Pardon me,' the banker says, 'But I can't help wondering why you bothered with a 2000 franc loan – a man of your obvious means.'

'Very simple,' he replied, 'Where else could I have stored a Rolls for a month for 24 francs?'

LOGGING OFF

Why did Maria Schriver marry Arnold Schwarzenegger?

They're trying to breed a bullet-proof Kennedy.

Bill Gates died and went to Heaven. On arrival, he had to wait in the reception area. This was the size of Massachusetts with literally millions of people milling about, living in tents with nothing to do all day. Food and water were being distributed from the backs of trucks; staffers with clipboards were fighting their way through the crowd. Booze and drugs were being passed around. Fights were commonplace. Sanitation conditions were appalling. It looked like Woodstock gone metastatic.

Bill lived in a tent for three weeks until, finally, one of the staffers approached him — a young man in his late teens with acne scars wearing a blue T-shirt with the words TEAM PETER on it.

'Hello,' said the staffer, in the bored voice of a bureaucrat. 'My name is Gabriel and I'll be your induction co-ordinator.'

Bill started to ask a question but Gabriel interrupted him. 'No, I'm not the Archangel Gabriel. I'm just a guy from Philadelphia named Gabriel. I died in a car wreck at the age of 17. Now, give me your name, last name first. Unless you're Chinese, in which case it's first name first.'

'Gates, Bill.' Gabriel checked his clipboard.

'What's going on here?' asked Bill. 'Why are all these people here? Where's St Peter? Where are the Pearly Gates?'

Gabriel ignored the questions until he located Bill's entry. 'It says here that you were the president of a large software company? Is that right?'

'Yes.'

'Well then, do the massive chip-head! When Heaven opened for business, only 100 people or so died every day. Peter could handle it all by himself, no problems. Now there are over five billion people on Earth. Jesus, when God said to go forth and multiply he didn't mean like rabbits! Now 10 000 people die every hour, over a quarter of a million people every day. Do you think Peter can meet them all personally?'

'I guess not.'

'You guessed right. So Peter had to franchise the operation. He's now the CEO of Team Peter Enterprises Inc. Just sits in the corporate headquarters and sets policy. Franchisees like me handle the actual inductions. Your paperwork seems to be in order and with a background like yours, you'll be getting a plum job assignment.'

'Job assignment?'

'Of course. Did you expect to spend the rest of eternity sitting on your arse and drinking ambrosia? Heaven's a big operation. You have to pull your weight.' Gabriel had Bill sign a triplicate form, then tore out the middle copy and handed it to him.

'Take this down to Induction Centre #23 and meet up with your Occupational Orientator. His name is Abraham.' Bill started to ask a question, but Gabriel interrupted. 'No, he's not *that* Abraham.'

Gates walked down a long, muddy trail until he came to Induction Centre #23. After a mere six-hour wait he met Abraham.

'Heaven is centuries behind in its data processing infrastructure,' explained Abraham. 'We're still doing everything on paper. It takes us a week to process new entries. Your job will be to supervise Heaven's new data processing centre. We're putting in the largest computing facility in creation. Half a million computers connected by a multi-segment, fibre-optic network, all running into a back-end server network with a thousand CPUs on a gigabyte channel. Fully fault tolerant. Fully distributed processing. The works!'

'Wow!' said Bill, 'what a great job! This really is Heaven!'

Abraham and Bill caught the shuttle bus and went to Heaven's new data-processing centre. It was a truly huge facility, a hundred times bigger than the Astrodome, with workmen crawling all over it. And in the middle, half a million computers, arranged neatly, row-by-row. Half a million.

'Macintoshes!' said Bill, horrified.

'All running ClarisWorks software! Not a single byte of Microsoft code!' said Abraham.

The thought of spending the rest of Eternity using products he'd spent his life working to destroy was too much for Bill. 'What about PCs?' he exclaimed. 'What about Windows? What about Excel? What about Word?'

'This is Heaven,' explained Abraham. 'We need a computer system that's heavenly to use. If you want to build a data processing centre based on PCs running Windows, then GO TO HELL!'

In Hollywood, every producer has his yes-man whose job is to follow the producer around and say, 'Yes, CB, Right CB,' and so on. Well, one of these yes-men got depressed, so down in fact that he was unable to function. So he consulted a psychiatrist. The psychiatrist quickly determined the problem, and told the yes-man that he just had to find a release for his negative feelings, and say no.

'But if I said no I'll get fired!' the yes-man protested. The psychiatrist said, 'Oh, I don't mean on the job, I mean go out to the Grand Canyon and find a ledge off the trail, and there you can yell no to your heart's content and no one will be any the wiser.'

Well, the yes-man decided to try it. He went to the Grand Canyon and found a spot off the trail, stood there and very timidly said no. It felt good, so he tried it a little louder. 'No!' Even better! Soon he was shouting, 'NO, NO, NO, NO!' at the top of his lungs and feeling great.

He went back to work a changed man, and said yes with all the proper enthusiasm, because on the weekend he could escape to the Grand Canyon and say no.

Other yes-men decided to try this also, and soon every weekend the Grand Canyon was crammed with yes-men shouting no.

A new yes-man came to Hollywood and he too felt the need for such a release, but when he tried to find a ledge in the Grand Canyon all of them seemed to be taken. He hunted and hunted, but every place he found was already taken by another yes-man. Finally he found a small ledge which had been overlooked because of its size. Thankfully he scurried out on it and stood there and said no. It felt great! So he wound up and released an enormous no and in so doing lost his balance and fell to his death.

Which just goes to prove that a little no ledge can be a dangerous thing.

There once was a little pink lady. She had a little pink house and a little pink dress and a little pink dog. This lady sold Avon.

One day the lady was walking down a street selling her Avon when she came across a little red house. She pressed the doorbell. In the little red house lived a little red man. He was having a bath in his little red bathtub when he heard his little red doorbell ring.

'There goes my doorbell!' he said to himself as he clambered out of his little red bath. He grabbed a little red towel and put it around his waist and walked down his little red stairs to his little red door.

But, when he opened the door, his little red towel slipped and fell off. The little pink lady screamed and ran out across the street. A car coming down the road hit her and she died.

Moral: never cross the street when the little red man is flashing.

As a part of a funeral package, an undertaker agreed to provide a seven-word notice in the local paper for a frugal woman who was making arrangements for her recently deceased husband. She was asked what she'd like to say. She thought about it for a while, and then said, 'John is dead.'

The undertaker reminded her that she had paid for seven words.

The woman pondered a bit more, then with a very serious expression said, 'John is dead. Pickup truck for sale.'

A very old man was walking the grounds of a retirement home. He staggered up to another resident and said, 'Hello, my name is Charlie. How old do you think I am?' The resident looked him up and down and said, '80.' Charlie said, 'Nope, 95,' and staggered on.

He approached another resident. 'Hello, my name is Charlie. How old do you think I am?' The second resident looked him over and guessed 86. Again Charlie said, 'Nope, 95,' and walked on.

He approached an elderly woman and asked her how old she thought he was. The woman unzipped his fly, reached into his pants, felt his private parts for a few minutes and said, '95.' Amazed, Charlie exclaimed, 'How can you tell?'

The old woman said, 'I heard you tell those other guys.'

The old age pensioners' club of a small English town are boarding a coach for the annual trip to the seaside at Whitby. As the last old chap is walking along the aisle to his seat, the vehicle lurches into motion. He stumbles and lands in the lap of an octogenarian lady. During the resultant struggle, his elbow pokes the old woman in the left breast.

Back on his feet he says, 'I'm sorry about that, my dear, but if your heart is as soft as your breast, I'm sure I'll see you in Heaven.'

To which she replies, 'And if your dick is as hard as your elbow, I'll see you in Whitby.'

A couple of dear old ladies were sitting on a patio in their twilight home. Both were very, very bored. One turned to the other and said, 'Nothing happens here. All the men are half dead. There's no fun.'

The other said, 'Okay, let's do something to liven the place up.'

So they agreed to streak along the verandah to attract the attention of the old blokes who were sunning themselves.

One of them looked up and said to the other, 'Did you see that?'

The other said, 'I think so. Couldn't say for sure. My eyes aren't too good these days. What were they wearing?'

'Couldn't say for sure. But whatever it was, they needed ironing.'

Finally, Fred's family has had it. They take him out to the retirement home and install him. After a few hours a lovely young nurse comes and asks if he'd like to spend some time on the verandah. Fred says, 'Sure.'

Fred and the nurse are on the verandah enjoying the sun when Fred begins to lean to his left. The nurse, thinking he's going to fall, pushes him back upright. A few moments later Fred begins to lean, this time to his right. The nurse pushes him back upright. After a few minutes the scene is repeated. Finally she takes Fred back to his room. The next day Fred's friend Bob comes to visit. 'How do you like it here?' asks Bob.

'Well,' says Fred, 'it's fine, I suppose. The bed's not too soft and it's not too hard. The food is reasonable. The people are pleasant, but they won't let you fart on the verandah.'

I finally stopped grandma from sliding down the bannisters.'
'How?'
'I wrapped barbed wire around it.'
'That stopped her?'
'Not entirely. But it sure slows her down.'

Three old blokes are sitting on the porch of a retirement home.

'Fellas, I've got a real problem,' says the first. 'I'm 70 years old, and every morning at 7 a.m. I get up and try to pee. All day long I try to pee. They give me all kinds of pee medicine but nothing helps.'

The second old man says, 'You think you've got problems. I'm 80 years old. Every morning at 8 I get up and try to move my bowels. I try all day long. They give me all kinds of laxatives but nothing helps.'

Finally the third old man speaks up. 'Fellas, I'm 90 years old. Every morning at 7 sharp, I urinate. Every morning at 8 sharp, I move my bowels. And every morning at 9 sharp, I wake up.'

Why is it good to have Alzheimer's Disease?
You can hide your own Easter eggs.

RUBBER BULLETS, PAPER PLANES

'**M**en,' says the sergeant to the new recruits, 'you've been placed under my supervision so I can teach you sissies how to do one of my favourite things. Kill! Unfortunately the army is under-funded these days, so I'll have to furnish you with these high-quality broomsticks. What I want you to do with them is point at your target and yell, Bangety-bang.'

The men did this for the rest of the week.

'Now you'll be taught how to kill close up. I don't have the money to buy you bayonets so I'm providing you with these plastic combs. What you need to do with them is to tape them to the end of your broomsticks and practice using them by yelling, Stabbety-stab!'

They practised this for a week and became quite good at it.

Suddenly training was over and they were told it was time to defend their country. Though they were afraid, they followed their sergeant into battle.

Eventually they worked their way up to the front line. With nothing but a comb taped on a broomstick in their trembling hands and fear and doubt in their hearts, they pointed at the oncoming enemy and yelled, 'Bangety-bang.' Surprisingly, it worked. They fought fiercely and their enemies dropped like flies. When the enemy got too close, they used their combs and yelled, 'Stabbety-stab.'

The battle raged on and the loss of life on both sides was significant.

Finally it was down to only two men. One from each side. The man from the USA raised his comb-broomstick and pointed it at the unarmed man shuffling towards him and yelled as loud as he could, 'Bangety-Bang!' It didn't work. Finally the man got so close that the US soldier could use his comb directly on him. He jabbed at the enemy and yelled, 'Stabbety-Stab!' That didn't work either.

Indeed, the enemy knocked him down and ran right over him. The fallen US soldier couldn't figure it out until he heard the enemy repeating, 'Tankety-tank, tankety-tank.'

A senior pilot was explaining his emergency equipment to some cadets touring a US Air Force base. He showed them his parachute, emergency radio, signal mirror and other survival items. A cadet noticed a pack of playing cards and asked what they were for.

'Oh,' replied the pilot, 'these are my last resort. If nothing else works and nobody comes to the rescue, I take these, lay out a game of patience and wait. In a few minutes someone will be looking over my shoulder saying, "No – put that card over there." '

Two heavily bemedalled gentlemen are sitting in a hotel bar late at night reminiscing over the old days. The first had been in the army, and insisted that that service had the greatest reputation when it came to womanising, that he'd slept with hundreds during the war. The other had been an admiral, and insisted that the navy had a greater tradition of virility.

'Crap,' said the general, 'I just know Iza slept with mow women than youse!'

'Sheeet, no!'

'Okay, when did you last sleep with a woman?'

'About 1945.'

'You call that virile!'

The admiral looked at his watch. 'Well, it's only 2130 now.'

A young soldier lost his bayonet. Rather than face the consequences of this misdemeanour, he carved an excellent imitation of the missing blade. For months he went about his duties with the wooden weapon in his scabbard. Finally the inevitable order came. 'Fix bayonets!' He could do nothing but stand there, his scabbard untouched. The sergeant

401

demanded an explanation. 'Sir, it's a promise I made to my dad,' said the soldier, 'as he lay on his death bed. I told him I would never bear a bayonet on the anniversary of his death.'

'That's the damndest story I've ever heard,' roared the sergeant, 'let me see that bayonet!'

'For breaking a solemn promise,' said the soldier as he drew it out, 'may the Lord turn this to wood!'

The captain and several of his officers were returning to the ship after an evening ashore. As they climbed the gangway the captain threw up all over his uniform. Pointing to a young seaman at the head of the gangway he shouted, 'Give that man five days in the brig for vomiting on his captain.'

Next morning the captain was checking the log and saw that the young seaman had been sentenced to ten days. He asked the chief mate why. 'Well, Cap'n, when we got you undressed we found he'd also shat your underpants.'

'Well,' snarled the marine sergeant to the cowering private, 'I suppose when you get discharged from the army you'll just be waiting for me to kick the bucket so that you can come and spit on my grave.'

'Not me, Sarge,' the private replied, 'once I get

out of this man's army, I ain't ever going to stand in line again.' '

A navy squid returned home to visit his father the day after he was supposed to have had his first parachute jump. 'Dad, I was real scared up there. Everyone was going out before me and I just couldn't bring myself to jump out of that plane! So finally my commander comes up behind me as I'm looking out the plane door and says, "Son, if you don't jump right this instant, I'm going to fuck you up the ass!" '

His father asks, 'Well, did you jump?'

The son replies, 'A little, at first.'

The Central Intelligence Agency ran a Help Wanted ad for new recruits. Three men answered the advertisement and were invited to the office for an interview. After filling out their applications, they were taken, one at a time, into another room. Here an interviewer told them, 'One of the requirements for joining this organisation is that you prove your unswerving loyalty to us. We want you to take this gun, go into the other room and shoot your wife.'

The first job-seeker refused. 'Sorry, I can't do that. We just got married.' The interviewer asked him to leave.

The second applicant was then taken into the room and given the same instruction. 'I can't do that,' he protested, 'we've been married ten years and have two lovely children.' So he was rejected as well.

The last applicant was presented with the ultimatum in the same monotone, to which he replied, 'Sure, I'll do it.' And he marched into the other room.

Shots were fired. Then all sorts of noises came from the room as if a brawl were ensuing. There were screams, kicking and thumping. Finally the third applicant returned and was asked what had happened. He said, 'Some jerk put blanks in the gun. So I had to strangle her.'

World War III. The USA have succeeded in building a fantastic computer that is able to solve any strategical or tactical problem. The military leaders are assembled in front of the new machine. They describe the situation to the computer and then ask it, 'Shall we attack? Shall we retreat?'

The computer computes for an hour and then comes up with the answer, 'Yes!'

The generals, rather stupefied, look at each other. Finally one of them asks the computer, 'Yes, what?'

After another 15 minutes the computer replies, 'Yes, sir!'

A British officer spotted a busker at the bottom of the escalators of a London underground station.

The busker had a sign which read: VETERAN SOLDIER OF THE FALKLANDS WAR. The officer thought, Poor chap. I was there and it was hell. Feeling sorry for his fellow veteran, he took £20 out of his wallet and gave it to the busker, who responded with a hearty, 'Grazias, señor.'

Did you know the Shuttle commander was on the radio when the shuttle blew up?

And on the walls, and on the windscreen, and on the ceiling.

How do you fit 11 astronauts in a VW Bug?

Two in the front, two in the back, and seven in the ashtray.

A 747 is flying over the Atlantic and the pilot finishes a routine announcement over the intercom. When he puts the mike down he forgets to hit the off switch. 'Take over for a while, Dave,' he says to his co-pilot. 'I'm going to take a shit and then bang that new stewardess.'

Needless to say, the passengers are enormously amused and intrigued by this revelation. The stewardess is so embarrassed and indignant that she hurries towards the cockpit. In her haste, she trips and falls to her knees in the aisle. The sweet old

405

lady in 7F says, 'Don't rush dear. He said he had to take a shit first.'

A man travelling by plane was in urgent need of the toilet. But each time he looked up the illuminated sign proclaimed that it was occupied. The stewardess, aware of his predicament, suggested that he use the plane's new prototype women's loo. But he mustn't press any of the buttons inside. They were labelled WW, WA, PP and ATR.

The man's curiosity got the better of him and he started pressing the buttons. When he pressed WW, warm, fragrant water was sprayed all over his entire bottom. He thought, Wow, the women really have it made. Still curious, he pressed the button marked WA, and a gentle breeze of Warm Air quickly dried his hindquarters. He thought this was fantastic and reached for the button marked PP. This yielded a large Powder Puff that delicately applied a soft talc to his rear. Naturally he couldn't resist the last button marked ATR.

When he woke up in the hospital, he buzzed for the nurse. 'What happened to me? The last thing I remember is that I was in the new ladies' room on a plane.'

'Yes. Apparently you were having a great time until you pressed the ATR button, which stands for Automatic Tampon Removal. Your penis is under your pillow.'

Sue and Bob, a pair of tightwads, lived in the Mid-West and had been married for years. Bob had always wanted to go flying. The desire deepened each time a barnstormer flew into town to offer rides. Bob would ask, and Sue would say, 'No way, $10 is $10.'

The years went by, and Bob figured he didn't have much longer, so he got Sue out to the show, explaining that it was free to watch. And once he got there his desire became even stronger. Sue and Bob started to argue. The pilot, between flights, overheard, and said, 'I'll tell you what, I'll take you guys up flying, and if you don't say a word the ride is on me, but if one of you makes one sound, you pay $10.'

So off they flew, the pilot doing as many rolls and dives as he could. Heading for the ground as fast as the plane could go, he pulled out of the dive at the very last second. Not a word. Finally, he admitted defeat and went back to the field. 'I'm surprised, how could you not say anything?'

'Well, I almost said something when Sue fell out, but $10 is $10!'

You are one of a group of people on a malfunctioning aeroplane with only one parachute.

PESSIMIST: You refuse the parachute because you might die in the jump anyway.

OPTIMIST: You refuse the parachute because people have survived jumps just like this before.

BUREAUCRAT: You order a feasibility study on

parachute use in multi-engine aircraft under code red conditions.

LAWYER: You charge one parachute for helping sue the airline.

INTERNAL REVENUE SERVICE: You confiscate the parachute along with their luggage, wallet, and gold fillings.

ENGINEER: You make another parachute out of aisle curtains and dental floss.

MATHEMATICIAN: You refuse to accept the parachute without proof that it will work in all cases.

PHILOSOPHER: You ask how we can know the parachute actually exists.

PSYCHOANALYST: You ask what the shape of a parachute reminds them of.

DRAMATIST: You tie them down so they can watch you develop the character of a person stuck on a falling plane without a parachute.

ARTIST: You hang the parachute on the wall and sign it.

REPUBLICAN: As you jump out with the parachute, you tell them to work hard and not expect handouts.

DEMOCRAT: You ask them for a dollar to buy scissors so you can cut the parachute into two equal pieces.

LIBERTARIAN: After reminding them of their constitutional right to have a parachute you take it and jump out.

SURGEON GENERAL: You issue a warning that skydiving can be hazardous to your health.

ASSOCIAITON OF TOBACCO GROWERS: You explain

very patiently that despite a number of remarkable coincidences, studies have shown no link whatsoever between aeroplane crashes and death.

NATIONAL RIFLE ASSOCIATION: You shoot them and take the parachute.

ENVIRONMENTALIST: You refuse to use the parachute unless it is biodegradable.

OBJECTIVIST: Your only rational and moral choice is to take the parachute, as the free market will take care of the other person.

BRANCH DAVIDIAN: You get inside the parachute and refuse to come out.

The Greatest Lies in Aviation:
I'm from the FAA and am here to help you.
We'll be on time, maybe even earlier.
I only need glasses for reading.
If we get a little lower, I think we'll see the lights.
I'd love to have a woman co-pilot.
All you have to do is follow the book.
Sure I can fly – it has wings, doesn't it?
I'm *sure* the gear was down.

An experienced skydiver is about to jump when he notices that he's sitting next to another guy, obviously outfitted to dive, but wearing dark glasses, carrying a white cane, and holding the leash of a seeing-eye dog.

After some hesitation, he speaks to the blind guy,

expressing his admiration for his courage. He then asks him how he knows when the ground is getting close. The blind guy replies, 'When the leash goes slack!'

●nce upon a time there were three brothers who were knights in a certain kingdom. Now there was a princess in a neighbouring kingdom who was of marriageable age. The three brothers decided to travel there and see if one of them could win her hand. They set off in full armour, with their horses and their page. The road was long and there were many obstacles along the way, robbers to be overcome, hard terrain to cross. As they coped with each obstacle they became more and more disgusted with their page. He was not only inept, he was a coward, he could not handle the horses, he was in short a complete flop. When they arrived at the court of the kingdom, they found that they were expected to present the princess with some treasure. The two older brothers were discouraged, since they had not thought of this and were unprepared. The youngest however, had the answer: Promise her anything, but give her our page.

What lies at the bottom of the sea and whimpers?
A nervous wreck.

Someone scrawled the following on a wall at a university.

Is there intelligent life on Earth?

A week or so later someone else tacked on: Yes, but we're only stopping to refuel.

A man is on a package tour of the USA. On day one, the bus goes to Mexico. He's looking forward to wild, decadent times but the bus drops him at a sleepy pueblo with a population of three people and one tumbleweed. The bus departs with the driver shouting something about returning in three hours.

The man decides to make the best of it. Surely he can amuse himself for three hours. The man heads for a bar and tries to talk to the patron, who turns out to be the most boring person on earth. Five minutes feels like three hours, so the man makes his excuses and departs. Next he sees a sleepy hombre sitting against the wall in his sombrero. '*Quel estas 'l'hora?*' he asks in his best Spanglais.

'You want man?' replies the hombre.

'No, no. The time, what is it?'

The hombre reaches out to a mule, lifts its scrotum and then lets it drop. 'About 2.30,' he says.

'Astonishing,' says the tourist, 'how did you manage that?'

Once again the hombre reaches out and lifts the donkey's scrotum. 'You see that clock tower over there?'

411

'Yes.'
'So can I, now.'

A spaceship from the planet Zong lands in Farmborough in the middle of the night. The town is deserted as the aliens descend from their ship. They wander around for a while until they come across a garage and what they perceive to be intelligent life – a petrol pump. The chief Zong greets the petrol pump. 'Greetings, I am Zong, a Zong from the planet Zong. We have come in our spaceship, the Zong, to meet Earth people. Take me to your leader.'

The Zong receives no reply, so he repeats his demands using shorter words: 'Take me to your leader.' The petrol pump, unsurprisingly, says nothing. By now, the short-tempered captain of the Zong is getting a bit annoyed at being ignored. He levels his ray gun at the petrol pump, much to the distress of his first mate, and demands, 'Take me to your leader, insolent scum, or I will blow you to pieces!'

Of course, the petrol pump remains silent. His Zongian shipmates try to restrain him, but the leader fires. There is an almighty explosion as the petrol pump bursts into a huge ball of flames and the crew are hurled hundreds of metres into the air. They land in a nearby field with a bump. 'What the hell happened?' shouted the Zong captain. 'I tried to warn you,' said the first mate, 'You just don't mess with a guy who can wrap his penis around his waist and stick it in his ear.'

GIGGLE-BYTES

IBM:

I Beg Mercy
I Blame Microsoft
I Bought Macintosh
Idiots Become Managers
Idiots Bewilderment Machines
Idiots Bought Me
Illustrative of Bad Marketing
Immense Bins of Money
Immense Bucket of Manure
Imperialism By Marketing
Impractical But Marketable
In a Befuddled Manner
In Business for Money
Incredible Bunch of Muffinheads
Incredibly Big Machine
Industry's Biggest Mistake
Insipid Brainless Monster
Insolence Breeds Mediocrity

Installed By Masochists
Institute of Broken Minds
Intensely Boring Machines
Intergalactic Brotherhood of Motherfuckers
International Bureaucracy Merchants
Involuntary Bowel Movement
It Beats Mattel
It's Broken Mummy
I've Been Misled

Aphorisms

I bet I can quit gambling.

A closed mouth gathers no feet.

A journey of a thousand miles begins with a cash advance.

A king's castle is his home.

A penny saved is ridiculous.

All that glitters is a high refractive index.

Ambition is a poor excuse for not having enough sense to be lazy.

Anarchy is better than no government at all.

Any small object when dropped will hide under a larger object.

Be moderate where pleasure is concerned, avoid fatigue.

Of the choice of two evils, I pick the one I've never tried before.

Death is life's way of telling you you've been fired.

Do something unusual today – accomplish work on the computer.

Don't hate yourself in the morning – sleep till noon.

Earn cash in your spare time – blackmail friends.

Entropy isn't what it used to be.

Familiarity breeds children.

Health is merely the slowest possible rate at which
one can die.

History doesn't repeat itself – historians merely
repeat each other.

It's a miracle that curiosity survives formal education.

It works better if you plug it in.

Life is what happens to you while you're planning
to do something else.

Quoting one is plagiarism. Quoting many is
research.

Reality is the only obstacle to happiness.

The attention span of a computer is as long as its
electrical cord.

The only difference between a rut and a grave is
the depth.

The only way to get rid of temptation is to yield to
it.

The road to success is always under construction.

To be, or not to be, those are the parameters.

To err is human – to really foul things up requires a
computer.

Blessed are they that run around in circles, for they
shall be known as wheels.

Charity: the thing that begins at home and usually
stays there.

Drawing on my fine command of language, I said
nothing.

Every absurdity has a champion to defend it.

Everything you know is wrong.

Take care of the luxuries and the necessities will take care of themselves.

The universe is laughing behind your back.

To think is to be human, to compute divine.

There are no saints, only unrecognised villains.

The light at the end of the tunnel is an oncoming freight train.

Nothing is true. Everything is permitted.

Just because everything is different doesn't mean anything has changed.

The opposite of a correct statement is a false statement. But the opposite of a profound truth may well be another profound truth.

Never invest your money in anything that eats or needs painting.

Tip the world over on its side and everything loose will land in Los Angeles.

Any smoothly functioning technology will have the appearance of magic.

I think that in creating man, God somewhat over-estimated his ability.

We are what we pretend to be.

Time is an illusion perpetrated by the manufacturers of space.

A physicist is an atom's way of knowing about atoms.

We don't know who discovered water, but we are certain it wasn't a fish.

I either want less corruption, or more chances to participate in it.

If the Aborigines drafted an IQ test, all of western civilisation would flunk it.

The meek shall inherit the earth, but not its mineral
  rights.
A man without religion is like a fish without a
  bicycle.
The unnatural – that too is natural.
I used to be indecisive: now I'm not so sure.
I'd give my right arm to be ambidextrous.
Science has proof without any certainty. Creationists
  have certainty without any proof.
Logic is an organised way of going wrong with
  confidence.
An intellectual is someone whose mind watches
  itself.
A little caution outflanks a large cavalry.
The only remedy for sex is more sex.
Everyone is entitled to my opinion.
He who laughs last didn't get the joke.
Atheism is a non-prophet organisation.
Gravity brings me down.
Help stamp out and abolish redundancy.
Where there's a will, there's an inheritance tax.
If everything is coming your way, you're in the
  wrong lane.
While money can't buy happiness it certainly lets
  you choose your own form of misery.
Two is company, three is an orgy.
Xerox never comes up with anything original.

As much use as:

A one-legged man in an arse-kicking contest.

A chocolate teapot.

Milk shoes.

A nuclear-powered computer controlled intercontinental ballistic duck.

A flammable fire extinguisher.

A glass cricket bat.

A gelignite suppository.

A coal-powered frog violin.

Granite sugar cubes.

Pasta audio wire.

A pastry telephone.

Ice-cream gloves.

A sugar surf board.

Span windscreen wipers.

A blind lifeguard.

Wooden soap.

Shortbread tyres.

A whipped-cream jet engine.

A knitted light bulb.

A plate-steel trampoline.

An invisible traffic light.

A bread boat.

Plasticine wire cutters.

A neon pink secret door.

Chocolate staples.

A lead balloon.

A latex multi-storey car park.

A margarine turbocharger.

Custard floorboards.

Gravy ceiling tiles.

A fried motor boat.
A mud monitor.
A silent telephone.
A velvet TV set.
A concrete engine.
An exploding bassoon.
A stone cigarette.
Syrup underwear.
A plastic oven.
A wax truss.
A licquorice suspension bridge.
Soap false teeth.
Asbestos water wings.
A lemonade roof.
A pair of jelly wellingtons.
A jam cardigan.
A paper bicycle pump.
Non-stick cellotape.
A sponge radar.
Anti-matter sun-tan lotion.
A soluble drain pipe.
A cubic ball bearing.
An inflatable dartboard.
A glass hammer.
A packet of rubber nails.
Elevator Earth shoes.
Heat'n'eat popsicles.
A see-through mirror.
A revolving basement restaurant.
A G-rated porn flick.
Roll-on hairspray.
Braille speedometers.
A screen door on a submarine.

An ejector seat in a helicopter.
Waterproof teabags.
Solar-powered torches.
A pocket in a pair of underpants.
A chocolate dick.
An ashtray on a motorbike.
A sodium submarine.
Tits on a bull.
A condom with a hole in it.
A box of matches in the desert.

Collectibles

Why do you need a driver's licence to buy liquor when you can't drink and drive?

Why isn't phonetic spelled the way it sounds?

Why are there interstate highways in Hawaii?

Why are there flotation devices under plane seats instead of parachutes?

Have you ever imagined a world with no hypothetical situations?

How does the guy who drives the snowplough get to work in the mornings?

If 7-eleven is open 24 hours a day, 365 days a year, why are there locks on the doors?

If you're in a vehicle going the speed of light, what happens when you turn on the headlights?

Why do they put Braille dots on the keypad of the drive-up ATM?

Why is it that when you transport something by

car, it's called a shipment, but when you transport
something by ship, it's called cargo?

You know that little indestructible black box that is
used on planes – why can't they make the whole
plane out of the same stuff?

Why is it that when you're driving and looking for
an address, you turn down the volume on the
radio?

PC:

Piece a Chit
Primitive Calculator
Pseudo Computer

Condom slogans

Before you attack her, wrap your whacker.

Don't be silly, protect your willy.

Cover your stump before you hump.

Don't be a loaner, cover your boner.

If you're not going to sack it, go home and whack
it.

Before you bag her, sheath your dagger.

You can't go wrong if you shield your dong.

It'll be sweeter if you wrap your peter.

Wrap it in foil before checking her oil.

Elephant books

The French book: *100 Ways to Cook Elephants*

The English book: *Elephants I have Shot on Safari*

The Welsh book: *The Elephant and its Influence on Welsh Language and Culture. Or, Oes ysgol tocynnau eleffant llanfairpwll nhadau coeden*

The American book: *How to Make Bigger and Better Elephants*

The Japanese book: *How to Make Smaller and Cheaper Elephants*

The Greek book: *How to Sell Elephants for a lot of Money*

The Finnish book: *What Do Elephants Think About Finnish People?*

The German book: *A Short Introduction to Elephants, Vols 1–6*

The Icelandic book: *Defrosting an Elephant*

The Swiss book: *Switzerland: The Country Through Which Hannibal Went With His Elephants*

The Canadian book: *Elephants: A Federal or State Issue?*

Forty-six things that never happen in *Star Trek*

1. The *Enterprise* runs into a mysterious energy field of a type that it has encountered several times before.

2. The *Enterprise* goes to check up on a remote outpost of scientists, who are all perfectly all right.

3. The *Enterprise* comes across a Garden-of-Eden-like planet called Paradise, where everyone is happy all the time. However, everything is soon revealed to be exactly as it seems.

4. The crew of the *Enterprise* discover a totally new lifeform, which later turns out to be a rather well-known old lifeform, wearing a silly hat.

5. The crew of the *Enterprise* are struck by a strange alien plague, for which the cure is found in the well-stocked sick-bay.

6. An enigmatic being composed of pure energy attempts to interface with the *Enterprise's* computer, only to find out that it has forgotten to bring the right leads.

7. A power surge on the Bridge is rapidly and correctly diagnosed as a faulty capacitor by the highly-trained and competent engineering staff.

8. A power surge on the Bridge fails to electrocute the user of a computer panel, due to a highly sophisticated 24th century surge protection feature called 'a fuse'.

9. The *Enterprise* ferries an alien VIP from one place to another without serious incident.

10. The *Enterprise* is captured by a vastly superior alien intelligence which does not put them on trial.

11. The *Enterprise* separates as soon as there is any danger.

12. The *Enterprise* gets involved in an enigmatic, strange and dangerous situation, and there are no pesky aliens they can blame it on in the end.

13. The *Enterprise* is captured by a vastly inferior

alien intelligence which they easily pacify by offering it some sweeties.

14. The *Enterprise* is involved in a bizarre time-warp phenomenon, which is in some way unconnected with the 20th century.

15. Somebody takes out a shuttle and it doesn't explode or crash.

16. A major Starfleet emergency breaks out near the *Enterprise*, but fortunately some other ships in the area are able to deal with it to everyone's satisfaction.

17. The shields of the *Enterprise* stay up during a battle.

18. The *Enterprise* visits the Klingon Home World on a bright, sunny day.

19. An attempt at undermining the Klingon-Federation alliance is discovered without anyone noting that such an attempt, if successful, would represent a fundamental shift of power throughout the quadrant.

20. A major character spends the entire episode in the Holodeck without a single malfunction trapping him/her there.

21. Picard hears the door chime and doesn't bother to say, 'Come.'

22. Picard doesn't answer a suggestion with, 'Make it so!'

23. Picard walks up to the replicator and says, 'Coke on ice!'

24. Councillor Troi states something other than the blindingly obvious.

25. Mood rings come back in style, jeopardizing Councillor Troi's position.

26. Worf and Troi finally decide to get married, only to have Kate Pulaski show up and disrupt the wedding by shouting, 'Did he read you love poetry? Did he serve you poisonous tea? He's MINE!'

27. When Worf tells the bridge officers that something is entering visual range no one says, 'On screen.'

28. Worf actually gives another vessel more than two seconds to respond to one of the *Enterprise's* hails.

29. Worf kills Wesley by mistake in the Holodeck.

30. Wesley Crusher gets beaten up by his classmates for being a smarmy git, and consequently has a go at making some friends of his own age for a change.

31. Wesley saves the ship, the Federation and the Universe as we know it, and EVERYONE is grateful.

32. The warp engines start playing up a bit, but seem to sort themselves out after a while without any intervention from boy genius Wesley Crusher.

33. Wesley Crusher tries to upgrade the and they work better than ever.

34. Beverly Crusher manages to go thr whole episode without having a h getting breathless every time Pica room.

35. Guinan forgets herself, and brea up comedy routine.

36. Data falls in love with the rep

37. Kirk (or Riker) falls in love w

planet he visits, and isn't tragically separated from her at the end of the episode.

38. The Captain has to make a difficult decision about a less advanced people which is made a great deal easier by the Starfleet Prime Directive.

39. An unknown ensign beams down as part of an away team and lives to tell the tale.

40. Spock or Data is fired from his high-ranking position for not being able to understand the most basic nuances of about one in three sentences that anyone says to him.

41. Kirk's hair remains consistent for more than one consecutive episode.

42. Kirk gets into a fistfight and doesn't rip his shirt.

43. Kirk doesn't end up kissing the troubled guest-female before she doesn't sacrifice herself for him.

44. Scotty doesn't mention the law of physics.

45. Spock isn't the only crew member not affected by new weapon/attack by alien race, etc. due to his darn green blood or bizarre Vulcan physiology and thus he cannot save the day.

46. The episode ends without Bones and Kirk laughing at Spock's inability to understand the joke, and he doesn't raise his eyebrow.

edical terminology
the layman

RY: The study of fine paintings

What you do when CPR fails

CAESAREAN SECTION: A district in Rome

COLIC: A sheep dog

COMA: A punctuation mark

CONGENITAL: Friendly

DILATE: To live longer

G.I. SERIES: Baseball games between teams of soldiers

GRIPPE: A suitcase

HANGNAIL: A coat hook

MEDICAL STAFF: A doctor's cane

MINOR OPERATION: Coal digging

MORBID: A higher offer

NITRATE: Lower than the day rate

NODE: Was aware of

ORGANIC: Musical

OUTPATIENT: A person who has fainted

POST-OPERATIVE: A letter carrier

PROTEIN: In favour of young people

SECRETION: Hiding anything

SEROLOGY: Study of English knighthood

TABLET: A small table

TUMOR: An extra pair

URINE: Opposite of you're out

VARICOSE VEINS: Veins that are close together

A code of ethical behaviour for patients

1. DO NOT EXPECT YOUR DOCTOR TO SHARE YOUR DISCOMFORT: involvement with the patient's

suffering might cause him to lose valuable
scientific objectivity.

2. BE CHEERFUL AT ALL TIMES: your doctor leads a
busy and trying life and requires all the
gentleness and reassurance he can get.

3. TRY TO SUFFER FROM THE DISEASE FOR WHICH
YOU ARE BEING TREATED: remember that your
doctor has a professional reputation to uphold.

4. DO NOT COMPLAIN IF THE TREATMENT FAILS TO
BRING RELIEF: you must believe that your doctor
has achieved a deep insight into the true nature
of your illness, which transcends any mere
permanent disability you may have experienced.

5. NEVER ASK A DOCTOR TO EXPLAIN WHAT THEY
ARE DOING OR WHY THEY ARE DOING IT: it is
presumptuous to assume that such profound
matters could be explained in terms that you
would understand.

6. SUBMIT TO NOVEL EXPERIMENTAL TREATMENT
READILY: though the surgery may not benefit
you directly, the resulting research paper will
surely be of widespread interest.

7. PAY YOUR MEDICAL BILLS PROMPTLY AND
WILLINGLY: you should consider it a privilege to
contribute, however modestly, to the well-being
of physicians and other humanitarians.

8. DO NOT SUFFER FROM AILMENTS THAT YOU
CANNOT AFFORD: it is sheer arrogance to
contract illnesses that are beyond your means.

9. NEVER REVEAL ANY OF THE SHORTCOMINGS THAT
HAVE COME TO LIGHT IN THE COURSE OF
TREATMENT BY YOUR DOCTOR: the patient-
doctor relationship is a privileged one and you

have a sacred duty to protect your doctor from exposure.

10. NEVER DIE WHILE IN YOUR DOCTOR'S PRESENCE OR UNDER HIS DIRECT CARE: this will only cause him or her needless inconvenience and embarrassment.

Mistakes made by Adolf Hitler

Leaving his little moustache.

Not buying lifts for his shoes.

Chose the swastika as the party symbol rather than the daisy.

Lost the Ark to Indiana Jones.

Chose unfashionable blacks and browns rather than trendy plaids.

Referred to Stalin as 'that old Geogian fart'.

Bad toupé.

Chose Italy as ally.

Made pass at Eleanor Roosevelt during 1936 Olympics.

Always got Churchill out of bed for conference calls.

Never had fireside mass rallies.

Told Einstein he had a stupid name.

Used SS instead of LAPD.

Admired Napoleon's strategy.

Strong fondness for saukraut and beans made staff avoid him.

Failed to revoke Rudolph Hess's pilot licence.

Pissed off Jesse Owens at 1936 Olympics.

Passed in Finnish 'tanks with snowshoes' offer before invasion of USSR.

Blew nose on Operation Barbarossa maps, forcing extemporaneous invasion of Soviet Union.

Took no steps to keep Neville Chamberlain in power.

Came off as poor loser when *Triumph of the Will* failed to win Oscar for Best Foreign Film.

Got drunk on schnapps and told Tojo to attack the US, saying, 'The US has only 20 times your industrial power. What are you, a wimp?'

Listened to too much Wagner and not enough Peter, Paul and Mary.

Being born.

Kept Colonel Klink in command.

Used same astrologer as the Reagans.

Not the full quid

A couple of slates short of a full roof.

A couplet short of a sonnet.

A day late and a dollar short.

A few beers short of a six-pack.

A few ears short of a bushel.

A few feathers short of a duck.

A few peas short of a pod.

A few straws shy of a bale.

A few tiles missing from his space shuttle.

A few yards short of the hole.

A kangaroo loose in her top paddock.

A pane short of a window.

A semi-tone flat on the high notes.
A span short of a bridge.
Airhead.
Bubble brain.
All foam, no beer.
All hammer, no nail.
All hat and no cattle.
All the lights don't shine in her marquee.
All wax and no wick.
An experiment in Artificial Stupidity.
Answers the door when the phone rings.
As focused as a fart.
Bad spot on the disk.
Batteries not included.
Bright as Alaska in December.
Bubbles in her think tank.
Can't count his balls and get the same answer
    twice.
Cart can't hold all the groceries.
Cheats when filling out opinion polls.
Chimney's clogged.
Clock doesn't have all its numbers.
Couldn't organise a piss-up in a brewery.
Couldn't pour water out of a boot with instructions
    on the heel.
Couldn't write dialogue for a porno flick.
Cranio-rectally inverted.
Deep as her dimples.
Defective hard drive.
Dock doesn't quite reach the water.
Doesn't just know nothing; doesn't even suspect
    much.

Doesn't know whether to scratch his watch or wind his balls.

Elevator doesn't go all the way to the penthouse.

Elevator goes all the way to the top but the door doesn't open.

Elevator is on the ground floor and he's pushing the DOWN button.

Enough sawdust between the ears to bed an elephant.

Goalie for the dart team.

Got into the gene pool while the lifeguard wasn't watching.

Has all the brains God gave a duck's arse.

Has an IQ one point lower than it takes to grunt.

Has his brain on cruise control.

Has no upper stage.

Has the personality of a snail on Valium.

Having a party in his head, but no one else is invited.

He's so dense, light bends around him.

Her modem lights are on but there's no carrier.

His head whistles in a cross wind.

His IQ is a false positive.

His spark can't jump the gap.

If brains were taxed, he'd get a rebate.

If his brains were money, he'd still be in debt.

If his IQ was two points higher he'd be a rock.

If you stand close enough to him, you can hear the ocean.

In the shopping mall of the mind, he's in the toy store.

Informationally deprived.

434 | Inspected by #13.

IQ lower than a snake's belly in a wagon-rut.
It's hard to believe he beat 100 000 other sperm.
Knitting with only one needle.
Left the store without all of his groceries.
Levelled off before reaching altitude.
Lights are on but nobody's home.
Lives in La-la-land.
Living proof that nature does not abhor a vacuum.
Missing a few buttons on his remote.
Mouth is in gear, brain is in neutral.
Moves his lips to pretend he's reading.
Nice house but not much furniture.
No coins in the fountain.
No grain in the silo.
No hay in the loft.
No one at the throttle.
Not the brightest bulb on the Christmas tree.
Oil doesn't reach his dipstick.
One bit short of a byte.
One board short of a porch.
One bun short of a dozen.
One hot pepper short of an enchilada.
One node short of a network.
One pearl short of a necklace.
Ready to check in at the Ha-Ha Hilton.
Running on empty.
Serving donuts on another planet.
She wears a ponytail to cover up the valve stem.
Short-circuited between the earphones.
Sloppy as a soup sandwich.
Slow as molasses in January.
Slow out of the gate.
Smarter than the average bear.

Smoke doesn't make it to the top of his chimney.
So boring, his dreams have Muzak.
So dim, his psyche carries a flashlight.
So dumb, blondes tell jokes about him.
So dumb, he faxes face up.
So dumb, his dog teaches him tricks.
So slow, he has to speed up to stop.
So stupid, mind readers charge half price.
Someone blew out his pilot light.
Suffers from Clue Deficit Disorder.
Switch is on, but no one's receiving.
Takes her 1.5 hours to watch *60 Minutes*.
The cheese slid off his cracker.
The wheel's spinning but the hamster's dead.
Thick as pig dung and twice as smelly.
Thinks cellular phones are carbon-based life forms.
Thinks Moby Dick is a venereal disease.
Three chickens short of a henhouse.
Toys in the attic.
Travelling without a passport.
Two chapters short of a novel.
Uses his head to keep the rain out of his neck.
Warranty expired.
Wasn't strapped in during launch.
Whole lotta choppin', but no chips a flyin'.
Zero K memory.

Top 17 children's books not recommended by the National Library Association

Bob the Germ's Wonderous Journey Into and Back Out of Your Digestive System.

The Little Engine that Became Intoxicated and Killed Civilians.

Rudolph the Rednosed Reindeer's Games of Revenge.

Clifford the Big Red Dog Accidentally Eats His Masters and is put to Sleep.

Valuable Protein and other Nutritional Benefits of Things from your Nose.

A Pictorial History of Circus Geek Suicides.

Charles Manson Bedtime Stories.

Daddy Loses His Job and Finds the Bottle.

Babar Meets the Taxidermist and Becomes a Piano.

Controlling the Playground: Respect Through Fear.

David Duke's World of Imagination.

Curious George and the High-Voltage Fence.

The Boy Who Died from Eating All His Vegetables.

Teddy: The Elf With the Detached Retina.

The Pop-up Book of Human Anatomy.

Things Rich Kids Have, But You Never Will.

Let's Draw Betty and Veronica Without Their Clothes On.

The Care Bears Maul Some Campers and are Shot Dead.

Useful phrases for Arab travel

AKBAR KHALI-KILI HAFTIR LOFTAN:
Thank you for showing me your marvellous gun.

FEKR GABUL GARDAN DAVAT PAEH GUSH DIVAR:
I am delighted to accept your kind invitation to lie down on the floor with my arms above my head and my legs apart.

SHOMAEH FEKR TAMOMEH OEH GOFTEH BANDE:
I agree with everything you have ever said or thought in your life.

AUTO ARRAREGH DAVATEMAN MANO SEPAHEH-HAST:
It is exceptionally kind of you to allow me to travel in the trunk of your car.

FASHAL-EH TUPEHMAN NA DEGAT MANO GOFTAM
CHEESHAYEH MOHEMARA JEBEHKESHVAREHMAN:
If you will do me the kindness of not harming my
genital appendages, I will gladly reciprocate by
betraying my country in public.

KHREL, JEPAHEH MANEH VA JAYEII AMRIKAHEY:
I will tell you the names and address of many
American spies travelling as reporters.

BALLI, BALLI, BALLI:
Whatever you say!

MATERNIER GHERMEZ AHLIEH, GHORBAN:
The red blindfold would be lovely, Excellency.

TIKEH NUNEH BA OB KHRELLEH BEZORG VA KHRUBE
BOYAST NO BEGERAM:
The water-soaked breadcrumbs are delicious, thank
you. I must have the recipe.

Why did the chicken cross the road?

PLATO: For the greater good.

KARL MARX: It was a historical inevitability.

MACHIAVELLI: So that its subjects will view it with
admiration, as a chicken which has the daring and
courage to boldly cross the road, but also with
fear. For whom among them has the strength to
contend with such a paragon of avian virtue? In

such a manner is the princely chicken's dominion maintained.

HIPPOCRATES: Because of an excess of light pink gooey stuff in its pancreas.

JACQUES DERRIDA: Any number of contending discourses may be discovered within the act of the chicken crossing the road, and each interpretation is equally valid as the authorial intent can never be discerned, because structuralism is dead, dammit, dead!

THOMAS DE TORQUEMADA: Give me ten minutes with the chicken and I'll find out.

TIMOTHY LEARY: Because that's the only kind of trip the Establishment would let it take.

DOUGLAS ADAMS: Forty-two.

NIETZSCHE: Because if you gaze too long across the Road, the Road gazes also across you.

OLIVER NORTH: National security was at stake.

B.F. SKINNER: Because the external influences which had pervaded its sensorium from birth had caused it to develop in such a fashion that it would tend to cross roads, even while believing these actions to be of its own free will.

CARL JUNG: The confluence of events in the cultural gestalt necessitated that individual chickens cross roads at this historical juncture, and therefore synchronicitously brought such occurrences into being.

JEAN-PAUL SARTRE: In order to act in good faith and be true to itself, the chicken found it necessary to cross the road.

LUDWIG WITTGENSTEIN: The possibility of 'crossing' was encoded into the objects 'chicken' and 'road', and circumstances came into being which caused the actualisation of this potential occurrence.

ALBERT EINSTEIN: Whether the chicken crossed the road or the road crossed the chicken depends upon your frame of reference.

ARISTOTLE: To actualise its potential.

BUDDHA: If you ask this question, you deny your own chicken-nature.

HOWARD COSELL: It may very well have been one of the most astonishing events to grace the annals of history. An historic, unprecedented avian biped with the temerity to attempt such a Herculean achievement formerly relegated to homo sapien pedestrians is truly a remarkable occurrence.

SALVADOR DALI: The Fish.

DARWIN: It was the logical next step after coming down from the trees.

EPICURUS: For fun.

RALPH WALDO EMERSON: It didn't cross the road; it transcended it.

JOHANN FRIEDRICH VON GOETHE: The external hen-principle made it do it.

ERNEST HEMINGWAY: To die. In the rain.

WERNER HEISENBER: We are not sure which side of the road the chicken was on, but it was moving very fast.

DAVID HUME: Out of custom and habit.

SADDAM HUSSEIN: This was an unprovoked act of rebellion and we were quite justified in dropping 50 tons of nerve gas on it.

JACK NICHOLSON: 'Cause it (censored) wanted to. That's the (censored) reason.

RONALD REAGAN: I forget.

JOHN SUNUNU: The air force was only too happy to provide the transportation, so quite understandably the chicken availed himself of the opportunity.

THE SPHINX: You tell me.

MR T: If you saw me coming you'd cross the road too!

HENRY DAVID THOREAU: To live delibeately ... and suck all the marrow out of life.

MARK TWAIN: The news of its crossing has been greatly exaggerated.

MOLLY YARD: It was a hen!

ZENO OF ELEA: To prove it could never reach the other side.

Index